The Teacher of Teachers

The Teacher of Teachers

Frontiers of Theory and Practice
in Teacher Education

HAROLD RUGG

Professor Emeritus of Education
Teachers College, Columbia University

HARPER & BROTHERS, PUBLISHERS, NEW YORK

Library of Congress catalog card number: 52-5728

To

my wife, Elizabeth,

who always helps

CONTENTS

Preface

The Teacher of Teachers was approximately finished when I
left the United States in the summer of 1951 for the Middle East,
as Fulbright Lecturer on education and changing culture; the
concluding chapter was written in Cairo. I returned just in time
to read proof. The year with my Arab colleagues has not led me
to modify the thesis of the book, or its major concepts; on the
contrary, it has underlined my conclusions by placing them in a
larger world and historical context. While the West is now well
into the *second* stage of those intellectual, technological, social
and moral revolutions that have been transforming our society,
the East has barely entered its *first* stage; it lags fifty years, perhaps a century behind us. A billion men east of Suez, bogged
down in a primitive agrarianism and burdened by a massive
pyramid of theological dogma and ancient custom, are just now
building their new nationalisms and asserting their political independence. But their leaders stand baffled by the vicious circle of
self-defeating factors that strangles all efforts to industrialize their
economy and democratize their authoritarian way of life. To be
an eye-witness of this process is to see more clearly than one can
at home America's critical role in the world crisis, and within it,
the powerful role of the American Teacher of Teachers. The
latter is the chief theme of my book.

The prior thesis of this book—that our western liberal arts
education, and the First Draft of its teacher education, did not
fit the needs of our people—received a dramatic confirmation as
I came face to face with the British-French version of it in the
countries of the Middle East. I had become sceptical of it first, in
1924 and 1925, as a member of government educational survey
commissions in the Philippines and Puerto Rico. Scepticism became documented conviction in the next twelve years as I developed my program in the social sciences, and served as educational
consultant in China, Japan, and Hawaii (1931-1932), South
Africa (1934), New Zealand and Australia (1937), and in countries of Western Europe over a quarter century. The Middle East

experience clinched the generalization. In a dozen roundtables, from Cairo to Damascus since October 1951, my Arab colleagues agreed to a man that this same limited literacy education, which had been imposed upon them by Britain and France, does not fit the needs of their awakening peoples, and the mass American form was little better. I abandoned any concern that I might have had, lest I had been too hard (in Chapter II) on my elder brothers, or that I had condemned too harshly the First Draft of teacher education which they had devised between 1880 and 1920. I have not changed a line of the writing.

I had the definite advantage of writing the final chapter (VIII) in the midst of the stirring changes in the Middle East. There I put the whole story together in briefer synthesis. Reviewers and others-in-a-hurry may wish to scan it first.

What single fact stands out from my past year's experiences? The fact of America! It is breath-taking! To the people of Asia, and all others who live in scarcity and fear, its abundance and security are incredible. Even its generous motive of "live-and-help-live" is beyond their belief. For these 1,500 million people, two-thirds of human-kind, are still being ruled by selfish and arrogant men who neither treasure human life nor respect the personality of the individual. Here in our favored America, we come closer than anywhere else on the earth to doing both. For thirty years, in all my books, I have affirmed this fact, and the corollary that follows from it: America, its goal focussed more on men than on goods, is the promise of the world. It has fallen to her lot to lead mankind; if she denies her responsibility there is no other nation to take her place. But to take up this leadership will require the courageous and self-sacrificing teamwork of both the Practical Men and the Creative Men, who occupy central places in my book, and foremost among them, the Teacher of Teachers.

So, I have returned to my country proud and happy in its record, and humbly grateful for the opportunity to live and work in a democratic society.

HAROLD RUGG

Woodstock, New York
June 12, 1952

Part I

THE TEACHER OF TEACHERS
Leader or Follower?

CHAPTER I

The Penalties of Leadership

I

This is a book about the Teacher of Teachers in America, and this is the principal thesis:

Theoretically, in a democratic society, the Teacher of Teachers should prove to be a man whose resources match the penalties of leadership. In a dynamic society he is the chosen change agent, the clear guide for the culture-molding process. Potentially, I say, he is one of the true creatives of the people. But actually, in our society, matters have turned out otherwise. Instead of leading, he is following. Instead of creating the new he is reciting the categories of the old. The cause resides in the development of Euro-American industrial culture. Its history, in all continents and all epochs, gave the leadership to the Practical Man. Western culture today, as it was in every century of its growth, is still marked by a deep dichotomy between the Practical Man and the Creative Man. The former, man of action, has always been regarded as the safe and efficient leader and has risen to the top of the ladder of prestige and power; the latter was merely tolerated on the lower rungs as an inferior follower and echoer of his superior.

This selection from the reservoir of our resources of energy and design was not only accepted by the people; they pointed to it with pride. In spite of the tragic crescendo of the business cycle of economic chills and fevers, the slack was so great and the cultural expansion so rapid that the erroneous guesses of the Practical Man could be assimilated without too great pain. And so the people continued to follow him.

But in the twentieth century of World Wars and Great Depressions the lag in the institutional and moral culture behind technology has become so great, and the creative tasks so baffling, that even the man on the street has begun to sense that the penalties

3

of leadership are too great for the meager resources of the Practical Man. His heavy industry, supplied by the Creative Man with all the makings of automatization—radar, the feed-back, the vacuum tube, sequential analysis—has now reached the verge of manless production. Alternative vistas confront him: a society of robots operating clever machines, men with full stomachs and empty hands and minds; or, happy men engaged in creative labor. The people must choose soon which they want most.

Thus mid-century America has come out upon a new frontier and must chart a new course. It is a psychological frontier, an unmarked wilderness of competing desires and possessions, of property ownerships and power complexes. It is also a jungle of power politics, in which momentous decisions must be made from drastic alternatives. They must be made by the people—the democratic principle requires it—and creative persons are now needed to lead them. Creative, I say. Neither technical efficiency nor political cleverness will serve; only creative imagination can see us through these next twenty-five years.

This compels a reconsideration of the resources of leadership. The Creative Men must now rise to the top and the Teacher of Teachers looms prominently among them. As they face their overwhelming tasks, however, they do not start from scratch. A company of imaginative older brothers, in the fifty years just passed, has blazed a creative path through the intellectual jungle of the modern world. The conceptual gifts of the great age of expression, in which they have built a new Science and Art of Man, will serve us now.

Have the Teachers of Teachers had access to these great concepts that guide our trends? They could have had, for the scholars were laying them bare, all through the decades from the 1890's to the 1950's. But throughout that time most of them ignored the resources of the creative revolution. Between the 1890's and World War I, the first professors of education improvised the nation's first draft of teacher education without any reference to this body of knowledge. These professors were the spokesmen for the Practical Men and got their education as worshipful students of the Victorian exponents of the liberal arts. Thus teacher education had little to do with the changing civilization surrounding the teachers colleges. The rank and file of the Teachers of

Teachers continued in the Conforming Way throughout the Long Armistice and the Forties.

But World War I brought a small company of brave and imaginative ones to the Creative Path where, in the second generation, the 1920's to the 1950's, they found conceptual keys to the problems of our times. It is from the actuality of their magnificent leadership that we know that the Teacher of Teachers can now become one of the sure pilots through the storms of our day.

This is the dominant thesis of my book.

Several minor theses, presented briefly, will supply the prologue to the little-known drama of teacher education.

II

I begin with the centuries-long split in the culture. Western civilization has run its course in two streams of life. One has been the practical, get-it-done, efficiency strand, which I call the Practical Tradition, and its leaders the Practical Men. The other is the stream of creative thought and feeling which received its impetus from the idealization of the Good Life. This strand I call the Great Tradition, and its leaders, the Creative Men. The credit for building the magnificent physical structure of modern civilization goes to the two traditions, jointly; neither one alone could possibly have done it. As we appraise it today the results are both good and bad. On the good side is the powerful industrial producing system that gives our people the best physical life of any nation on earth; given a good distributing mechanism, it could now bring the abundant life to all. But the bad is mixed in with the good—an uncontrolled price and distribution system, horrid slums, great depressions of unemployment, racial tensions, a general acceleration of mental disturbance in the population, and inability to achieve permanent peace.

Whenever the Practical Men were given their head, they carried on without conscience; the ensuing climate of opinion I call the Exploitive Tradition. Under its drive the Practical Men preempted the land for the strong, aggressive first-comers, and exploited it without let or hindrance. This denied the sustained-yield principle and produced individualism on the march—a ragged as well as rugged individualism. It was this Exploitive Tradition that has gripped most of the practical men throughout much of recorded history. An unending conflict developed around their struggle to control property and government. In the long run the clever ones always came to control the property and hence the government and the cycle of war and peace. In modern times this conflict has been marked by the rise and fall of economic and social classes and of governments, and resulted in the destruction of whole peoples.

The impasse between the Practical Men and the men of creative feeling and thought has existed throughout the centuries, dividing the men of energy and productiveness in every modern industrializing nation. It was long in England, France, Germany, Italy, Scandinavia, Spain. It is now showing itself in China and in the changing Latin-American countries. And I feel sure that if we could penetrate the Iron Curtain and gain the confidence of the men of integrity and creative energy in the Soviet Union, we would find it there also. It is a culture-wide, a world-wide split.

The split is still deep in our culture. It shows itself in the contempt of the town for the gown, and in the casual epithet of the practical men for the teachers and the artists—"They've never met a pay-roll"; for all those, in fact, who have never made much money or achieved positions of public prestige. In World War I the army men referred to us as "the damned psychologists"; today, irresponsible, demagogic Congressmen generalize about "the damn professors." Among the Teachers of Teachers the effect of living in such a climate of opinion is clear—not a platoon in an army of them is concerned with either the theory or the practice of reconstruction.

The impasse is in fact over the ordeal of ideas. The Practical Men give themselves to organization—to pushing things and men around into categories and grooves. Catching glimpses of the ordeal of thinking and imagining, by trying it a bit here and there and backing away from it, they shun any problem that involves more than one-step perception. If they should be confronted by a hierarchy of concepts such as those we are compelled to deal with in this book, they would run as from the plague, denouncing those who indulge in such study as subversive. Expressing this split in psychological terms, the Practical Men are men of percept—the Creative Men, men of concept. They can be visualized on a continuum from the one-step perception of the Conforming Way to the complex conceptual relationships of the Creative Path.

This is the cultural stage set, sketched in its bold contours, in Chapter II of my book.

III

In this tragic moment in world history,
In the midst of dire national danger . . . of bewilderment
    . . . of defeatism,
Creative Americans are drawing the curtain aside
    on a vista of world communal life
    . . . of a civilization just over the horizon
    whose wealth, beauty and spirit
Will stagger the imagination and dwarf anything that has
    gone before.

My lines are truer today than they were when written a decade ago.

This will either be our most creative moment, or our country will be turned into another tyrannical fascist state. The supreme need will be imagination, based on encyclopedic knowledge of the new university disciplines. Not skill, not efficiency, not even inventive ability will suffice. The building of technical know-how, important though that may be, will take second place. The engineers, especially those of electronics, will be important, but only those equipped to do really creative jobs. Among the men of imagination the Teacher of Teachers will be called upon to put his talents to work far beyond the conventional fields of education.

The novel problem of world history today—certainly it is a frightening one—may turn out to be the imaginative task of creating a totally new conception of work. Tens of millions of men will be permanently excluded from the mechanized industries, and nonmechanized jobs must be evolved for them. It is now in the technological cards that all heavy industry will become "automatic"—that is, relatively operable *without men*—within a determinable number of years. The electronics men (Wiener, Bush, Leaver, *et al.*) base their time estimates on what happened in World War II. Under the terrifying impetus of the Battle of Britain, the successful invention of radar and its fusion with the vacuum tube, feed-back, sequential analysis, and other principles *took place in less than two years!* If World War III comes, these men agree, all heavy industry *will become automatic—approximately manless—in five years!* If my estimate is correct that we will go on with the cold war, that we will continue to live for a generation on borrowed time, automatization will come about anyway within twenty-five years.

The key idea here is the insistent concept of *"technological unemployment,"* that is, the displacement of workers by machines. During a century and a half, new mechanized industries have arisen each time to absorb those displaced by some major invention. But a new and revolutionary factor has now been introduced: the displacement this time *will be in enormous units and will be permanent.* These technologically unemployed will not find work in new industries because *the latter will be automatic at their birth.* The reason is that the mathematician-engineers have now licked the key theoretical problem of communication-control of the machine and the factory. Given time (either five years of hot war, or twenty-five years of cold war) and they will have built the necessary know-how. So rapidly have scientific factory organization and the necessary electronic instruments been developed since World War II, that it is now possible to build a single giant factory which can manufacture and assemble all of the nation's requirements for a complex commodity. This automatic control of industry has already come into extensive use in such continuous-process industries as paper, canning, steel-rolling, wire and tinplate, oil-cracking, chemical works, in the handling of the dangerous materials of atomic energy, and in the mechanization of office work.

The prospect for man's work is ugly. The persons displaced from all work will be men with food, shelter, and clothing in abundance, but they will be idle men; men with all-day "leisure" and with nothing to do; men degenerating, their souls and their minds inert. In a society which has never accepted the concept of the dole, or the notion that men who do not work can receive support from government, such a condition is unthinkable.

There are three alternatives before us: first, a society of robots, operating clever machines on the order of George Orwell's *1984;* second, a society of idle degenerates, stomachs full, but minds and souls empty; third, a society of happy craftsmen engaged in labor adapted to their creative abilities, but *not competing with the standardized products of the automatic factory!* There are no other choices. In the next generation we have to decide which we want.

IV

The engineers are convinced that the trail now being followed by the industrializing nations of mixing men and machines together in the same factory will lead to some kind of robot society. The recent proposals of the electronics men show that they see the problem clearly and know how to build a production system which will stop the mixing of men and machines and leave the men free for a craft and creative life. This is heartening but does not go far enough. The engineers leave us with the mere hope that men may have "an era of peace and creative human development."

But we shall not have it unless we create it. Who among us can do it? The cue to the answer, it seems to me, lies in the inevitable fact of the mechanization of most of the jobs of the current factory system. There is no use in persuading displaced workers to go into new mechanical industries, for those are being mechanized too. The task is clear: *we must invent jobs that cannot be mechanized.* The necessity for this is clarified by studying just what it is the new "giant brains," computing machines, cannot do. Dr. Vannevar Bush, the distinguished inventor of the modern analogue computer, makes their limitations very clear. It is established that the computer *can* "think"; that is, it can solve in one minute problems that would take two mathematicians six months. But it is equally clear that it can do that only if a human mind—a creative mind—can build the coded premises of the problem into the machine. *The machine cannot think creatively.*[1] It is clear, therefore, that even in heavy industry there will be some demand for men of imagination. Their numbers are today severalfold larger than twenty years ago; but, compared to the total number that will be displaced, the number of creatives needed in industry will be infinitesimal.

Nothing will be more important in the era of the society which lies ahead of us, therefore, than the concept of creative labor.

[1] See Norbert Wiener's *Cybernetics: Communication Control in the Animal and the Machine,* and his *The Human Use of Human Beings;* also Vannevar Bush's *Modern Arms and Free Men;* and many others in the technical literature.

As I said at the trough of the depression: "Our social order will
be great not because the twelve-hour day becomes the four-hour
day but because work of any prolongation becomes a happy and
creative experience." Not leisure but labor must become the psychological focus both of life and of education. *Our chief cultural
goal is not goods, but men.* Thus the emphasis will be upon the
process of creation, not upon the product itself. Goods of high
quality will, of course, be an outcome from all labor, but they
will be by-products; the mind and personality of the craftsman
are the true objects of concern.

V

In the course of the next twenty-five years our people will be
compelled to confront another novel problem that will, perhaps,
be as baffling as that of creating a wholly new theory and practice
of work. It too is a problem that magnifies the tasks of statesmanship that the Teacher of Teachers must now take up. Our people
will be forced to use their national system of schools and colleges
as a free forum for the study and discussion of the crucial issues
dividing mankind today.

This affirmation may be questioned by some of my readers, for
national school systems have never been employed as public
forums on issues of deep controversy. They are a nation's chief
instrument for indoctrinating the dominant beliefs and values of
the way of life. Their function has been to pass *on* the culture,
not to *pass* on it. That is the tradition, but it will now be changed.
As I said, we have already passed out onto a new frontier and our
problems are matters of *mass psychology.* We have reached a
point of inflection on the curve of industrializing culture—the
opening years of a new stage of history. Finding themselves in
this position, the people are warned that they must take account
of their ways of living, assess their concepts, and make conscious
decisions concerning new directions.

It becomes inevitable if we are to prevent our democracy from
turning into a fascist state that the schools and colleges must
become public forums on public issues. The chief task is to
change men's minds, for the impending decisions must be made
by the people. If fundamental changes in control and organization
are to be brought about, the people must believe in them and

want them. It is clear, therefore, that new public minds are to be created. New climates of opinion must be formed in the neighborhoods of America. This can be done only by creating millions of new individual minds and welding them together into a new social mind. Old stereotypes, outmoded by the changing culture, must be uprooted; new ones, grounded in documented fact, appropriate to our times and our needs, must be established.

But this is the task of education, and the Teacher of Teachers is the only potential leader on the horizon who can promptly make himself competent to guide this public process. He is the only man among us with the needed combination of competencies. The engineer, the industrial researcher, the student of government, the public health leader, and the social welfare worker—all these and others have powerful qualifications for special tasks that lie ahead. But they lack the integrating knowledge and experience of design and guidance in the crucial task, which is education. Even the practical men in business and politics have been heard to mutter recently, as though it were a new idea, that perhaps we will have to rely on education as the hope of democracy. The evidence of recent American history denies, however, that they will welcome the use of the schools and colleges as forums for controversial discussion. But the leaders in the foundations of education, and some astute students of government, have long known that government in a democratic society cannot stop short of education itself. Government must include the collective study, discussion, and decision of men concerning their public affairs, and that is a day-by-day self-educative process. In a democracy government and education are synonymous.

VI

This brief glimpse of two of the baffling problems of our crisis culture will document sufficiently, perhaps, for the purposes of this introductory chapter, the thesis that America's dire need is for leaders of creative imagination. Since there is no shred of evidence in history that they can be found, in any numbers sufficient for our purposes, among the Practical Men, we must look for them among the new profession of students of the culture and the Person. We have the needed competence in the men who are building the new disciplines, including the Foundations of Education. Some are already competent in the Social Foundations, others in the Bio-Psychological study of the Person, still others in the new Esthetics.

It is a central premise of my book, therefore, that in the tumultuous scene of the next twenty-five years, the Teacher of Teachers can and must take his proper place among the creative leaders of western culture. To most of our people this will sound like wishful thinking; to some it will seem silly. The Teacher of Teachers—a national leader! In the average community he is but a faint echo of the practical men who regard him as a nonentity and tell him what not to teach. To their cloistered spokesmen in the liberal arts colleges he is uncouth and illiterate, dumb in the company of Latinists, the scorned foster-child of the graduate school. Can this embarrassed barbarian become the pilot guiding us surely through the storms of our day?

Yes, he can, and will. My premise emerges straight from the logic of our needs, a review of the competencies of men today, and the heartening instances of educational leaders living in our midst. This book is primarily an effort to hold before the Teacher of Teachers a mirror that will awaken in him a consciousness of his destiny.

VII

We who devote ourselves to the professional study and practice of education must first make clear to our people that they must give up their naïve belief that there is some inherent magic in education. For over a century they have relied upon it as the guarantee of the treasured democratic way of life. Yet the western world's recent experience should teach us that we must be critical of that assumption. Since 1920 we have learned that dictators as well as democrats can use "education" to build fighting allegiances; witness the success of the mass-education programs of the totalitarian rulers of Italy, Germany, Japan, and Russia. Not less than a hundred million youth—perhaps two hundred—have been indoctrinated in the last thirty years with unthinking allegiance to the discarded concept of a ruling élite class. Instead of education being the instrument with which catastrophe would be avoided, as H. G. Wells predicted at the close of World War I, the race has actually proved to be, as he said when Hitler went into Poland, "a walkover for disaster." The frightening fact is that while attendance in high schools and colleges in democratic states has probably advanced the understanding of democracy, a corresponding increase in the mass education of millions of fascist youth led them to fight on the battlefield, with fanatic zeal and brutality, for fascist ideas and values.

We may as well face it: education can be used to teach *any* shibboleth, to advocate *any* side. It can build stupid robots, create a false sense of understanding, or befuddle men into thinking they are free even while they are slaves of degenerate sadists. It can be so innocuous that it leaves the people inert, bewildered, uncertain of their problems, their resources, or the paths they may choose. Or, it can build intelligently informed citizens who make decisions grounded in knowledge. I repeat, we must define our democratic education boldly and in the concrete terms of our problems and issues. We dare no longer avoid the traditionally shunned and neglected areas in the curriculum. *To keep issues out of the college and the school is to keep life out of them.* The center of "social study" must be the actual root problems of the civilization—not merely the superficial matters of "reform." The curriculum must employ the history of the actual trends and forces that brought about these problems. Teachers must critically confront and teach all the proposed solutions for the issues of our times. This brings controversy into the college, but that is unavoidable if we are to practice the essence of the democracy which we preach.

VIII

I can hear some of my readers protesting: This reliance on study and planning is all very well in a time of peace and complacency, but this is a moment of tragic crisis. Have we time for the long-term tasks of design? Will we be engulfed, bombed out of existence by a shooting World War III, before the peoples of the world, and particularly our own people who must lead, can come to understand the problems sufficiently to solve them peaceably?

I am one of those who, from the study of the social forces and factors in the past fifty years, and of the zigzag turning of events since World War II, have concluded that the third quarter of the twentieth century will constitute a great "breathing space" for the study and answering of these questions. I hasten to add that we may possibly be wrong. History indicates that in the years ahead there will be no interludes in which economic change will slow down and wait for our institutions to catch up. And common sense warns that the blunderings of our politicians and ignorant business and political bosses, who doggedly attempt to administer modern production on the *laissez-faire* principles of the eighteenth century, may not leave us an opportunity to work for the New Day. Hence we must not teach our youth, too glibly, that the New World will inevitably be better than the old one. Social change is man-made, and man himself must create intelligent institutions to cope with the problems of social control created by the incredible changes in technology. But, I repeat, there is a possibility that there may not be time.

There are signposts in the record of recent history. When the confused aftermath of World War I turned the defeated nations of Germany and Italy away from the long mainline of democracy into tragic fascist régimes, many thoughtful men regarded it merely as a short interregnum of dictatorship. They knew, and they were right, that America's giant armament industries could, and would if called upon, knock out the Fuehrers. They assumed that society would then take up the march toward democracy at the point where it had been interrupted in the Twenties. But they were wrong. For one thing, they misjudged the speed of the first technological revolution. They were, indeed, unaware that a novel second phase was already underway, and that the centralization and concentration of industrial control, together with the limitless physical power of production, was forcing the swift acceleration of monopoly. But that is what happened: political revolution began to catch up with technological revolution. The historic fact is that the chief outcome, outside the United States, of the concurrent operation of these factors has been the swift advance of public monopoly. Although the instrument of political change was, in the 1940's, the series of dictated Communist revolutions that swept across middle Europe, it was, more fundamentally, the longer-timed product of "the social organization of the world." Perhaps that accounts for the fact that so few frontier students of society anticipated the speed with which political revolution would roll up after World War II. Nevertheless, it happened, and instead of leaving another full generation for the growth of popular understanding of these social trends, and the consequent invention of new social controls, the preliminaries of the "struggle for the world," which many thought might come near the close of the twentieth century, seem to confront us now. Their focus is in the cold war—USSR *vis-à-vis* USA, with western Europe and the British Commonwealth of Nations on the fringe—and in such trial-balloon, undeclared shooting wars as that in Korea.

These comments are a mere hint of the trends and the critical lineup of forces implementing our warning that there may not be time to use education in building popular understanding. Time may be too short for the people to learn through mass education that they must choose leaders of wisdom and understanding who will build the necessary social controls to keep the world system running and to preserve the indispensable amount of the individual's freedom.

I recognize all these conditions and possible eventualities, yet the positive answer—"Yes, there is time"—emerges from the careful study of the curves of social change in the USA and the USSR since 1917. This convinces me that there will be no shooting World War III in this period. The chief reason is that the USSR simply will not have sufficient heavy industry to fight our utterly fantastic "arsenal of democracy." Not only are we the mightiest technological state of human history; our might is at this moment accelerating at incomprehensible rates. The example I have cited of the automatization of heavy industry brings up a shocking picture of the potential destructive power of our production system, as well as of its power to produce the abundant life. These facts of the rate of acceleration of our heavy industry are convincing to me, and I find confirmation in the current technical literature, that for twenty-five years the hard-boiled realists of the Politburo will not initiate a full-scale world war.

Moreover, as long as we put 20 per cent of our national income, as we are doing today, into the heavy industry of armament we shall not even have that promised Great Depression with 25,000,000 out of work. The social engineers felt sure this would come at the close of World War II. I understand that some among them prayed for it almost nightly in the belief that nothing else would awaken the American people to the basic changes they must make in their social system. The seventy or eighty billions of annual purchasing power that is now being distributed by the armament industries is the governor of the economic machine.

Thanks to that and to the possibility of using the Public Debt we are, for the moment, secure. But when that governor fails to rise and fall with the pressure we shall either solve the key occupational problem of an automatic heavy industry, or we will face social degeneration and possible economic collapse and political revolution. That day, however, is still many years ahead—perhaps fifteen, perhaps twenty-five.

So, I conclude that men of intelligence are given a "time-out" period, not for escape or relaxation—I warn even the middle-aged ones of sixty-five!—but for intense study and the creative tasks of design. *The next twenty-five years should bring forth the most important body of mature design, and reveal the most intense preoccupation with ideas, in the history of our nation.* Progressive educators have a moral obligation to take a leading part in this adventure.

IX

Assuming, then, for the purposes of this book, that I am correct in saying "there is time"—where shall the Teacher of Teachers take hold of his task? He begins where he has the greatest competence and where his influence will radiate most widely. He works at the reconstruction of teacher education.

His prior task is to develop an adequate theory which will organize our wisdom and provide the motive power to put it to work. That we have the ingredients of wisdom is clear, but they must be organized in a great design, on which a program of education can be erected. But every technologist, businessman, artist, every thoughtful citizen who is to build anything knows that before he can design he must have a theory. For example, an owner-designer wishes to plan his house, but he stands impotent until he answers the prior *theoretical* question: What kind of life is going to be lived in it? Answering it, he can design the structure and build. The order of work falls into three steps and these steps are in an imperative sequence—theory, design, building.

This is the thesis dealt with in Chapter IV, but to clear the way for the positive and exciting task, I must introduce a negative note. I fear that before we can have a renaissance in creative theory building in education we shall have to awaken our colleagues to the imperative demands that it makes of us. The most depressing fact encountered on my recent rendezvous with my

colleagues in teacher education is an abysmal indifference to problems of theory. Among a thousand professors who gathered under
their own power to discuss the reconstruction of the *Foundations*
of teacher education, hardly a dozen were actively devoting themselves to rethinking and rewriting the theory of education. The
few that are at work are, I am convinced, beginning to bring
about a new and profound shift in thought. But if some wealthy
"foundation" were prepared today to organize an Institute for
Advanced Studies in Education and Related Sciences, comparable
to the well-known institute at Princeton, it would not be easy to
find a score of students of educational theory with which to staff it.

To the world-shaking intellectual changes of modern times
most of the teachers of teachers appear to present a bland indifference. They teach as though the five-century-long shift in
thought had never taken place. The danger to cultural progress,
including educational reconstruction, of such indifference to indispensable theory is thrown into sharp relief when we consider
the degree to which it is a chronic condition in our profession.
Ever since the first draft of our undergraduate program in teacher
education was written our institutions have tended to be trade
schools rather than centers of thought. We are concerned with
the "know-how" rather than with the "know-what," with the formula rather than the first principle and the equation. Yet this
whole history of modern science should teach us that we shall
not succeed in producing properly designed and organized
teacher-education programs until we first succeed in developing
a sound theory of society—of the nature, behavior, and expression
of man—as foundations of education. It was not until Maxwell,
Hertz, Einstein, *et al.*, succeeded in building a sound theory of
energy (one based on organic explanations), and in discovering
and describing in equational form the electromagnetic field, that
their engineering collaborators were able to build the technical
know-how which solved the electronics problem of the source of
atomic energy and of communication. The "know-what" had to
be conceived in imagination before the "know-how" could be
designed and built. We in education shall be well advised to learn
this lesson that theory and design must precede construction, that
first principles must be discovered and put to work before the
formulas of teaching can be derived. This means that our teacher-
education institutions must rid themselves of their traditional

trade-school temper and become centers of ideas. I take us out to three frontiers of theory in Chapter IV.

X

This brings us to the problem of design and control of the program within the colleges and to another major thesis. Note that the tasks of design and control must be joined. It is a truism of design in technology, business, government, art, or education that the adequate design of anything requires total control of it. The designer and the builder must have control of the entire enterprise—whether it be a factory, an electric power plant, a dam, the government of the community, a corporation, or a river valley like that of the Tennessee. The key to construction is design and the key to design is control. We can generalize the experiences of the communities of men: no true design without control. I was drastically reminded, for example, in conferring with some of the opponents of my treatment of the problem of social planning in my social science textbooks, that it was not "planning" they were afraid of; it was *control*. They recognized that the social system of the country could not be planned and operated without control.

The principle applies to the design of an integrative program of teacher education in a college. I cannot say too emphatically that *the present plan of control will have to be drastically changed if a truly adequate program is to be developed in the teacher-education institutions.* In the state universities and the liberal arts colleges control today resides in the faculties of the sciences and the arts. The educationalists' control over teacher education is almost universally restricted to a minor share in the planning of the program in the junior, senior, and masters' years. Only in the Teachers Colleges, and in those "State Colleges" which have recently developed out of the former teachers colleges, does the education faculty share with the liberal arts faculty in the control and design of the entire undergraduate program. And in only a few of those—where the president and the key administrative group profoundly believe in such unified control and design—does that occur. There are, happily, striking exceptions and I shall discuss these in Chapter V.

The present plan puts the control in the hands of the wrong people. It is in the hands of the professors of the academic subjects who traditionally have been untrained and inexperienced to handle it. It puts control in the hands of those who are confessed opponents of dealing with the problems of modern life in the college and the school, and the died-in-the-wool enemies of "education," which they contemptuously denounce as a cult of "presentism," a cult of "scientism," a cult of "uncertainty."

My thesis is that *no important step can be taken until those who are competent to design the total program of teacher education, from the freshman to the masters' year, are given control of it.* Of all the members of the university community, a nucleus of the younger professors of the Foundations of Education have proved during the last fifteen years that they are competent to do it. But these professors do not now have control, and the design of teacher education is hamstrung. I discuss in Chapter V instances in which the members of the most competent "social foundations of education" group in the United States are being stymied from doing what they need to do, and want to do, by the fact that they do not have control over their own curriculum and teaching. In Chapter IV, in my preface to a Theory of Teacher Education, I deal with this prior problem of control.

XI

These are the principal theses of the book. In the setting of the major premise they describe the tasks for which the Teacher of Teachers must prepare himself in the most creative age in human history. The problem now is to defend these theses with as much documentation and logic as I can command. Material for an article was expanded into a short essay and has now become a small book. To prevent it from becoming a large one, I have deliberately cut the negative materials to leave room for more of the positive achievements of our creative age, and for the positive statement of the problems ahead of us. But the prior task is the awakening of the Teacher of Teachers to his great opportunity and responsibility to lead America in creative reconstruction while there is still time. How can that be done? I have asked myself that question many times since I came home last year from my nation-wide meetings with the teachers of teachers.

I have a cue to the answer in a page in Richard Tawney's *Religion and the Rise of Capitalism*, which I discovered a long time ago. It was a description of:

. . . a magic mirror in which each order and organ of society, as the consciousness of its character and destiny dawns upon it, looks for a moment, before the dust of conflict or the glamour of success obscures its vision. In that enchanted glass, it sees its own lineaments reflected with ravishing allurements; for what it sees is not what it is, but what in the eyes of mankind and of its own heart it would be.

Like the Britain of the early seventeenth century of which Tawney was writing, the dominant orders of American society, even to the twentieth century, have had their magic mirrros. As in England and western Europe, so in America the middle classes saw the great power of their modern Puritanism in their own enchanted glass and rose triumphantly to build the industrial civilization of today. Five advancing frontiers were given vigor by the sober exaltation that those neo-Puritans sensed. For seven "zealous, Godly" generations their emigrant children were "punctual in labor, constant in prayer, thrifty and thriving, filled with a decent pride in themselves and their calling, assured that strenuous toil is acceptable to heaven." Their adamant conquest of the land—by hand!—was propelled on all the new continents by the terrific explosive energy in the doctrine of *laissez faire*.

So in the twentieth century the American business-politician-descendants of those Puritan leaders are still moved by the reflection of the power, the comfort, and the glory in those magic mirrors. During the Great Depression we saw the reflection of the Great Tradition in the words and acts of Franklin Roosevelt, as he gathered and spurred on his National Council of Design at Washington. One senses a similar force inspired from some hidden reservoir of power in the lifelong statesmanship of Jefferson, and in Walt Whitman's great symphonic poem.

But if the teachers of America ever had such a magic mirror, its reflecting power has long been obscured by the low esteem in which they have come to be held. While such other orders of our society as militant labor and dominant business seem to have their respective enchanted glasses through which to renew their energy, the teachers stand impotent. There was a time perhaps when the leaders—Horace Mann and James Carter of Massachusetts, to name only two famous ones—turning their backs on law and moneymaking, saw in the new democracy's mirror their great instrumental function—the education of the teachers who would guide the youth of the future America. But today, when access to such sources of stored energy is needed above all, a profound sense of inferiority in a tense and hysterical society dims the sight of all but a few of acute vision.

This, then, is one of the purposes of my essay—to hold a magic mirror before the teacher and especially before the Teacher of Teachers, in which he can see an image of what, in America's great hour of need, he might become.

CHAPTER II

The Conforming Way:
Teacher Education Improvised, 1890–1920

I

One who visits the universities and liberal arts colleges today senses a widespread inertia among those who are training our teachers. This inertia should really cause little wonder. It is the product of recognizable forces in the culture and the perpetuation of the basic pattern that has been fastened on teacher education for fifty years. The forces surrounding the teachers have conspired to make them timid about making over the schools, or the teacher-education program. The communities in which they went to school and the climate of opinion in their colleges warned them not to be too active. The standard pattern of teacher education taught that the school was to pass *on* the social heritage; it was not to appraise the social order, let alone try to change it. Teachers were to fit into the society. It was a good society, probably the best man had yet produced. If it had weaknesses, let the town fathers correct them. They were practical men. Let the teachers stick to their Three R's.

The confused, transitional nature of our times created many occasions for active groups in the community to reiterate this passive role of teachers. Too many *new* things happened at once in the years between 1900 and 1950; the town fathers could not understand them. I recall the conspicuous ones quickly: totally new ways of producing goods . . . vast "technological" forms of unemployment, in the midst of astonishingly increasing and efficient production . . . a multitude of new uses of government in the social system . . . new and menacing forms of totalitarian dictatorship which tyrannized over half of humankind . . . barbaric mass murders by degenerate fascist and communist leaders . . . new and incomprehensible discoveries in the sciences . . .

one of the world's greatest ages of expression, which produced new—and equally shocking—forms of "modern art" . . . disappearing religious loyalties unaccompanied by clear moral mooringmasts which could take their places . . . and—to top it all—a host of new experiments in education! It was all too much for the Practical Man. The penalties of leadership were too great for his meager resources.

But such a period of confusion has been a gorgeous field day for the clever, self-seeking profiteers and patrioteers of the two world wars and the long armistice. These postwar years of mounting social unrest and hysteria were made to order for the witchhunters. Money was easy to get for rooting out the subversives, whether from a baffled Congress for one un-American committee after another, or for the fine-sounding "National Economic Councils," "Pro-Americas," "National Councils for Education," or "Friends of the Public Schools." Thus, for a generation, we have had one attack after another on good schools: the Red Scare of 1921 to 1924 . . . the Merchants of Conflict manufacturing "treason in the textbooks" from 1938 to 1941 . . . and the current destruction of good education in Pasadena and other progressive cities.

And so fear was bred among the teachers and their teachers. And so also among them grew the mood of let-well-enough-alone. The teachers went back to their Three R's. Too many of them were not too unwilling.

II

The timidity of the Teachers of Teachers would not be a matter of such vital concern if the original pattern of teacher education had really fitted the changing civilization and the needs of our people. But the tragic fact is that the national program of education, including teacher education, created before World War I had little to do with the real world of the twentieth century. It was improvised fifty years ago by men brought up by Victorian defenders of the liberal arts tradition. These classicists utterly ignored—if they were not oblivious to—the devastating social changes taking place around them. And while the program that they fastened upon the youth and the young teachers was adorned with modern sounding labels, it was actually devoid of the true concepts of man and his changing civilization, his behavior and expression, which were already emerging in the scholars' multiplying studies.

III

Another fact of importance is the speed with which the first real program of teacher education was thrown together. The Teacher of Teachers has had to do his work in a period in which changes in education, as well as in the culture, were brought about with great dispatch. A half century ago the American school system had no graduate program of teacher education. There was only the "normal school," a twelve-week to two-year short cut to teaching. By that time an occasional university had included on its faculty a Professor of the History and Art of Teaching, such as Paul Hanus of Harvard, or a Professor of Philosophy and the Institutes of Education such as Nicholas Murray Butler of Columbia. But the more popular label in the few universities that admitted the education of teachers to their higher academic realms was "Professor of Pedagogy."

Some university leaders had been urging the incorporation of "Departments," even "Schools" and "Colleges" of education in their programs for forty years. In 1850 President Wayland of Brown had succeeded in establishing a "course of instruction in the science of education" and another in "didactics," as pedagogy was frequently called, but these were short lived and are interesting only because they seem to be the first courses in education given in an American university. Antioch College, under the presidency of Horace Mann, offered instruction in education, but of not much better than "Normal School" grade, as early as 1853. Between 1856 and 1873, the State University of Iowa tried several times to establish courses, finally getting a "Chair of Mental Philosophy, Moral Philosophy, and Didactics." A group at the University of Missouri agitated unsuccessfully for such instruction in 1867.

The country was becoming teacher-education conscious. Susan Blow and other European advocates of the new principles were developing kindergarten clubs in the larger cities, and making the influence of Herbart and Froebel felt throughout the United States. A "new education," built around the "object lessons" of Froebel and the educational principles of Herbart, was being widely discussed through the National Herbart Society.[1] This had been organized in 1895 under the leadership of United States Commissioner of Education William T. Harris, and of Charles de Garmo, Charles and Frank McMurry, and others. The name of John Dewey appears in its early reports, but a close reading gives us the picture of a cautious and critical appraiser of their ideas standing on the sidelines of the discussions. The widespread and growing interest in Herbartian ideas is shown by the publication of de Garmo's *Essentials of Method* (1890) and his *Herbart and the Herbartians* (1898) the same year the McMurry's best-selling *The Method of the Recitation* and N. M. Butler's *The Meaning of Education* were published.

Finally, in 1879, under the encouragement of President Angell, who had formerly been a student and colleague of President Wayland's at Brown, the University of Michigan succeeded in establishing permanently what is regarded as the first university chair in "Education."[2] Seven years later, 1886, the University of Indiana established a Department of Pedagogy. In 1888 Northwestern University organized "lectures on teaching." In 1889 the University of New Mexico developed a "Normal School" as a part of its regular program. New York University created a school of pedagogy in 1870, the University of Texas, a "school" (really a department) in 1891, Leland Stanford, Jr., University, a full department, and the University of Rochester, a "course" in the same year. The University of Illinois, under the leadership of Frank M. McMurry, and the University of California created departments of pedagogy in 1892.

In spite of all this sporadic activity, even in the late 1890's there was no planned undergraduate or graduate degree course in "education." Educational Psychology did not exist. Educational Sociology had not been conceived. There was no History of Education and no School Administration. Even a definite ordering of

---

[1] This society changed its name in 1902 to National Society for the Scientific Study of Education, the word "scientific" being dropped later to give the name "National Society for the Study of Education." For a half century this has been one of the most influential educational organizations in the history of the nation. As I write, the *Fiftieth Yearbook* (Part I) has just arrived, dealing with the problem of the "Graduate Study of Education."

[2] Actual priority in the western world goes to the two Chairs in Education in Edinburgh and St. Andrews, Scotland.

the principles of education was lacking. In fact, the very university disciplines from which sound Foundations of Education could have been developed had not been conceived. Lacking these, there could be no organized professional knowledge of curriculum, teaching, guidance, and evaluation.

But by the end of World War I all these things had been improvised, hurriedly and enthusiastically put together. All but a few states had degree-granting teachers colleges created out of the normal schools by their ambitious administrators. Graduate colleges of education had been organized in a score of state and private universities. Within one short generation the First Draft of a national program of teacher education was written.

IV

To ascribe this physical achievement to the period between the 1890's and the 1920's does not ignore the magnificent *building* job that had been done by Horace Mann, James Carter, Henry Barnard, Calvin Stowe, and their associates in the preceding half century. These were the pioneers who had fought the battle for free and compulsory universal education, establishing the principle that "the wealth of the State must educate the children of the State." These rid the young country of the pauper-school idea and the Rate Bill, and established the right to tax property generally for the support of public schools. These sufficiently modified the deep-seated American belief in local control to set up state supervision of public schools. These broke down the traditional union of Church and State and eliminated sectarianism from public education. To cap it all, these created free compulsory high school education. In 1850, there were still 6000 private "academies" and only 600 free public schools: by 1900 the private academies had dwindled to 1300 and the free high schools had increased to 7000. At the outbreak of World War I the number was 12,000.

To describe this achievement as a magnificent job of *physical* construction is to praise rather than demean. In an infant democratic society the building of the first schools, colleges, and normal schools was a prior demand upon a people who had little understanding of their problems or of the indispensable role of education. A continental clearance job was being done, and towns and cities were growing. Schools for children and training schools for teachers were imperatively required. For the first time in history men and women, mostly women, were gathered from the homes of farmers, shopkeepers, mechanics, and clerks to learn as best they might in a few months of "normal school instruction" how to teach all the children of all the people.

As we approach the appraisal of teacher education in America, therefore, we must not forget that its entire history is, even in eastern America, little more than a century old. It dates from the first "normal schools" of Massachusetts (Lexington, 1839, Barre and Bridgewater, 1840) of Pennsylvania (1848), of Connecticut (1849), and of Michigan (1850). Not until 1900, when there were 170 institutions, could it be said that each state had a system of "normal education." Even as late as 1913 Professor Strayer,[3] appraising the situation, could say:

Many of the men and women now teaching in the public schools in the United States have never had any definite professional training in preparation for teaching. It is still possible in many states for those who have completed an elementary school to be certified as teachers after a minimum of preparation, consisting largely of a review of the subjects commonly taught in the elementary school.

But the prior legal and physical job had been done.

It was indeed a typical American achievement of swift physical construction. Fifty years of battling for free public schools, followed by twenty years of improvisation, produced the First Draft of teacher education. It was the pattern of this First Draft that molded the Teacher of Teachers throughout the past generation. But the First Draft was a rough improvisation, rather than a true design. The tragedy was that the dominance of the Practical Man over the American climate of opinion, the inexorable processes of cultural change, and the devilish work of the patrioteers did their work too well. The American teacher was made into an echoing follower, not a leader. And the Teacher of Teachers was too ignorant or too timid to endure the ordeal of design.

It is of the utmost importance that we understand, not only the haste in which the first program of teacher education was thrown

[3] In Paul Monroe, *Cyclopedia of Education,* Vol. IV, p. 481.

together, but also the conditions in the civilization, and in the colleges and schools, in which it was done. To do that we must know the men who made it and the forces in home, school, and civilization which made them.

V

Fewer than two scores of men improvised the first teacher-education program. They formed a compact little group, the product of a special culture and outlook on life and of a theory of education based upon it. Twenty-two of the improvisers did their major work in one institution—Teachers College of Columbia University. Eighteen or twenty others were scattered across the country in half a dozen other institutions, but the leadership and the responsibility was in Teachers College.

For clarity I divide the twenty-two into two groups: fourteen outstanding leaders in building the first "Educational Foundations" program; eight others who built the first "Professional Program" in methods and teaching of the school subjects.

1. BUILDERS OF THE FIRST FOUNDATIONS OF EDUCATION

Of the fourteen pioneers who built the original program in Educational Foundations, there were five older and nine younger ones. Arranged in order of birth, the five older ones were:

Charles de Garmo   (1849–1934)
Samuel Train Dutton   (1849–1919)
Charles McMurry   (1857–1929)
Frank N. McMurry   (1862–1936)
James Earl Russell   (1864–1945)

All but Dutton studied in European centers of Herbartian philosophy, getting their doctor's degrees at Halle, Jena, Berlin, or Leipzig.

One of them, James Earl Russell, became—as Dean of Teachers College, Columbia, from 1898–1927—the outstanding administrative builder of the first teacher-education program. Two of the other four men were associated with him in the development of Teachers College. All but one of the nine younger ones (Charles H. Judd) were either students or professors, or both, at Teachers College. Repeating the Dean's name, they were:

At Teachers College since 1898

	AS A STUDENT	AS A PROFESSOR
James E. Russell (1864–1945)		1897–1926 (Dean, 1898–1927)
Ellwood P. Cubberley (1868–1941)	1902–1905	
David Snedden (1868–)	1901–1907	1905–1909, 1916–1935
Paul Monroe (1869–1947)		1897–1923
Ernest N. Henderson (1869–1938)	1901–1903	1915
Edward L. Thorndike (1874–1949)		1901–1940
William C. Bagley (1874–1946)		1917–1940
William C. Ruediger (1874–1947)	1907	
George D. Strayer (1876–)	1903–1905	1905–1943
Charles H. Judd (1873–1946)	Ph.D., Leipzig, 1896	U. of Chicago, 1909–1938

2. BUILDERS OF THE FIRST PROFESSIONAL CURRICULUM IN EDUCATION

Contemporary with these fourteen men were eight others who were pioneers in the development of educational method and school administration. All of these were connected with Teachers College, Columbia, either as students or as professors, or both:

At Teachers College

	DEPARTMENT	AS A PROFESSOR
David Eugene Smith (1860–1944)	Mathematics	1901–1926
Franklin T. Baker (1864–1949)	English	1893–1933
Henry Johnson (1867–)	History	1906–1933
John F. Woodhull (1857–1941)	Physical science	1888–1922
Maurice Bigelow (1872–)	Biological science	1899–1939
Gonzalez Lodge (1863–1942)	Latin and Greek	1900–1930
R. E. Dodge (1868–)	Geography	1897–1916
Thomas D. Wood (1865–1951)	Physical education	1903–1932

These eight men, with the collaboration of Charles and Frank McMurry, largely created the first *professional* curriculum in

teacher education and its books and teaching methods in the
various school subjects of study. Five others from the foregoing
lists—Dutton, Snedden, Cubberley, Strayer, and Judd—collaborated in creating the first graduate study of the administration,
organization, and supervision of schools.[4]

VI

By the 1880's the way was prepared for the strategic institution to take the leadership in building a full-fledged program of
undergraduate and graduate education of teachers. It was in the
cultural cards of the 1880's and 1890's that a new "teachers college" should rise at Columbia to do that. Advantaged by the
attractions of New York City, the nation's metropolis, world
entrepot and cultural center, and by the drawing power of one
of the country's largest institutes of graduate study, no other
urban and education center could rival it. Its tenth president,
Frederick A. P. Barnard (1809–1889) was certainly aware of the
need and the opportunity. As early as 1881 he had responded to
the growing demand for the college education of teachers by
sketching in his Annual Report, "the organization and work of
'a university department of the history, theory, and practice of
education'; and added that, 'education is nowhere treated as a

[4] A dozen others, contemporaries of the twenty-two, collaborated in the
new program in several other universities: Paul Hanus (1855–1941), Professor of History and Art of Teaching, Harvard, 1891–1921; Michael Vincent
O'Shea (1866–1932), Professor of Education, University of Wisconsin,
1897–1932; W. W. Charters (1875–), Professor of Education, in the University of Illinois, Carnegie Institute of Technology, and the Universities
of Pittsburgh, Chicago, and Ohio, from 1917–1942; Walter Jessup (1877–
1944), Ph.D., Teachers College, Columbia, 1911, Professor, Dean of Education and President, State University of Iowa, 1912–1934; Lotus D. Coffman
(1875–1938), Ph.D., Teachers College, 1911, Professor of Education, University of Illinois, 1912–1915, Dean of Education and President, University
of Minnesota, 1915–1938; Edward C. Elliott (1874–), Ph.D., Teachers
College, 1905, Professor of Education in University of Wisconsin, 1907–1916,
Chancellor, University of Montana, 1916–1922, President of Purdue Uni-
versity, 1922–1945; Junius L. Meriam (1872–), Ph.D., Teachers College,
Columbia, 1905, Professor of Education, University of Missouri, 1904–1924,
University of California at Los Angeles, 1924–1943; Ernest Horn (1882–),
Ph.D., Teachers College, Columbia, 1914, Professor, State University of
Iowa, 1915–1951; Lewis M. Terman (1877–), Ph.D., Clark University,
1905, Professor, Stanford University, 1910–1942; Frank N. Freeman, Ph.D.,
Yale, 1908, Professor of Educational Psychology, University of Chicago,
1920–1939, Dean, College of Education, University of California (Berkeley),
1939–1948. And there were others.

science, and nowhere is there an attempt to expound its true philosophy.' "[5]

Money was available in New York, and the trustees of Columbia and their friends had it. Enormous fortunes were being accumulated in the new industrial expansion. Their "Gospel of Wealth," which Carnegie was rationalizing in his autobiography, set the doctrinal tone for the college men. It taught in sermon, lecture, and textbook the obligation of each American to work hard to own property, and to protect it for moral ends. Offspring of a half-dozen generations of Puritanism, Carnegie's secular form of the Gospel was fourfold: individualism, private property, the "law" of accumulation of wealth, and the "law" of competition. He preached for his "capitalist Utopia" the Darwinian concept of the survival of the fittest, "the strong shall inherit the earth." But he accompanied it by the concept of "stewardship"— that is, the obligation of charity. The pursuit of wealth for itself was considered ignoble, but as a means to social ends it could become "a glorious adventure." By the 1880's and 1890's the adventure had already brought about expensive investments by the masters of capital in the humanitarian and philanthropic movements of the day—in social settlements, in colleges, and a wide variety of experiments to "help the masses" of the people. But the "stewardship" of financial help from the practical men carried with it implicitly the right to determine the kind of education the masses got. *The new "teachers college" therefore, owed its origin in large part, and much of its slant for fifty years, to this interest of moneyed people in a "practical" education for the people.* Moreover its leaders' conscious theory of education was definitely given this slant.

This was shown in the initial steps. In 1877 Miss Emily Huntington started several successful "kitchen-garden" schools in New York City, leading to the forming of the Kitchen-Garden Association in 1880. Recognizing that the Kitchen-Garden interest was but a phase of a broader conception that was coming to be called "industrial education," the Kitchen-Garden Association was dissolved on March 21, 1884, and, at the same meeting, the Industrial Education Association was created under the presidency of the young Dr. Nicholas Murray Butler, a Columbia University Fellow

[5] Quoted in Walter S. Hervey, "Historical Sketch," Volume I of the *Teachers College Record*, 1900, pp. 12–35.

in Philosophy. Butler felt keenly the growing demand for the professional education of teachers. He says in one of his essays in the 1890's:

I offered in 1886 lectures in education given on Saturday mornings in the College buildings in 49th Street for teachers and those who were preparing to teach. It was predicted that this undertaking would be futile . . . What happened, however, was that the largest room which the College (Columbia) could then provide was crowded with an interested and attentive audience, chiefly public school teachers, and *more than two thousand requests for tickets of admission had to be declined.* (My italics.)

By 1886 interest had grown to such a point that the Association had committed "to his care the organization and guidance" of a "proposed training college."

That institution, the New York College for the Training of Teachers, with Dr. Butler as President, was opened in September, 1887. He continued to be President until 1891 on which date Dr. Walter Hervey, a professor in the College, was appointed President. On December 14, 1892, the name was changed to Teachers College.[6] Dr. Hervey served until 1897 when Professor James Earl Russell was made Dean of Teachers College and commissioned to reorganize the institution as a degree-granting four-year "professional school for teachers." Promptly he developed it into the first major graduate teachers college in America. James E. Russell[7] served as its Dean from 1897 to 1927, when his son, William F. Russell, was made Dean. (He changed the title to "President" in 1950.)

But by far the most dominating person in the original development of Teachers College and its theoretical orientation was the young Fellow in Philosophy who, by 1890, was Dean of the

[6] The Charter was made absolute, and the name was changed by mutual consent to "Teachers College." The next step was effective July 1, 1893, " 'for the purpose of securing to the students of Columbia College, Barnard College and the Teachers' College reciprocal advantages and opportunities, an agreement . . . was entered into between the above named institutions.' " (Teachers' College, *Circular of Information,* 1893–1894, p. 7.)

[7] Dr. James Earl Russell was a teacher in public schools in the late 1880's; student in German universities in 1893 and 1894, Ph.D., Leipzig, 1894; Professor of Philosophy and Pedagogy in the University of Colorado, 1895–1897; and a professor in the New York College for the Training of Teachers, 1897–1898.

Faculty and Professor of Philosophy and Education and, who twelve years later, began an administration lasting forty years as President of Columbia University—Dr. Nicholas Murray Butler.

The practical arts emphasis in the program, to the neglect of social theory, was established at the very beginning; three of the first five departments in the New York College for the Training of Teachers, in 1887, were called respectively: mechanical drawing and woodworking, domestic economy, and industrial arts. By 1910 these had evolved into a School of Household Arts and a School of Industrial Arts under a single director, the work still being essentially undergraduate. The professional work for teachers steadily increased in importance and step by step the undergraduate years were eliminated and the faculty concentrated on graduate study. In 1923 the School of Practical Arts had become a professional school of technical education on a graduate basis, meeting the standard for graduate work which had been set a decade before by the college's "School of Education," which had, almost from the beginning, housed the foundational and professional courses in the graduate study of education. The "practical" slant persisted in the whole college, consciously cultivated throughout the elder Dean Russell's administration. Not only is this evident as one works his way through the first twenty-seven bound volumes of the *Teachers College Record*, in which much of the accumulating theory and practice of the faculty has been published, but some of us who lived long in the institution,[8] also felt it at close range. Almost every year from 1920 to 1926, the "younger" professors were gathered by the dean at the Faculty Club in small evening conferences and admonished to preserve the "professional and practical" character of the institution. The "academic" work—philosophy, principles, psychology, and history of education—is important of course, he added, but Teachers College is primarily a "professional" school for teachers.

What Dean Russell used to call "academic work"—that is, the phases of study grouped today in Division I of Teachers College, as "Foundations of Education"—and those phases of "professional work" involved in the subject matter and teaching of "the school

[8] I have recently completed my thirty-first and last year, as a professor in Teachers College. I joined the staff, January 1, 1920, and was retired July 1, 1951. My first seven years were in the administration of James Earl Russell, the last twenty-four in that of his son.

subjects," developed in the same years into the College's School of Education. The first volume of the *Teachers College Record,* 1900, presents the syllabi for four of the academic departments: (1) "Principles of Education" (the first form in which Philosophy of Education was offered), by Professor Nicholas Murray Butler; (2) "History of Education," by Professor Paul Monroe; (3) "School Administration," by Professor Samuel Train Dutton; and (4) "National Education Systems," by Professor James E. Russell. The last course developed later into the department called Comparative Education. The first major course in educational psychology was organized in 1901 by Edward Lee Thorndike, a young graduate of Columbia and an assistant of McKeen Cattell who had given some instruction in general psychology. Thus by 1901 four of the six major Foundations of Education courses had been improvised: Philosophy, History, Psychology, and Comparative Education. There was no educational sociology, no educational economics, and no educational esthetics. The study of society was lacking.

VII

So much for the origin and the early structural development of the strategic center in which the First Draft of the nation's teacher-education program was improvised after 1890. Certainly by the moment of the formal opening of Teachers College in 1898 the stage had been set for the swift improvising of the nation's first systematic teacher-education program. Before the close of World War I, in the next twenty years, the structure was set up essentially under the leadership of the two scores of men whom we have named. It was they, in a dozen institutions, who set the mold of teacher education in which the present staff of teachers of teachers grew up. These built the dominant American beliefs and values into the teacher-education program. These made the college courses, wrote the textbooks, and graduated the dozens of doctors in education who built the new state colleges of education. These designed the new educational measuring instruments, made the school surveys, and led in organizing most of the million teachers of the nation into educational associations.

Viewed from our vantage point at the mid-century it was another spectacular building job. Hats off to these men for an efficient piece of *physical* construction. They transformed the trade of teaching into the *profession of education.* Certainly, on the quantitative side, their achievement is important. Begun as an undergraduate college of a few hundred students, Columbia's Teachers College, by the end of World War II, had become a physical giant of more than 8000 graduate students, granting 2000 Masters and 50 Doctor's degrees a year. The massive character of the output is reflected on a smaller scale in other institutions. I felt it as much as any did for I practically lived in Horace Mann Auditorium after 1934. "Classes" of 500 were common; one of 900 (caused by the G. I. influx of 1946) was I guess "the record," but "educationally" not much to be proud of, I fear.

Hats off, I say, to our elder brothers, for an important contribution to American civilization. These were good men and men of good will and they are to be credited with an impressive improvisational achievement. I say this emphatically because I must find severe shortcomings in their achievement. Viewed from our knowledge today of what the vital need for design was in 1900, it fell far short of what America and her children should have had during these past fifty years. Moreover, it fell far short of what the professors could have produced, had they been truly aware of their world.

The tragedy is that, on the whole, these sincere, hard-working Men of the First Draft listened to the wrong people, both in the society and in the college. They listened to the rank and file of the professors of the liberal arts and sciences, who were the spokesmen for the Practical Men and their Gospel of Wealth. I shall give many documentary illustrations in this book. All their lives these men were exponents of the *status quo* and stayed securely within the Conforming Way. They accepted, most of them unquestioningly, the liberal arts curriculum which the same professors, constituting a majority of the NEA's Committee of Ten, were then fastening on the American high school. They became defenders of the conventional faith in every phase of the culture.

It is true that they vaguely sensed that part of the "first" intellectual revolution which produced Pestalozzi, Rousseau, Herbart, and Froebel. But they totally missed the study of society and of behavior, and of the expressive arts, and hence the truly significant things that were being said and done all around them. Had they found the Creative Path, as some of their younger brothers actually did after 1920, they would have built into the national pattern of teacher education the point of view and the key concepts of the "second" intellectual revolution, which was at that moment moving across the western world of scholarship. It was this second intellectual revolution, which I discuss in Chapters III and IV, that was already beginning to produce a new technological revolution and drastic social change throughout the society and the culture.

VIII

Working beside these Men of the First Draft,[9] in the same towns and colleges, was a little band of brave, free, and imaginative men who did not miss these vital materials of education. So important are they and their teachers to my story that I must at least set the conspicuous older ones among them in the record before I deal more fully with the works of the Thirty.

Francis Wayland Parker (1837–1902), first progressive Superintendent of Schools (at Quincy, Mass., 1870–1875); Principal, Cook County (Illinois) Normal School, 1883–1901. Regarded as "Father of Progressive Education."

John Dewey (1859–1952), Professor and Director, Laboratory School, University of Chicago, 1894–1904; Professor of Philosophy, Columbia University, 1904–1930.

William Heard Kilpatrick (1871–), Professor at Teachers College, Columbia, 1909–1938.

Boyd Henry Bode (1873–), Professor at University of Illinois and Ohio, 1909–1944.

Francis Parker—"The Colonel" as he was almost always affectionately called by the thousands who loved him—was the great evangelist of the new education of our times. John Dewey was the profound student and critic of what the improvisers were doing. Kilpatrick and Bode, freeing themselves by 1920 from the blinders of conformist Americanism and education, became the great teachers and interpreters of the movement led by Dewey for the reconstruction of the life and teaching method of the schools.

[9] To avoid the awkwardness of the long phrase: "those who prepared the first draft of teacher education in America," I will refer to them as the Men of the First Draft.

It will make for clarity, therefore, as we study the dominant improvising work of the thirty Professors of Education, to keep the image of this other little group in the background of our minds. It was their theories and experimental practices, and those of the younger men who joined them after 1920, that came to guide the real and deeper attempts at reconstruction of teacher education after 1920.

IX

At this point I must stress the fact that even in the 1880's and 1890's American thought and feeling did *not* present a united front. It was split between a conservative and overwhelmingly majority opinion reflecting the broadly accepted beliefs and values of the nation and a tiny minority opinion of the few thinking people who were even then studying the root factors in the culture and who had come to question seriously some of the accepted ideas and beliefs. The dominant mass opinion, seldom questioned, essentially buttressed the *status quo* in the culture. I call this *The Conforming Way*. The outlook and values in thought and feeling of the creative minority I call *The Creative Path*. The split between them was reflected in the instruction of the colleges and university faculties as well as in the practical political life. The rank and file of the new professors of education followed the dominant majority—the social-political leaders of the community and the liberal arts professors of the colleges. The little group of progressives that, after 1920, gathered around Dewey, followed the students of the new revolutions in thought, technology, and social institutions.

For twenty years—nearly thirty—there was no split in thought and feeling in Teachers College or in most of the other teacher-education institutions of the country. The reason is clear—the professors all thought alike. There was no real minority. Not until the 1920's did one appear and then it was tiny. But steadily it grew in unity and in clearness and conviction and in adamant-ness of purpose and direction. By 1935 to 1940 it was influencing the entire profession. Then, as World War II came and social hysteria and liberal-baiting developed after 1945, it disintegrated, broke into isolated fragments. Individuals went their separate ways. Unity was lost. As I write the men of the Creative Path are scattered and my book has been written to hearten, to help coalesce them, to let them know how right they always have been —and still are.

But the dominant word of the Teachers of Teachers from 1900 to this day has been that of The Conforming Way.

X

The devotees of both majority and minority opinions—that is, Butler's men and Dewey's men—were contemporaries. They were all born just before, during, or after the Civil War. They grew up in the same American communities, they sat in the same college classrooms at about the same time. The older ones got their doctor's degrees in the 1890's, the younger ones just after 1900. Thus their formative and productive years were lived in the great industrial expansion between the Civil War and World War I.

The two groups went to school and college in the midst of the same stir of industrialization, political activity, and changing town and city life. They heard their elders discuss the same problems of local and national government and, so far as their elders were sufficiently educated to do so, appraise the same books and problems. Their childhood was lived at the moment of the passing of the last frontier, at the end of clearance and settlement. Action-expansion-growth was the keynote. Hamlets were becoming towns, and towns, cities; population was doubling every twenty years. Tiny hand forges were being transformed into United States Steel, a few scattered oil wells became the world-ramifying Standard Oil. These young men grew up seeing their lusty third-rank debtor country become World Economic and Military Power No. 1, creditor to the earth, possessor of a giant, technically efficient producing system and the predominance of mankind's developed natural resources. The people were becoming convinced that they could conquer any physical problem. Had they not hacked down a continent's forests by hand, dug a billion dollars in gold and silver by hand, built a transcontinental transport and communication system by hand? They had indeed— and by the American Way. It was a good way; they knew because they had found it good and it was their way. If the world tried to impose another way, they could, if necessary, lick the world or would shortly if that was required to persuade the world to go the good way.

It is a truism to all who today are conversant with the anthropologists' findings about the culture-molding process that home, community, school, and colleges made these drafters of mass teacher education into what they were. In company with 80 per cent of the people they had grown up in middle-class families and middle-class neighborhoods and had been taught by other middle-class teachers. Even though they were elevated to the higher academic realms, most of them continued to reflect middle-class attitudes throughout their lives. I have never been able to escape the conviction that the group, and most of their students and colleagues throughout the country, have always been bogged down by the provincialism from which they sprang.

They were typically American in their beliefs and values. They grew up convinced of the Supreme Value of the Individual, free and equal, but not even vaguely glimpsing the trends toward what Mr. Justice Holmes was just then calling "the social organization of the world." They were convinced that the unique brand of American individualism marked the hope of mankind. It was a reciprocating culture; it promised opportunity and demanded obligation. It was marked by a deep sense of equality and freedom for each individual to grow to his highest potentiality. But the Bill of Rights in this "American Dream" had its corollary Bill of Duties. It was hoped that its very balance would produce balance in its individuals.

Most of these men had been brought up in "the West." Theirs was the third generation of an open society in which the people had restlessly striven for a better life on a succession of frontiers. It was still one of the western world's great success societies; the possession of money and things was quietly held to be the primary measure. The spirit of economic freedom had taught each generation the principle of *laissez faire*—every man for himself. Even down to 1900 it was still a scarcity society and youth were taught the necessity for hard work, thrift, and fair play if they were to climb the ladder of opportunity.

Moreover, it was the most dynamic state of man's entire history and its ideology made men of action of these Men of the First Draft. I do not remember seeing a lazy man—and only one really leisurely man—among them. It was a sensate culture which placed great value on Things, and they were go-getting men. Worry about economic security bothered most of the people, including our professors, most of the time. Property and freedom to own it, to develop it, or to withhold it from use, was central in their creed. Hence property and security came first in the thought of most of these improvisers of teacher education. I doubt if any of them consciously rationalized the concept, but all found security by staying carefully within the Conforming Way. The record is clear that not one of them stepped out of the main line.

They believed in the freedoms—including the freedom to say what they thought. But thinking was to be done in the framework of what the community held to be the American Way. That was never questoined.[10] Listening to them thirty years, I never heard one of them say anything that ran counter to the conforming opinion, and constantly, after 1925, I was publicly made to feel the sting of their rebuke. So they recited the categories of free speech, movement, assemblage, public discussion, the suffrage, and worship—the civil and political rights. But it never occurred to them to question the lack of such economic and social rights in the basic law of the land, as constituted by the National Resources Planning Board's "New Bill of Rights," or the "Nine Freedoms" in the era of the New Deal.

They were all urged by family, school, and town to make the most of themselves. In the 1880's individual success was held before youth as the supreme measure of social progress. Each generation was not only to be on its own, and to bring up its next generation in the conforming climate of opinion, but each one, by capitalizing on the funded experience of its predecessor, was expected to excel the latter's physical achievements. This was Progress—moving higher up the social scale, having more money, comforts—even luxuries—certainly achieving a higher order of education.

But progress, to be good, must come slowly. Although the fathers of our Professors saw many signs of changing physical life around them, they feared social change, especially if it was rapid. Changes in institutions were to be brought about slowly, by consensus, by "town meeting." Gradualness became the theme. Only fifty years before, Jefferson had pronounced for "revolution" every twenty years. But he had just lived through one; his own security had just been brought about by armed

[10] At Dartmouth, from 1904 to 1909, of all the faculty I knew, only George Ranger Wicker, economics instructor, ever questioned.

revolution. In two generations his grandchildren had come to feel that their security required the perpetuation of the *status quo*. The figurative admonition of elders to their sons: "Don't step over the traces," kept the youth in the Conforming Way. Though social institutions as well as technology were being transformed before their very eyes, and it troubled them vaguely, there was little discussion of it.

Even the alternation of fevers and chills in the economic system could not kill the optimism that was bred in the youth by this go-getting culture. Each not only knew that he had a chance to make the most of himself, but he knew also that he was responsible for himself. It never occurred to him that he could turn to the government for help in getting or keeping a job or for any other kind of economic security. In 1900 most young Americans still believed that "the less government, the better." There was little talk about democracy; it was simply accepted, no need to talk about it. In fact, there was not too much confidence among the people in the capacity of most of the people to govern. There was lip service to democracy—meaning with the French, "liberty, equality, and fraternity"—but a feeling also that the American political structure was a "republic," and in the long run government would be more properly conducted by "representatives" who would be chosen more largely from the "better classes." But with the ladder of opportunity available, and conventional higher education (including the doctorate) among the "better classes" as the conforming way to its top, the prospective education planners felt secure about that.

This did not mean that America, in the late nineteenth century, was a class society; no single distinguishing mark of a precisely ordered class society could be discerned. But it was a "rank-order" society, and one of great mobility, a constantly shifting welter of interest-groups—economic, political, social. Status was appraised on the basis of "What does he do?" "What has he done?" Even the son of the upper-uppers had to do something to be accepted. Children in school, youth in college, and grownups generally were measured on the questioning yardstick: "Have you done it better than these others?"—not, "Have you done it as well as you can?" After 1910 the first school surveyors and test-makers measured the achievements of school systems and of individual children on this rank-order principle.

This whole way of life in which the prospective teachers of teachers were brought up was the Conforming Way. They were taught by the parental and community culture to conform as well as to compete, to fit into the neighborhood and the town, to accept the common mores and codes of behavior, to become substantial citizens. "Keep off your neighbor and keep your neighbor off" was the precarious goal set before them. Although the climate of opinion was sentimental about the underdog, youth were warned that the rungs of the ladder of opportunity grew smaller as they climbed toward the top. If there was not room for all, it might be necessary, while striving to *serve* their neighbors, to fight them for a place on the ladder. Compete and conform! Inevitably the concept of personal integrity suffered.

XI

Going to college in the 1870's and 1880's did not lift my older brothers out of the deep ruts of the Conforming Way. On the contrary it confirmed their acceptance of it. The same traits and beliefs that had been cultivated by family and community were still further nourished in their colleges and the graduate schools. Most of them had their undergraduate studies in such small colleges as Wesleyan in Connecticut and the Wesleyan in Ohio, and western state universities—Indiana, Wisconsin, Michigan, Illinois, Minnesota, and California. A few found their way to private institutions—Johns Hopkins, Yale, Columbia, Syracuse, and Chicago. But the dominant tone in all of these, even of the new "scientific" universities—Johns Hopkins and Chicago—was in keeping with the pervasive overtone in the culture, "thoroughly Christian, and distinctly and earnestly evangelical." Most of the private colleges had been developed from frontier days for just such theological purposes; they were denominational institutions. But as the state universities were established, the climate of opinion— even in graduate classrooms—was also marked by an authoritarian and theological spirit. Johns Hopkins in 1876 and Chicago in 1893 also reflected the clerical mood; science and mathematics classes were opened with prayer and a third of the professors had received their degrees in theology. G. Stanley Hall, the leader of the new "scientific" psychology at Johns Hopkins and Clark, also a degree-holder in theology, maintained that the new psychology should be "Christian to its root and center." The science that

Thorstein Veblen studied at Carlton, at Yale, or at Cornell in the 1880's explained the uniformities of nature as the operation of "final causes"; even the physical sciences found the order in the universe to be teleologically controlled. As late as 1910 the teaching of "Natural Philosophy" was obsessed with "predestined forms" guided by the "unseen hand of an overruling Providence."

The split in the "American mind" to which I have referred was duplicated in the college faculty mind. Veblen and his biographers speak constantly of the fact that his generation was taught "two incompatible habits of thought." One was the scientific trend, thoroughly materialistic, at the very center of which was Darwin's evolutionary ideas. The other was a "personal, animistic point of view." This was further complicated, and certainly confused, by the utilitarian philosophy in economic life—the college professors' rationalization of *laissez faire*. While on the one hand they insisted that "unrestrained human conduct makes for the general welfare," their minds were also asked to balance it with the dictum that "its ultimate axiom is an uncritical natural law which inscrutably coerces the course of events." This was the doctrine that Butler, Russell, Monroe, Dutton, Thorndike and Judd, Charters and Henderson, Ruediger and Bagley (and Dewey, Parker, Bode, and Kilpatrick too) heard in their lecture rooms and from the pulpit, while its reverberations were felt in the business life of the nation, in legislatures, courts, and press. Moreover, some of these young men had personally felt the inexorable workings of the theory. Sons of landowning farmers, they had seen their elders dispossessed of their lands by transplanted New England Calvinist lawyers, bankers, and finance promoters. Veblen makes this clear.

The striking contrast between the major and the minor points of view—the Conforming Way and the Creative Path—is shown by what the two groups took from Darwin's theory of evolution. All of the older men—Butler, Russell, Dutton, *et al.*, and Dewey, Veblen, Robinson, Boas, *et al.*—had grown up and gone to college in the midst of the Darwinian controversy. By the time they were in graduate school their professors had generally come to accept certain implications of the theory of evolution. The effect upon the college textbooks in the natural sciences and in history was dramatic. As Randall said of the trend, "every history blossomed out into an 'evolution.'" Even though the historical method they exhibited was little more than a routine chronological survey of the obvious and innocuous events and facts of political life, most histories of that day excluded economic, social, and psychological materials. Thus when Butler wrote *The Meaning of Education,* and Monroe and Graves wrote their histories of education, and Bagley, Henderson, Ruediger, Thorndike, and Strayer, their various *Principles of Education,* they all "accepted" evolution, as did of course Dewey, Veblen, Robinson, *et al.*

But from the writings of the professors of education it is clear that evolution meant to them "adjustment," "adaptation"—that is, conformity. In fact the textbooks in education and psychology from 1900 to World War I were built very largely around the concept of adaptation, their leading theme being "education as adjustment." O'Shea's book carried that title, and the theme and the words were all through Bagley's *Educative Process* (1905), Ruediger's *Principles of Education,* Henderson's *Textbook in the Principles of Education,* Strayer's *Brief Course in the Teaching Process*—all of which were published in 1910.[11]

XII

The chief formative influence was Butler's. Because of his tremendous personal energy, initiative in launching and organizing new enterprises, and the range of the sounding board which was given to his voice—the presidency of the New York Training College for Teachers and (after 1902) of Columbia University—his pronouncements were listened to all over the country. In the famous publishing year of 1898, his addresses, given before the NEA and other regional and national organizations in the 1890's, were gathered together in a volume entitled *The Meaning of Education.* My own graduate study of "education" in Illinois (1911) began with the reading of this book, and I think it is fair to conclude that at that time it constituted generally the student's first "Introduction to Education." A comparison of its doctrine with the principles of education stated in a dozen volumes of the Teachers College group before World War I shows its formative influence.

Its basic concept was "a gradual adjustment to the spiritual pos-

---

[11] The reader is urged to look forward to my discussion (in Chapter V) of Van Wyck Brooks's attack on this concept of the practical men and their college spokesmen in 1915.

sessions of the race." This emphasis upon adaptation had come down through three generations from Charles Darwin's grandfather Erasmus, and Lamarck, and through Lyell and his *Principles of Geology* (1830) to Butler and the professors of philosophy and pedagogy in the 1890's. Its theme was: "Education is the adjustment of the individual to his world," not the building of the mastery of control over his world, as Dewey, Veblen, Robinson, *et al.*, maintained. The child, says Butler, must understand "that although he is an individual he is also a member of the body politic, of an institutional life in which he must give and take, defer and obey, adjust and correlate." There is a constant emphasis upon the "defer and obey, adjust and correlate," as there is upon the religious inheritance of the child without which he cannot become "a truly educated or cultivated man." Answering Spencer's famous question: "What knowledge is of most worth?" he said, "The highest and most enduring knowledge is of things of the spirit," meaning by it "that humanism which Petrarch and Erasmus spread over Europe." And he concludes that section of his book with a peroration, "that while no knowledge is worthless . . . yet that knowledge is of most worth which stands in closest relation to the highest forms of that spirit which is created in the image of Him who holds nature and man alike in the hollow of His hand."

These "Spiritual possessions of the race" are to be passed on through the seven liberal arts, which proclaim the majesty of the humanist culture of western Europe. This message of the greatness of the cultural heritage and the best of all possible educational media—namely, Europe's medieval seven liberal arts—was reflected also in the writings of Russell, Dutton, Monroe, Strayer, Henderson, Bagley, and the other new professors of education. In Butler you were told that western civilization developed a "wonderful institutional heritage." When one searches for the documentation, he finds it in the "right of private property, common law, the state, the Church." The new pedagogues came into the higher realms of education holding themselves to be the defenders of property rights and the "republic" conception of government by an élite. Butler distinguishes between the education of the better classes and "an educated proletariat—to use the forcible paradox of Bismarck—[which] *is the continuous source of disturbance and danger to any nation.*" (My italics.)

Acting on this conviction, *"the great modern democracies . . . are everywhere having a care that in education provision be made for the practical, or the immediately useful."* He was writing such things at the very moment when Thomas Bailey Aldrich, editing *The Atlantic* in Boston, "as Lowell wished it kept," was referring to the men of organized labor as *"the lazy canaille . . . the spawn of Santerre and Fouquier-Tinville."* And across the Charles River, Harvard's literary professor Paul Elmer More, praising a society ruled over by the "natural aristocracy" of economic power, was frankly revealing the attitude of his class toward the people: *"Looking at the larger good of society, we may say that the dollar is more than the man and that the rights of property are more important than the right to life."* (My italics throughout.) Property more than life itself? Incredible? Perhaps, but there it is for all who can read to ponder.

Here was the beginning of the view that was consciously taught the teachers: education is to transmit the culture, not to criticize it or rebuild it. It is to pass *on* the culture, not to *pass* on it. Nowhere in Butler, or in Monroe, Strayer, Ruediger, or Thorndike, or in Henderson—whose book is by far the best of these earlier ones—is there the slightest intimation that the student of education is to be a critical student of civilization. The all-pervasive tone is that he is to understand it, accept its beliefs and loyalties— that he is to conform.

Creative reconstruction is not in the plan for American education as developed in the first quarter of our century by these men of the Conforming Way. It was, however, all through Dewey, and in his younger associates in the *Social Frontier* group thirty years later. It was in Veblen, Robinson, and Beard, Thomas and Boas, and in all the leaders of the Creative Path. From the study of the Darwinian concepts they got the great idea of growth and development. With a thrill of admiration for Darwin's use of the scientific method, they got the idea of a direct, first-hand analysis of the actual conditions and problems of industrial society. More than any other single event, the concept of evolution led these young men of the 1890's to put the scientific method to work in the study of our civilization, to find out by face-to-face analysis the meaning of the problems of men and the resolution of the actual forces at work in the American scene, and to find out that light could be thrown on these by the discovery of all the tabooed strands of history that had never been taught before. Here were the makings of a new science of man—in Veblen, Turner, Robinson, *et al.*

But not in Butler, *et al.* Forty years after my first reading of it, I found *The Meaning of Education* on my library shelves and read it again, marveling that so many nice words could express so few important ideas.

XIII

The failure of Butler and his contemporaries does not excuse us from not seeing our problems clearly or for failing to be critical of our elders' failure. We have no business in teacher education today if we cannot recognize our basic problem. That basic problem today is the same as theirs was in 1900. It is to build a great theory and program of education from the scholars' most profound knowledge of the actual conditions and trends of our society and culture and of human behavior and expression. That was the problem of Butler, Russell, Dutton, Monroe, Thorndike, *et al.*, fifty years ago. The need in 1900 was to see Young America, living in the first transitional years of a rapidly changing society, and to face it boldly and competently from the new knowledge that was springing to life. There were five frontiers of the imagination then, as now, and there were scholars working on each of them:

1. *The Social Frontier:* The study of man and his society, the foundations of every aspect of the culture—its economics, geography, anthropology, sociology, politics, history.

2. *The Human Frontier:* The physiological and psychological study of man, his nature and conduct—all as a part of the expanding study of the organic life of the living creature—his health and its betterment through a better agriculture, medicine, hygiene, sanitation, and diet.

3. *The Frontier of the Expressive Arts:* The study of man's esthetic statement of his view of life, and his attempt to portray it through every conceivable medium of expression.

4. *The Frontier in Philosophy and Religion:* The study of man's objects of allegiance, his methods of inquiry and ways of working—the Great Tradition.

5. *The Educational Frontier:* The application of the foregoing in the conscious design and construction of a better education.

The need was there in 1900, as in 1950: first, to build five great Foundations of Education: Social Foundations, Bio-Psychological

Foundations, Esthetic Foundations, and Historical and Philosophical Foundations. Second, on these to erect the Professional Program in curriculum, guidance, teaching, and administration that would put the theory and the knowledge to work.

Did they meet this need? A brief appraisal for each of these areas will set the stage for our discussion in Chapter III of what they might have done.

Social Foundations? They built nothing worthy of the name.

Bio-psychological Foundations? "They" (Thorndike almost unaided) created the first Educational Psychology, original and provocative in scope, useful as a guide to many important problems of teaching, but utterly inadequate in content, and definitely out of step with the major shift in thought from mechanism to organism that was transforming all of the sciences and arts.

Esthetic Foundations? Nothing, absolutely nothing! They totally ignored one of the world's greatest expressive ages in which they were living, and set a mold of hyperintellectualism in which teachers have been cast to this very day.

Historical Foundations? They labored mightily and brought forth conventional academic studies which as Cubberley said in 1918, had "little relation to present day problems in education, and . . . failed to function . . . in orienting the prospective teacher."

Philosophical Foundations? Encyclopedic courses in and books on "Principles of Education" galore, but until Dewey—who was not of their company—produced *Democracy and Education* (1916), nothing worthy of the name.

XIV

At this point a bit of documentation about each of these will suffice. The cumulative evidence and argument on the point will, I think, be clear by the end of Chapter V. The sources for the generalizations are the professors' syllabi and their textbooks, which came from the presses between 1900 and the beginning of World War I. It was by these texts that they exercised such nation-wide influence in giving teacher education in our time its formative stamp. They taught the doctors and the masters who went out and built the normal schools and schools of education over the country and passed on the New Word to other young doctors and masters, who then went out and passed it on to tens of thousands of others. *The nature of that Word became of the greatest importance.* The thing snow-balled up and out until it became the essentially standardized teacher education of our times.

The formative influence of a few men of great energy and initiative was even deeper, for they not only wrote the widely used textbooks; they stimulated the strategically placed professors to write the books and brought authors and publishers together in popular "Educational Series." N. M. Butler had two series in the 1890's and early 1900's: "The Great Educators" and "The Teachers' Professional Library." Dean James E. Russell had one, "The American Teacher Series." Paul Monroe had two—one for major textbooks entitled "The Text-book Series in Education," and one entitled "Brief Course Series in Education." W. C. Bagley gathered a group of authors for another: "The Modern Teachers Series." Perhaps the most influential one was Ellwood P. Cubberley's "Riverside Textbooks in Education," which covered the entire field of education and psychology and included scores of authors from universities and colleges over the nation. Two of my first books were published in it—*Statistical Methods Applied to Education* (1917), and *A Primer of Graphics and Statistics* (1925). So lucrative was the series, and so wisely did Dr. Cubberley invest his royalties, that at his death he was able to bequeath to Stanford University nearly half a million dollars for the erection of Cubberley Hall, the new education building.

XV

FIRST: THE SOCIAL FOUNDATIONS

I said they produced nothing worthy of the name. No other conclusion can be drawn from their works for the first thirty years. By and large, they ignored society; as for "the culture," they wrote and taught as though they were unaware of it.

In some of them, a single chapter in twenty was devoted to "education and society." But it was discussed in terms of the evolution of "social heredity," the "historical necessities of schools in modern civilization," "the school as the outcome of conscious socialization," or "education is necessary because of the necessity of social control." The content dealt with such vague general concepts as "sociality," "social ability," "the traits of cooperation, imitation, and sympathy." They all recognize the twofold aim of education—the social aim as well as the individual objective—but show no concern with building a fundamental understanding of, interest in, and tendency to act upon the problems and issues of American and world society in 1900. Their pronouncements provided "for the formation of habits which are socially desirable" and for the inculcation of "regularity, helpfulness, industry, fidelity, honesty, truthfulness, cleanliness . . . patriotism" (which should be made habitual). But the treatment of the "role of education in society" is little more than a brief description of how various types of societies have employed education. There was much concern in building "interest," or sympathy, in the welfare of society; the professors dwelt at great length on such questions as: "Is there any real opposition between . . . the welfare of the individual and the good of society." I can testify from being taught by them that they recognized vaguely the perennial problem of I and We, freedom and control, but the discussion never landed. There was no consideration of social problems and issues, or of alternative programs of action for improving society. For the teacher, action in community and national life was taboo. "The development of citizenship" was accepted as a goal of education but never implemented in educational theory or practice. Professors even criticized their own courses saying, as Strayer did: "We do much to arouse the sympathy of children in the general welfare; we give them little opportunity to form the habit of social service." And the general welfare was never clearly defined in terms of such issues of that day as the labor-capital struggle for power, the problem of property ownership, the issues of racial and religious conflict. In not one of the books which I studied and have recently re-examined, published between 1895 and 1915, was there any discussion of the actual transformation that was under way in technology and the increasing unemployment produced by it, the unionization of labor, the problem of strikes, the conflict between Negroes and whites, Jews and gentiles, either in the South or in the industrial cities of the North, the basic trends in socialization, the issues raised by extreme left political parties, the economic imperialism that had been rampant for a hundred years in the leadership of Britain, France, Germany, and other industrial nations. Neither did they deal with personal problems of frustration and anxiety, of the individual human being, and the factors producing them in home, neighborhood, community.

My reader may be thinking: "But there was no 'social science' worthy of the name in existence in 1900." That is true, at least there were no definitive tomes interpreting the economic, social, and political changes in the new industrial society. Being suddenly elevated to the higher realms of the university, the schoolmasters —the first professors of education—had been given the task of improvising a new body of subject matter that would be accepted as a university discipline. *But they were given this task at the very moment when the modern physical, natural, and social sciences, which constitute the current university disciplines and which have increasingly taken the places of the medieval seven liberal arts, were themselves only beginning to take shape.* At the turn into the twentieth century there was no social science; the work of Comte, Spencer, and Ward had, as Giddings said, "merely predicted sociology." Hence the first professors of education could not be expected to build an *educational* sociology—at least nothing beyond Comte-Spencer-Ward-like speculations, which most of them had studied in the graduate school.

But they *were* surrounded with scholarly and provocative studies, dealing with the critical issues, problems, and trends and they could and should have used them. As early as 1893 Robinson had published his essay in "The New History," and Turner his presidential address on "The Significance of the Frontier in American History." Veblen had turned out *The Theory of the Leisure Class* in 1899, but this was regarded throughout most of these years as an amusing satire on conspicuous waste in frivolous American society; only an infinitesimal group among the scholars understood that it was a profound interpretation of our economic-political epoch, and marked the beginning of modern *social psychology*. Not one in a hundred of the educationalists understood the significance, if they were aware of the event, of Supreme Court Justice Holmes's recurring reminder that "the world is being socially organized." Moreover, by World War I, at the very moment when most of the new textbooks on education were coming from the presses, a dozen major products of the new scholarship in the social sciences *were* available. To name but a few: Veblen's *Theory of Business Enterprise* (1903), Simon Patten's, *The New Basis of Civilization* (1909), Charles Cooley's *Human Nature and the Social Order* (1909), and his *Social Organization* (1909), J. Mark Baldwin's *Individual and Society*

(1910), Graham Wallas' *The Great Society* (1912), Franz Boas' *The Mind of Primitive Man* (1911), Charles Beard's *Economic Interpretation of the United States Constitution* (1913), John A. Hobson's *Evolution of Modern Capitalism* (1914), James Harvey Robinson's *The New History* (1918), and Frederick J. Turner's *The Frontier in American History* (1921).

I repeat, there were no *Social Foundations in Education* in the first improvisations of teacher education.

XVI

SECOND: THE HISTORICAL FOUNDATIONS OF EDUCATION

I have struggled for thirty years with the problem of how to incorporate history into the education of teachers and children. The experience convinces me that in no field have our efforts been more abortive. Even today, after fifty years, we have no clear prevision of how to use history in education. But we do know that we *must* use it, and that it must be the history of the vital movements of our changing civilization, the trends that have brought about our real conditions and problems and issues. That our elder brothers of 1895 to 1920—Dexter, Monroe, and Graves—did not understand it is very evident from their textbooks.[12]

Monroe's various texts set the mold for twenty-five years. They were straight, slow-moving, chronological accounts, most of the story dealing with primitive, ancient, and medieval education and eighty per cent of it set in the framework of the "educational classics" published before 1860. There was no analysis of the industrial developments in America or Europe in the nineteenth century. Superficial political events, but no significant ones, after 1870 were treated in ten pages. The book ignored the industrial expansion and corporate life (1865–1914), and the corresponding changes in government, the labor movement and its problems, and

[12] Dexter, E. G., *History of Education in the United States.*

Monroe, Paul, *A Textbook in The History of Education; Brief Course in The History of Education; Source Book of the History of Education.*

Graves, Frank P., *A History of Education* (3 volumes).

Cubberley, Ellwood P., *Public Education in the United States; The History of Education.*

The publication of the Cubberley books marked the beginning of a slightly new trend.

the rise of cities and the parallel problems of population. The role of the scientific revolution in creating the technological revolution was not referred to. The significance of the functional, "social use" climate of opinion that was sweeping across the nation in Monroe's day was not mentioned. There was no hint of the new bio-psychology of James and his contemporaries (in fact James got only a couple of quoted sentences), and no reference to the work of such thinkers as Baldwin and Cooley in the social-psycholgoical sciences. "Psychology" was dealt with in a chapter but only in terms of Pestalozzi, Herbart, and Froebel in the background of Rousseau and the "naturalistic" tendency in education. The "sociological tendency" was interpreted from the speculations and cosmogonies of Comte, Spencer, and Ward. The description of the movement for social reform was little more than a reference to the philanthropic movements of the late eighteenth and early nineteenth centuries.

My judgment is confirmed by Professor Butts's appraisal;[13] he notes two dominant characteristics: an exclusive concern with

. . . factual information about the history of schools, their organization, curriculum, and methods . . . Little attention was devoted to the study of the society and culture in which education operated or to the role of education in the culture . . . The history of education has been taught in a systematic chronological way that often failed to relate the past to the present and failed to indicate the meaning of historical generalizations for the present. Much of this emphasis stemmed from an overly academic view of historical research that borrowed its methods from the physical sciences and was concerned only with facts for their own sake to the exclusion of their meaning for present problems.

By the close of World War I, the more progressive professors in this field were themselves highly critical of the program. Cubberley, one of the most competent leaders of that day, in the preface to his own book *Public Education in the United States* (1919),[14] pointed directly to the glaring inadequacies of the courses in the History of Education. A study made under his direction showed that,

[13] R. Freeman Butts, in Chapter III, of *The Emerging Task of the Foundations of Education*, National Society of College Teachers of Education, 1950.
[14] Cubberley, Ellwood P., *Public Education in the United States*, Author's Preface, p. vii.

. . . of the dozen most commonly used textbooks, only three gave as much as twenty-five per cent of their space to the developments of the past fifty years; that most of them devoted the great bulk of their space to ancient and mediaeval education and European development; that most of them were cyclopedic in character and seemed constructed on the old fact-theory-of-knowledge basis; that only two or three attempted to relate the history they presented to present-day problems in instruction; that only one made any real connection between the study of history of education and the institutional efforts of the State in the matter of training; and that practically none treated the history of education in the light of either the recent important advances in educational practice and procedure or the great social, political, and industrial changes which have given the recent marked expansion of state educational effort its entire meaning.

He insisted that the history of education needed reorganizing, that "much old subject matter should be eliminated, much new subject matter added." As for the ancient history of education, the beginning student should go beyond "the Protestant revolt of the sixteenth century and the general awakening of Europe," and "much time . . . need not be spent on our development before the first quarter of the nineteenth century, when the forces—national, state, philanthropic, social, political, and economic—which were potent in our educational development first began to find expression." Cubberley did change the course in one fundamental way by his own books. He interjected what he called "the great milestones in our early national education history"—the story of America's great "battle" for free, compulsory public education—1840–1920. But even taking Cubberley and Eby and Arrowood into account, there was still a deep hiatus between what the history of education professors wrote in their textbooks and the life going on around them at the time they were writing.

XVII

THIRD: THE BIO-PSYCHOLOGICAL FOUNDATIONS OF EDUCATION

In the 1890's there was no organic biology beyond the pioneering of the Europeans with a descriptive physiology and endocrinology. Pavlov and Bechterev had just announced the first studies of the conditioned reflex; Cannon was beginning his researches on bodily changes in pain, hunger, fear, and rage, and was reaching for the great self-balancing concept—homeostasis. The physiology of drives, tensions, needs was, until the 1920's, still an unmarked frontier.

The first American psychological laboratories were hardly a decade old. The psychology of the day, the product of psychophysics, statistics, and exact measurement, was straight "mechanism." Wilhelm Max Wundt was still "the pope" issuing encyclicals of mechanical elementarism and training; J. McKeen Cattell, G. Stanley Hall, J. Mark Baldwin, Charles H. Judd, and a host of younger men were building the second line of measuring laboratories for the carrying on of perceptual studies of reaction and learning. This orthodox psychology—a rigid mechanical explanation of the human being as an assembly of parts—was spearheaded by Edward Bradford Tichener at Cornell from 1892 to 1927. It was he who trained William Chandler Bagley, Boyd H. Bode, Guy Montrose Whipple, Madison Bentley, and fifty other professors of psychology and education. Thus the psychology of the day, transferred into the new "educational psychology," was largely a paraphrase of the Wundtian studies of mental minutiae, measured reaction time, association time, tapping, and the like.

Freud's pioneer work in exploring and discovering the foundations of a true depth psychology was just beginning. The significance of the concept of the electromagnetic field—which had been mathematically described by Maxwell (1873) and shortly was to emerge in the epoch-marking energy equation of Einstein (1905)—was not appreciated by most college teachers of physics and chemistry. Dewey's reflex-arc article had just been published (1896) but even his armchair prevision of the organic concept in human behavior had not yet been given literate form. The "field" explorations of some of the Gestalt psychologists were a generation in the offing. The social anthropologists of the third generation (the Lynds, the Warner group, Jones, et al.) were not to begin their first-hand studies of American community life for twenty-five more years. Such psychology as was being incorporated in the curricula of the normal schools—coming to be known as "teachers colleges"—was of a thoroughly connectionist and conditioned-response nature.

Edward L. Thorndike, Adjunct Professor of Educational Psychology in Columbia's new Teachers College in 1901, was the

first to receive that title in America. Certainly he was the first to
build a systematic program of study in "educational" psychology.
Almost unaided, he built the content of the courses in that field
which have been taught to this day in the teacher-education institutions of America. My recent studies show that his is still the
dominating influence. His first book, *Educational Psychology*,
was published in 1903, his *Mental and Social Measurements* in
1904, and his *Elements of Psychology* in 1905. While I was doing
my graduate work in education and sociology at the University of
Illinois, his major three-volume work, *Educational Psychology*,
appeared (1913–1914). This became the "bible" of graduate students everywhere in the country for the next twenty years. A score
of new texts came from the younger men, but most of them were
built on Thorndike's framework.[15]

Looking back more systematically over the half century we can
say that three schools of thought, reflecting essentially the same
basic concepts, dominated the first "draft" of educational psychology. The first was the conditioned-response view initiated
in physiology in the 1890's by the Russians—Pavlov and Bechterev
—and developed in the United States in the last three decades
under such psychological laboratory workers as Clark L. Hull.
The second, and by far more influential theory, was the connectionist-trial-and-error view developed under the leadership of
Thorndike. The third, very different from the first two, was that
generally known as Gestalt, the product of four German psychologists—Wertheimer, Köhler, Koffka, and Lewin, and sponsored in
America primarily by R. M. Ogden, R. M. Wheeler, and George
Hartmann. It resembled Dewey's concept of "problem-solving
thinking," and stressed "insight" *via* the recognition of the "whole,"
the "pattern" or "configuration." Its thesis is that the meaning of
the part is determined by its relation with the whole. There were
other theories but they played a minor role during the era in
which educational psychology was being developed (1900–1930)
and before it had begun to change. A recent systematic appraisal
of the reading materials most widely used in educational psy-

[15] The great exception was Pressey and Robinson's *Psychology Applied to
Education*, but this was not published until 1933. Even this did not do the
total job of integrating the entire range of the scholarship of the human and
social sciences. Eighteen more years passed before that task was beautifully
done by Dr. Lawrence E. Cole in his *Educational Psychology* (1950).

chology, and in curriculum and teaching in the teachers colleges, showed that a very Thorndikian brand of psychology still rules the minds of most of the professors.

To state its characteristics briefly: It was a *"behavior"* and *action* psychology, resting on the *principle of active response.* Like the more organic view which developed in recent years, it accepted and built upon the *principle of association:* all learning is, in one way or another, "associative." It was both a *conditioned response* and a *"connectionist"* psychology, teaching that as the human being confronts any new situation he is conditioned to make new responses. It was the *first trial-and-error explanation of behavior,* pointing out that in the complex, problematic situations which baffle us and block our smooth progress in learning, behavior seems to plot its course in a blundering, random, trial-and-error way.

It clarified the fact of individual differences and studied mental work and fatigue. On the long-standing controversy over nature and nurture it was primarily for "nature," building on a list of "instincts" that outdid James's famous score. It emphasized the anatomy and physiology of original "satisfiers" and "annoyers," stressing inherited structure and minimizing environment.

In its latter days (in the 1930's) it stressed the role of motives, incentives, interests, and rewards and punishments, and there were signs that it was groping toward an understanding of the role of needs in learning. It stimulated a deep interest in the psychology of learning, but was concerned more with the statistical analysis of the development of learning than it was with the physiological and sociological factors which so vitally affected it.

Its general import for fifty years has been the support it has given to mechanistic and atomistic views of human nature and behavior. While it is possible to find in the writings of Thorndike and his associates much implied acceptance of the principle of generalization (witness their accounts of reasoning and thinking in the psychology of reading, arithmetic, and algebra), they are essentially concerned with structure, specific connections, habit, skill, and practice. From the first twenty years of their work, we get a picture of the infant discipline of Educational Psychology doggedly determined to be "scientific," rigorously applying concepts of *mechanism* to a complex human organism that is growing up and being molded by a powerful and complex organic culture, but without any real concern with the culture which is molding the organism and with an additive conception of the organism itself.

Nevertheless, the group following Thorndike's leadership did improvise the "first" educational psychology, and *it is important to remind ourselves that a "second" one, such as we are building today, could not be produced without it.* Moreover, they did contribute important psychological concepts which can help us create a more effective school today.

XVIII

FOURTH: THE ESTHETIC FOUNDATIONS OF EDUCATION, 1890–1920

There were no esthetic foundations in this period. There were professional courses galore—and textbooks in each "subject"—in the teaching of English, the teaching of art, music, and dramatics; but these were taken only by those special students who were going to be "supervisors" or teachers of what was always called, in those days, "The Special Subjects." For the administrators of schools, whose power and leadership over the life and program was greatest, and for the vast preponderance of teachers, there was no introduction to the greatest expressive age in the history of the nation. I can find no reference at all to the pioneering of Cézanne, Matisse, and the French and German expressionists of the late nineteenth century, or to the Americans—Louis Sullivan in architecture, Isadora Duncan in the dance, Alfred Stieglitz, Marin, *et al.*, in the graphic and plastic arts, Charles Ives, *et al.*, in music, Crane, Dreiser, Bourne, Brooks, Frank, *et al.*, in letters, and their contemporaries in the theater and other expressive fields. From that day to this, Esthetic Foundations has never been developed as an integral part of teacher education.

XIX

FIFTH: THE PHILOSOPHIC FOUNDATIONS OF EDUCATION

For twenty years after the establishment of Teachers College there was little agreement among the professors of education as to the building of a "philosophy of education" by the prospective teachers. Some said it could only be developed by the worker on the job through years of experience in teaching and administering schools. Others maintained that it was the task of a teachers college to organize the systematic study of philosophy and apply it to education. Still others said: "Send the prospective teachers to regular philosophy courses in the liberal arts college."

At Teachers College, Columbia, a course was improvised by Dr. Butler which, on his becoming President of the University in 1902, was taken over by Dr. John A. MacVannel. For many years it was called "Principles of Education." Herman Harrel Horne of New York University had just published a book called *Philosophy of Education* and Paul Hanus of Harvard one called *Educational Aims and Values*, both of which were used in such courses.

That the "Principles of Education" course was a kind of improvised catch-all for the problems of education is shown by Butler's catalogue statement and by his syllabus reprinted in the *Teachers College Record* for 1900. Its purpose, he says, is:

. . . to lay the basis for a scientific theory of education considered as a human institution. The process of education is explained from the standpoint of the doctrine of evolution, and the fundamental principles thus arrived at are applied from the three-fold standpoint of the history of civilization, the developing powers of the child, and the cultivation of individual and social efficiency.

It was also shown by the required readings: Butler, *The Meaning of Education;* Davidson, *Aristotle and the Ancient Educational Ideals;* Eliot, *Educational Reform;* Harris, *Psychologic Foundations of Education.*

The chief themes of such courses during the first twenty years— "adaptation," from the doctrine of evolution, and the "cultivation of indivdiual and social efficiency"—were prominent in Butler's course. It began with the "Study of Education as a Science," a pattern followed by MacVannel, Thorndike, Monroe, Strayer, and others. They reflected the tendency of all academic people at that time to try to make everything "scientific," even though neither the concepts nor the method were really established. The scientific method was literally "in the air." In every phase of the new education—history, psychology, school administration, and comparative education—the aspiration was to make education scientific. It is interesting to note that today, when we have vastly more valid materials and methods for a Science of Man, we move in the other direction and insist that education is not a science, but an art. It does not itself possess a unique body of primary concepts—the prior criterion for a science; it draws its concepts *from* the physical and natural sciences.

This was the nature and scope of "Philosophy and Principles of Education" up to World War I. It and the other courses in education gave the "Foundations" their slant for twenty-odd years. In one way they were very much alike. They showed their "firstness" by their all-embracing, encyclopedic character. Each professor dealt not only with his own area, but with *all* the other fields too, treating all in a meager fashion. They all dealt with "aims," they all made some reference to psychology, and methods of teaching (both in general and in the principal school subjects), to history, and to the organization and administration of schools. They all abounded in generalities. They were all "Idealistic" and Hegelian in philosophy. They all plugged for the "scientific" study of education.

XX

The bridge between them and Dewey and the Creative Path was William Heard Kilpatrick. He had first studied with Dewey at Chicago in 1898, then with De Garmo at Cornell in 1900, and then with Dewey again at Columbia from 1907 to 1910. He had "taught" Dewey's *Interest as Related to Will* at a Summer School of the South in Knoxville, Tennessee, in 1902. These experiences had turned him away from the formalities of mathematics teaching and "vice-presidencing" at Mercer University in Georgia. He came to Columbia in 1907, and was for a while assistant to Paul Monroe in the History of Education. On MacVannel's retirement he took over the work in the Philosophy of Education, a field in which he has continued to be one of the nation's leaders to this day.[16]

Kilpatrick's story does not really belong here in the Conforming Way. I shall merely note that it was he, and Boyd Bode (who

[16] As I write (1951) announcement reaches me of the publication of his new book, *The Philosophy of Education.*

In Teachers College Henry Suzzallo (Ph.D., Columbia, 1905) taught a mixture of "Educational Sociology" and "Philosophy of Education" in various years from 1909 to 1915. At that time he became president of the University of Washington and Kilpatrick became the center of philosophical development in Teachers College for the next twenty years.

went to Ohio from Illinois in 1921) who brought Dewey to the teachers of America. Dewey's *Democracy in Education*, first called *Philosophy of Education*, was written and included in Monroe's series as a direct result of Kilpatrick's prodding. Its publication in 1916 was epoch-marking in this field. For thirty-four years nothing as definitive appeared in its field. Then in 1950 came Theodore Brameld's *Patterns of Educational Philosophy;* this, I am convinced, will mark a new era in thought and practice. In 1918 Kilpatrick published a little monograph, *The Project Method,* which provoked widespread controversial discussion of the new theories and experimental practices in education and helped to introduce Dewey, his ideas, and methods to teachers generally.

XXI

A fuller appraisal of our mass teacher education than I have space for would include an account of the counterrevolution in the liberal arts between the two world wars. The defenders of the classical faith—having built our first schools and teacher-education institutions and, having become aware of the success of the progressive movement in American life in bringing about the progressive schools—decided that they had to fight the influence of these movements. They also seemed to sense the arresting signs of the nature of the scholars' multiplying studies and the emergence of the new university disciplines. Certainly the impressive and publicized advances of the General Education movement in the Twenties and Thirties warned them that their most sacred preserves were being attacked.

The story would be told of how they fought to keep themselves entrenched in control of the program of education, both in the colleges and in the schools. These liberal arts defenders of authority, heavily financed by the Rockefeller and Carnegie foundations, published a series of national survey reports.

The Mathematics Investigation, 1920–1923
The Classical Investigation, 1921–1925
The Modern Language Study, 1924–1927
The Preliminary Study of History and Related Subjects,
  1925–1927

The American Historical Association's Study by its Committee on the Teaching of History and Other Social Studies, a 16-volume report, in the 1930's. This proved to be no defender of tradition; three members of the Commission refused to sign the report.

In the Thirties and Forties the counterrevolution was given a new impetus by the widely publicized "Great Book" movement of Mortimer Adler and the "Neo-Scholastics," Messrs. Buchanan, McKeon, Barr, Van Doren, *et al.*, who had converted Robert Hutchins. I had planned to interpret their creed, works, and effects.

A fuller account would also appraise the tinkering of the professors of education with their programs in the mass Teachers Colleges. It cannot be doubted that, especially after 1935, many of the teacher-education institutions slowly came under the influence of both the General Education movement in the liberal arts colleges and a mild application of the teachings of Messrs. Kilpatrick, Bode, and the younger progressives. There has been no sound account of the spread of this influence; but that it was there we see reflected in the new curricula announcements and in the interest in the work of the Committees on the Foundations of Education of the National Society of College Teachers of Education. But from 1920 to 1935 there was comparatively little influence of these reconstructive movements. This is clearly established in the voluminous reports of the various national commissions on teacher education from 1920 to 1945, led by William Chandler Bagley in the 1920's, by Samuel Evenden in the 1930's, and by Karl Bigelow in the 1940's.

An interpretation of the personnel, aims, methods of work, chief findings, and actual effects on teacher education of the first two of these national commissions would certainly be as negative as that of the proposed interpretation of the counterrevolution in the liberal arts. The third, of which Karl Bigelow was "director," made a contribution on the *psychological side*. I have in mind such volumes as *Helping Teachers Understand Children*. In Chapter V I appraise also the Armstrong, Hollis, and Davis volume, which was a good descriptive account of the "general education" trend in the teachers colleges. But on the social side, this heavily financed and long-lived commission did little.

On the whole, therefore, the studies of these commissions were made by men brought up in the framework of the first professors of education and reflected their point of view. My reading of them reveals very little influence of the new university disciplines in the sciences and the arts (except in personality psychology) nor of the emerging social foundations of education. There is in them little concern with the problem of educational theory, and not even the rudimentary outlines of an esthetic foundation can be seen. The historical and philosophical foundations were little more than a modified "history and philosophy of education" of the 1920 vintage. "Practice-teaching" by which prospective teachers might engage in active experience, either in a school or in the life of the culture outside the teachers college, was offered as a part of the work of the senior year only, and continued to be a routine formula. The gains that I consider important in all these years of tinkering with the mass teachers college programs, lay in a slightly more personalized psychology and in a changing conception of curriculum and teaching.

XXII

I have far more important things to do in my small book than to appraise any further the limitations of our older brothers who improvised our first program of teacher education. I have given, to my best knowledge, their loyalties and beliefs, their ideas and values. I grew up in the same environment with them although a decade or two later than most of them. I was taught by them from 1911 to 1915. For fifteen years I worked either for their Economy of Time Committee, or as a member of their later measurement committees and curriculum committees. From being a naïve and enthusiastic devotee, I finally met and acknowledged a creative world that they apparently never encountered. I shall describe that world in Chapters III and IV. In the background of this close personal collaboration with them and of that creative world, I have more recently gathered their works again and made a searching study of them. That study is convincing that they lived throughout their lives in the deep rut of the Conforming Way. Neither they nor their intellectual offspring who lived under the shaking impact of the Great Depression ever gave even grudging admission that the minority of the Creative Path might have a point.

of education and reflection. The account of them . . . My . . . Many of them
reveals very little influence of the new university disciplines in
the sciences and the arts . . . except in personality psychology; nor
of the emerging social round demand education). There is so little
little concern with the problem of education) that they are, and not
even the intellectual utilities of my college foundations can be
seen. The historical and philosophical foundations were little
more than a modified "mirror" and philosophy of education of
the 1920 vintage. Teacher-teaching by which respects teachers mainly tinged their experiences rather in a school or in the
life or the culture inside the teachers college who offered, as
a part of the work of their nine year only and continued to be a
routine formula. The point that I consider important to all these
years of tinkering with the . . . teachers college persons, for
in a slightly more personalized psychology, and in a changing
conception of curriculum and teaching.

XII

I have far more important things to do in my small book than to
appraise any further the limitations of my other teachers who
impressed one fair program of teacher education. I am given
to my own knowledge of their loyalties and beliefs, their ideals and
values I grew up in the same environment with them although
a decade or two later than most of them. I was helped by them
from 1911 to 1945. For fifteen years I worked either for their
Reading, of Time Committee, or as a member of their larger
organizational committees and curriculum committees. Thus being
a native and entirely resolute. I finally met and not realized, in
a native world that they apparently have never considered, I shall
describe that world in Chapters III and IV. In the background of
this other personal collaboration with them and of that creative
world I have more recently gathered their work again and made
a searching study of them. That study is reminding that they
lived throughout their lives in the deep rut of the Conforming
Way. Neither they nor their intellectual displays who in abundant
declaiming impact of the Great Depression ever gave even
grudging admission that the minority of the Creative Path might
have a point.

Part II

THE CREATIVE PATH, 1920–1950
The Makings of Teacher Education Emerge in
New University Disciplines

CHAPTER III

The Science of Society and Culture:
The Social Foundations of Education

I

"Put yourself in the creative path."

If someone of prestige had said that to Butler and his men in 1900, and made it stick, the story of American teacher education *might* have been very different. If great teachers could have opened the educationalists' minds to the true meaning of the social analysis that Veblen, Robinson, and Turner were making, or have paraphrased for them the operational psychology of meaning which Peirce and Wright had created in their Cambridge Metaphysical Club, our first teachers of teachers might have been diverted from the Conforming Way that gripped them all their lives. If, on that visiting day in 1900, some wise guide had persuaded James Earl Russell to look below the surface of John Dewey's noisy schoolroom at Chicago, a whole generation of lag might have been cut out of progressive education. But actually no teacher had the insight to do these things—that is, none but Dewey himself, and he was busy creating the new idea. So the older professors of education either slept through the creative revolution of 1870 to 1920 or, superficially aware of it, shrugged it off.

It was the impact of World War I that shocked a few of us, among their students, out of our conformity and ignorance. It brought us into contact with distinguished minds that had long been aware of the epoch-marking changes in technology and social institutions and were making profound studies of their implications. We found our bearings through the researches of these scholars of the social scene. They set us firmly on the Creative Path.[1]

---

[1] I was plain lucky to find it at all, brought up as I had been in the Conforming Way, and complacent about it until I was more than thirty years

67

During the very years 1890–1920, in which the first systematic materials of teacher education were being hurriedly put together, the makings of a sound program had been gathering in a body of new university disciplines and expressive arts. A "second" intellectual revolution, unknown to most of us, had been underway throughout much of the nineteenth century. Its hypotheses were so opposed to current doctrines in the physical and natural sciences and in the expressive arts that the few scholars of the universities who were aware of them denied their validity. Actually the imagined concepts were so true that, even in the short span of our own half century, they have supplanted the Galilean-Newtonian theory in the physical and natural sciences, and have ousted the representative photography of the expressive arts, both of which have governed thinking-feeling men for three hundred years.

What Butler and his colleagues were insensitive to was nothing short of the modern cycle of man's recurring ages of expression. It is difficult to understand how they could have missed it for its outward manifestations surrounded them. Moreover, not less than ten groups of students and artists, in both western Europe and America, had been building the new Creative Day. To name the conspicuous men and their works:

In the physical sciences, the Oersted-Faraday-Maxwell studies of electromagnetism (1825–1875); the first discovery of the "field" concept.

In psychology, the theoretical founding of the operational psychology of meaning in the brilliant "Metaphysical Club" (1869–1874) of Cambridge, Massachusetts—Charles Peirce, Chauncey Wright, Oliver

---

old. I finally stumbled into it in the years after 1918. World War I had brought me to Washington to join Yerkes's and Thorndike's Committee on Personnel in the Army. They had gathered into one study and planning group, thirty top imaginative men of the research divisions of the country's industrial corporations and universities. I had just published *Statistical Methods Applied to Education,* which, Thorndike thought, made me eligible. In the group I found not only great imagination and technical competence; more important, I found through such persons as Arthur Upham Pope (later world authority on Iranian art, and Director of the Asia Institute) the creative writings of the new social analysis and criticism of the American statement. After the war I went on to explore the meaning of what the *Seven Arts* and *New Republic* groups in America, and Tawney, Hobson, Wallas, Laski, and the London School group were saying. Within three years I was weaned from the Conforming Way.

Wendell Holmes, Jr., William James, Frank Abbott, John Fiske, and Fitzhugh Green.

In physiology, the prevision of modern endocrinology in the work of Claude Bernard, *et al.*, at the College of France (about 1855), and the consequent brilliant homeostatic researches and theories of Walter Cannon and his associates at Harvard, after 1890.

The pre-psychiatric work of Charcot and Janet in France, which set Sigmund Freud, *et al.*, on their creative path after 1890, in Vienna.

In the social sciences, the creation of the now famous "Fabian Society" of Beatrice and Sidney Webb, Bernard Shaw, Frank Podmore, Graham Wallas, and H. G. Wells; this, in the 1890's, led to the founding of the London School of Economics and Political Science, from which epoch-marking studies of industrial society supplied many of the key concepts for a new university discipline in the social sciences.

In the sciences, mathematics, psychology, and philosophy, a brilliant group at Johns Hopkins—Rowland, Remsen, Sylvester, and Michaelson—were laying the foundation for the American version of a new mathematical physics; John Dewey, Thorstein Veblen, W. H. Burnham, Joseph Jastrow, and Christine Ladd-Franklin, were getting glimpses of the active, operational, and pragmatic psychology from Charles Peirce.

At the University of Chicago, in the 1890's, the now famous group of "functional" psychologists, social psychologists, economists, sociologists, and anthropologists were building an organic-action-psychology and social science—John Dewey, James Angell, William I. Thomas, George H. Mead, and Thorstein Veblen, with Franz Boas nearby at the Field Museum.

At Columbia, in the 1890's, at the very moment that Butler and Russell were organizing Teachers College, James Harvey Robinson was giving his famous course in "The History of the Western Mind" and Franz Boas, who had left Chicago, was building the new "School of American Ethnology."

Frederick J. Turner was at Wisconsin writing the first draft of his Frontier essay on "The Significance of the Frontier in American History."

During the same years there was tremendous awakening in western Europe and eastern America in the expressional arts, revealed through the work of Cézanne, Matisse, Picasso, "The Eight," Stieglitz, Marin, and others in the graphic and plastic arts; Whitman, *et al.*, in letters; Louis Sullivan and Frank Lloyd Wright in architecture; Charles Ives in music; Eugene O'Neill, *et al.*, in the theater; Isadora Duncan in the dance; and still others.

Thus by 1920 an international awakening, encompassing much of the western world, had been breaking out of the Conforming Way in every science and art, and for more than half a century. Barbarians, such as myself and my educationalist brothers—and I think that goes for most of the engineers, doctors, lawyers, and other professionals of that day—were innocent of it all. In 1910 the chief indoor sport among professors of the liberal arts was to spend an evening together laughing uproariously over the latest yarns—apocryphal they proved to be—of how Dewey was bringing up his children. The only true Laboratory School in the world meant no more to us than that! I know, for I was in those liberal arts professors' living rooms, looking and listening, a young engineer trying to discover what it was all about. As for the other creatives—the laughter of the New York art dealers at Stieglitz' showing of Cézanne, Matisse, and Marin in 1908, the "funny" Armory Show of 1913, matched the shocked denunciation of the people and the critics at Isadora Duncan's dancing without shoes and stockings. No one had heard of Charles Ives or his "American" symphonies. "The Eight" were known as the "Ash Can School." Einstein's energy equation (1905) affected few professors of mathematics or physics, and Charles Beard's *Economic Interpretation of the United States Constitution* (1913) was denounced by 90 per cent of the historians. In 1917 Butler fired Cattell and Harry Dana at Columbia and let Robinson and Beard resign.

II

It was the impact of the Peace Conference at Versailles in 1918–1919 that finally shocked some of us into an understanding that our world was being manhandled by economic and psychological forces of which we had hitherto no inkling. The record of history is convincing that great crises such as modern wars and depressions initiate what the old Chinese called "times of the greatest learning." That was true for my generation in the years immediately following 1919. Not only did our infant debtor country discover its enormous productive resources, speeding up its technological revolution fourfold between 1914 and 1918, and throwing off its subservience to Britain and western Europe to take its place as a great industrial power; those years were also astonishingly productive of creative intellectual stock-taking across the entire culture. Word had scarcely come through of the nature of the peace treaty that Clemenceau and Lloyd George had put over on Woodrow Wilson, when new interpretations of our industrial society began to come from the presses on both sides of the Atlantic. In Britain, the center of creative thought was the London School; the new interpreters were such persons as Hobson, Tawney, the Webbs, Wallas, Laski, and Keynes. In the United States, their counterparts were Walton Hamilton, Leon Marshall, Harold Moulton, William F. Ogburn, Charles Beard, Walter Lippmann.[2]

These new social syntheses jolted a few of us in college and school education into a more realistic interpretation of industrial civilization. They not only gave us an overview of the whole society, only isolated parts of which we had acknowledged before; they raised questions about the significance of hidden forces and factors in the social system and gave inklings of new concepts. Reading them all in three winters following 1919, as I tried to do, I was driven back to the studies themselves. I finally had to read all of Veblen's books; *The Theory of the Leisure Class* was merely an incitement to *The Theory of Business Enterprise*,

[2] The library of interpretation that the youngsters gobbled up included: Hobson's *Evolution of Modern Capitalism* (1906), a pioneer synthesis of the factors of industrial and finance capitalism, and his *Taxation in the State* (1920); Tawney's little *Acquisitive Society* (1920), and his classic *Religion and the Rise of Capitalism* (1926); Wallas' *Great Society* came in 1914, and his *Social Heritage* in 1920. The young Harold Laski published his *Studies in the Problem of Sovereignty in America* (1917), the *Foundations of Sovereignty in America* (1921), and his *Rise of Liberalism* (1923). John Maynard Keynes told the world what he thought of "the war and the peace" in *The Economic Consequences of the Peace* (1920); twenty-five years later he had become, as Lord Keynes, the leading economist of the British world. And there were others; E. D. Morel, for example, had foreseen, long before 1914, that the industrial race for resources, markets, and a place to invest surplus capital was bringing on a series of world wars.

In the United States, in the same years there were published: Walter Hamilton's *Current Economic Problems* (1914) and Leon Marshall's *Readings in Industrial Society* (1918). Harold Moulton (for the next twenty years Director of the Brookings Institution) published *The Financial Organization of Society* (1921). At Wisconsin, John R. Commons and his associates produced their two-volume *History of Labor in the United States*.

Most provocative of all were: Frederick J. Turner's *The Frontier in American History* (1920), Thorstein Veblen's *The Engineers and the Price System*, Robinson's *Mind in the Making* (1921), Charles Beard's *Cross-Currents in Europe*, Carlton Hayes's *Political and Social History of Modern Europe*, and Sidney Fay's *Origins of the World War*.

and that in turn to the others.[3] Only then could a person brought up in the Conforming Way accept such shocking conclusions as found in Veblen's appraisal of the industrial system. Take these as examples: that while "relatively little . . . knowledge . . . is held by the owners . . . of typical large scale industries . . . these owners have a discretionary control of the technological proficiency of the community at large," that these owners *own also the working capacity of the community and the* [usufruct] *of the state* of the material arts." This, in more abstruse language, was Edward Bellamy's generalization that "He that owns the things that men must have, owns the men that must have them." This was the concept that Veblen had been so profoundly influenced by, thirty years before.

This generalization had been achieved independently, after 1890, by one after another of the "new historians." Turner had expressed it, in *The Frontier in American Life,* as "economic power secures political power," and Beard had documented it in the instance of the fifty-five men who made the United States Constitution. Schlesinger confirmed Beard in *New Viewpoints in American History,* saying: "Of the fifty-five members who attended the convention . . . at least five-sixths of the membership were directly and personally interested in the outcome of their labors through their ownership of property." It was such documented reiteration of generalizations encountered in volume after volume of *The New History* that began to open the eyes of a few—very few!—of the young pedagogues of the 1920's. But the older ones never blinked.

Moreover, as our studies broadened and deepened we slowly got a more integrated view of the several key factors in western culture that from 1870 to 1920 had brought about the new interpretation. The people had sensed the need for social control even if the professors of the liberal arts and sciences had not. A social and functional climate of opinion was spreading across America, bringing new legislation of social control; witness the Populist movement of the 1880's and 1890's. This was paralleled by changes in thought concerning the nature and behavior of

[3] *The Instinct of Workmanship and the State of the Industrial Arts, The Vested Interests and the Common Man, The Place of Science in Modern Civilization, The Engineers and the Price System,* and his last one (1923), *Absentee Ownership and Business Enterprise in Recent Times: the Case of America.*

the human organism; the inter-Atlantic discussion of Darwin's evolutionary views were put to work after 1890 in the face-to-face study of every phase of the new industrial society. Steadily these transformed mechanical explanations of human nature and behavior into thoroughly organic ones; even by 1890 they had been interpreted in James' *Psychology*. They were confirmed by such German precursors of Gestalt as Mach, Dilthey, and Ehrenfelds, and by Dewey's pioneering description of the organic nature of human response in his 1896 reflex-arc article. They were influenced also by the new European bio-psychology that was developing in France and by the expressionist trend that spread from France and Germany in the 1880's in all of the arts.

By the time Veblen, *et al.*—the first generation of true social scientists—had completed their work, that is, by the 1920's, a new picture of industrial society had been created. As we, their intellectual sons, applied it to the building of a new curriculum in the colleges and schools, we were able to write an account of our industrial social order that was a much closer approximation to reality than our teachers had taught us to see.

III

Looking back along the creative path of the thirty years just passed (1920–1950), we see three groups of imaginative men in the colleges and the universities who, catching the vision of the face-to-face study of human cultures, and applying the resultant knowledge to the reconstruction of life in America, *created a brilliant body of new university disciplines and made it possible for us today to build sound Foundations of Education.* They were few in number among the total academic personnel, but they were perceptive and they were tenacious. Their cumulating documentation gave their position the prestige of a growing consensus. The record of the thirty years has borne them out.

There was, *first*, the combined group of social scientists, psychologists, and artists who were creating a Science and Art of Man[4] that had been the goal of men of thought since Hobbes, Locke, Berkeley, and Hume. This first group comprised the stu-

---

[4] The label "Science of Man" is not forehanded presumption of mine. It comes from the anthropologists themselves; witness the symposium of thirty students Ralph Linton edited in his *The Science of Man in the World Crisis* (1945).

dents of man and his society, his behavior and expression. These were the true frontiersmen of thought and feeling.[5] I deal with them in this chapter.

The second group was composed of a few maverick professors in the colleges who returned from their World War I experiences determined to supplant the medieval "liberal arts" curriculum with a full and realistic introduction to the forces and factors in the modern world. These were the first creators of General Education in the colleges; it was they who put to work some of the great concepts of the emerging Science of Man. I deal with them in Chapter V.

The third group was made up of ourselves—the younger educationalists who gathered around Dewey, Kilpatrick, and Bode after 1920 and produced the "progressive" and "Social Frontier" movements in the schools and colleges. Their work was reconstructive in content and organization. To some extent it paralleled that of the second group, developing a new and vital General Education in a few schools and teachers colleges from the scattered and hidden researches of the scholars on all the frontiers. To interpret the creative revolution that built important examples of the new education in the thirty years from 1920 to 1950, I shall deal with the work of these three groups in Chapter V.

In this chapter and in Chapters IV and V I present the three Foundations of Education indispensable to a good college or school program.

> The Science of Society and Culture—The Social Foundations of Education.
>
> The Science of Behavior—The Bio-Psychological Foundations of Education.
>
> The Art of Expression—The Esthetic Foundations of Education.

From these, in their historical and contemporaneous perspectives, a great philosophy of education can be stated. Adding Historical

---

[5] I name them the Third Generation of the modern genealogy of thought. The First Generation was composed of those speculative forerunners, August Comte, Herbert Spencer, Lester Frank Ward, *et al.*, who "predicted sociology." The Second Generation included Veblen, Robinson, Turner, Boas, Dewey, James, Peirce, Freud, Cannon, Bernard, *et al.*, who made the first eye-witness analysis of society and a directly scientific study of behavior, 1890–1920.

and Philosophical Foundations of Education to these three, there-fore, we have the five irreducible foundations upon which a pro-gram of curriculum, teaching, guidance, administration, and appraisal can be erected.

IV

History will acknowledge the creative production of this gen-eration of students of the human sciences for they uncovered the key concepts that can now become the intellectual skeleton of the program in the Social and Bio-Psychological Foundations of Education. They produced a new Science of Man on which the underpinning of the whole educational program from nursery school to graduate university study can be built. The explosive preparatory work was done in the Long Armistice between the two World Wars. This was a period of creative imagination ap-plied to the whole culture—to the social system, to the study of individual and group behavior, and to the development of the expressional arts. I make much of the fact that in these years creative artists found themselves working side by side with scien-tific students of society. A statement of American life was being made by novelists, poets, essayists, painters, dramatists, and dancers, as well as by anthropologists, social psychologists, econ-omists, and students of government. I am confident that the pro-found meaning of several of our key concepts would not have been sensed in our day had not this conscious integration of fields of knowledge taken place. Masters of the ideas and techniques of special disciplines explored the no-man's land between the long-established academic areas of research and produced three new university disciplines for college and school.

The creative production of the Long Armistice breaks clearly into three phases dealt with in three decades. The decade of the Twenties was marked by the scholars' interpretive syntheses and preparatory studies. As far as popular understanding was con-cerned, the people, their politicians, and most of their professors were anesthetized by the deceptive paper-prosperity of the Harding-Coolidge-Hoover administrations. The second decade, the Great Depression Thirties, gave the world an historic experi-ment in the Welfare State, uniting astute political leaders and competent students of society in America's first attempt to design a Mixed Economy and to operate it democratically. Important social-educational syntheses were created, a novel body of social-psychological ideas discovered, and a dramatic literature of social expression built up by a dozen novelists, poets, and critics, a score of social painters, several creative dancers of the American theme, and an indigenous theater of social expression. The third decade—the Forties—marked by the latest shooting World War II and the Cold War of today, was a new period of intellectual inventory and of the current "Foundation" building in education itself.

V

THE NEW "POLITICAL ECONOMY"

Three major problems confront the democracies of the world and the students of the Science of Man that is being created by the scholars:

> The problem of government
> The problem of production
> The problem of the public mind

Each interpenetrates the other so fully that no fundamental solution of one will be achieved except in the light obtained from the others. This is so true of the first two that, with malice aforethought, I use the old-fashioned term "Political Economy" to set the stage for them. It centers attention on the single political and economic problem that will undoubtedly engage men's minds throughout the twentieth century: *What part shall Government play in bringing about uninterrupted full production and full employment in a democratic society?* We have been learning from the nation's social experience, as well as from the students' researches, that no good and sufficient answer can be obtained except by the closest union of Government and the economy. To bring that about permanently involves us in the problem of the popular mind. This is to build real understanding among the people of a private-enterprise capitalist system which is caught in an era of great transition. The problem is complicated by the fact that our system is changing into a Mixed Economy in a world of wide-spreading dictatorship, while we are adamantly striving to preserve the democratic way of life. And it is further complicated by the fact of our ignorance of what level of understanding of these modern problems can be achieved by what percentage of the people, or what the optimum percentage is in a democratic society.

Phrased differently, there are two choices before America and the democracies of the world:

Abundance *vs.* catastrophe. This is the production-employment problem.

Democracy *vs.* totalitarianism. This is the government problem.

To make these two choices will necessitate the study of an integration of political, economic, and social-psychological knowledge that has never been done before.

VI

The second baffling problem of our times is: What is happening to the historic American way of life in the long struggle over freedom and control? Particularly, what is social change doing to the mind and mood of our people? This problem is social-psychological. It involves the study of the ideas, values, and beliefs of our people; their sense of security; their traditional concepts of classlessness, equality, and freedom.

It is around these basic questions that our study of "Contemporary Civilization" in the colleges and of "Problems of Democracy" in the schools can now effectively be organized.

It was with a vague, perhaps naïve sense of these problems that the young builders of the new "social science" in college and school went to work in 1919 and 1920. Veblen's next to last book, *The Engineers and the Price System* (1921), took some of us directly to the nub of the task. Those who had been trained as engineers saw that the design task was a problem in social technology. Its true factors were: (1) the needs of the people for the highest standard of living the earth can supply, (2) the available natural resources, (3) the increasingly efficient machine-technology, (4) the available human resources—the scientific and technical personnel. The full scientific study of this problem had been anticipated in the analysis of the abundant energy resources in the North American continent which Veblen and his "Technical Alliance"[6] had made immediately at the close of World War I.

[6] This was a study and discussion group that gathered around Veblen in New York in 1919. It included such distinguished engineers as Charles P.

He had not only predicted that the resources and developing technology were adequate to produce a self-sufficient, high-level, industrial civilization, but he had also given a prevision of its statistical validation. Abundance *via* controlled design had been the theme of the social engineers since that day.

Other cues to the solution of the major problems came almost immediately from the integration of economics and government with sociology, anthropology, and social psychology. One of the most important ones was Ogburn's discovery and documentation of the concept of *cultural lag* in his little book, *Social Change*.[7] Here was the idea that in a *changing society*, technological inventions and factory production tends to far outrun changes in social institutions. It was a provocative cue to the explanation of the recurring periods of the business cycle of prosperity and depression, and to the other conspicuous stresses and strains in the new industrial society. Not much was done with the concept for ten years, although the anthropologists played with it. At the moment of the deepest misery of the nation's unemployed, and as the Roosevelt New Deal was ushered in (1933), the engineers clarified the concept. They defined the lag more sharply by their curve-fitting studies of a century growth of economic productivity,[8] population, and government controls.

By the closing depression years, many creative students of the economy were clear that we were not only living in the most dynamic state of all human history, but its equilibrium at a high-level of productivity could be guaranteed only when social institutions, popular understanding, and moral behavior kept pace with economic invention and production. That, they insisted, could be achieved *only by consciously planned design by an integrated team of competent social engineers*. This conception

---

Steinmetz of the General Electric Company, Richard Tolman, later Director of the California Institute of Technology, and Bassett Jones.

[7] I regard William F. Ogburn, for nearly thirty years Professor of Sociology at the University of Chicago, as the single most important mind that guided the social-economic studies and their practical application in government during the long armistice. He was Director of the now famous government-sponsored study of *Recent Social Trends* (1933); also of the epoch-making studies of the National Resources Planning Board, 1934–1940; see, for example, their *National Planning and Technological Trends, Problems of a Changing Population*, and *Our Changing Cities*.

[8] See Jones's *Debt and Production*, and my own *The Great Technology* (1933).

they put forward in a provocative and scholarly report—*Recent Social Trends*[9]—in that same fateful winter of 1933 when 15,000,-000 Americans were unemployed. The key idea of integration of indispensable bodies of knowledge was clear in their recommendation: a "National Advisory Council, including scientific, educational, governmental, economic (industrial, agricultural, and labor) points of contacts."

VII

The Thirties will be remembered as the time when an American President first attempted to create such a pioneer *National Council of Design*. There assembled in Washington from departments of the social sciences of the universities, from engineering and industrial research, from government research, and from social, religious, and educational organizations a remarkable body of students of social planning. To cite conspicuous examples: (1) The National Resources Planning Board, including the Harvard economist, Alvin Hansen (the "Keynes" of America, or was Keynes "The Hansen of England"?); Morris Cooke and Harlow Person, the industrial engineers; the Chicago political scientist-alderman, Charles E. Merriam; and Wesley Mitchell, the Columbia economist and historian of business cycles. (2) The Tennessee Valley Authority, led by the two Morgans—one an engineer and the other an educator—and the lawyer-publicist, David Lilienthal, later of Atomic Energy Board fame. (3) The extension of the Soil Conservation Service, under Hugh Bennett. (4) The six exciting WPA Federal Arts Projects, bringing together Hallie Flanagan, Holger Cahill, and other creative leaders, giving sustenance and creative life to America's artists in all media of expression and *building a new audience for them of tens of millions of people*. (5) The Federal Communications Commission of Messrs. Fly, Watson, Dodd; and there were others.

Here was a new phenomenon in government, an integration of competencies—scientific study, planning, and practical administration. Astute politicians and practical students of the public mind collaborated with top-ranking engineers, designers, and execu-

[9] By the government Committee of that name, under the leadership of Dr. Ogburn as Director of Research, this report expressed the point of view of a distinguished group of government and university specialists in the social sciences.

tives from industry. These joined hands with frontier students of society from the universities. I know no more important lesson to teach our youth about "Political Economy" than that recorded by this short-lived National Council of Design. For the first time in our history bold, disinterested, cooperative study of a "highly complex and rapidly changing society, advancing at uneven rates and causing great problems of unemployment and of class and racial conflict," was substituted for "tradition, unintelligence, inertia, indifference, emotion or the raw will to power," as Ogburn's Committee denounced the bottlenecks in government-by-the-Conforming Way.[10]

Steadily the Veblen "engineering" approach gained more and more adherents as students saw that the abundance-scarcity issue was the basic one. In the Thirties the researches of the economists, social engineers, and sociologists produced technically documented answers to the definite questions: (1) How much can the economic system produce, assuming no human bottlenecks? (2) How much has been actually getting to the American People? (3) In what directions are the basic social trends moving, and how closely are they keeping pace with one another? (4) What are the chief factors that are holding us back? And the ever-central question: (5) How much shall we depend on private enterprise and how much on government, to get full production and full employment while preserving as much freedom as possible?

I shall not repeat the documentation of these studies and findings, which I have already given in my earlier books.[11] Suffice it to say that the actual production history of the United States in the Forties, as well as the predictions of the current researches of the electronic engineers, has disposed of the persistent notion that modern American industrialism is a "scarcity society." Consider the bare facts of our national income. The maximum ever reached in the period of artificial prosperity was $89,000,000,000 (1929); five years later, at the depth of the Great Depression, it had dropped to an estimated $40,000,000,000! But eight years after that, under the enormous production demands of the continuous large-scale government buying in World War II, and

[10] For confirming evidence see the 20,000-page report of Congress's Temporary National Economic Committee and the Reports of the fifteen-year successful TVA.

[11] See my *Foundations in American Education*, Chapters VIII–XII.

even discounting the then slightly depressed value of the dollar, it had risen to $200,000,000,000. Such conservative government bureau heads as former Governor Chester Bowles, of Connecticut, asserted in print that the system has the capacity to produce a comparable $350,000,000,000 a year. This is nine times as much as it was at the trough of the Great Depression, and more than four times its earlier "prosperity" peak of 1929. (As I write, government reports indicate a 1951 annual income of more than $250,000,000,000.)

But to understand how inevitable was this abundant production we must join to the concepts of the new "political economy" still further concepts of a new discipline that was born of the Second Technological Revolution: electronic communication-control. Communication engineering, as one of its outstanding exponents, Dr. Norbert Wiener[12] calls it, has during the past thirty years produced

. . . communication machines, some of which have shown an uncanny ability to simulate human behavior, and thereby to throw light on the possible nature of human behavior. They have even shown the existence of a tremendous possibility of replacing human behavior, in many cases in which the human being is relatively slow and ineffective.

Its astounding results justify Wiener, *et al.*, in speaking of the new discipline as a "new and fundamental revolution in technique."

Conceived between Maxwell's (1870's) and Einstein's (1905) giant mathematical achievements, the initial development of electronics came at the turn into the twentieth century; witness for example, the vacuum tube, and the photoelectric eye, together with the standardization of straight-line continuous methods of factory production. It had an adolescent spurt under the frenzied production demands of the years during and following World War I. But its maturing was comparatively sudden in the creative Thirties and Forties. While it was enormously accelerated by the production demands of World War II, the real impetus was the despairing pleas of the Churchill government to "keep England from being knocked out by an overwhelming air attack." Success

---

[12] See his *The Human Use of Human Beings; Cybernetics and Society*, p. 1; see also his earlier book *Cybernetics; or Control and Communication in the Animal and the Machine.*

in the final perfection of radar was achieved in the short space of two years by a team of skilled mathematicians, physicists, and radio engineers. Another spectacular achievement was the building of a set of self-controls into aircraft cannon. In all this the principle of *the feed-back* (which James Clark Maxwell had designed mathematically as early as 1868), together with the newer uses of the *vacuum tube,* in sequential analysis, has brought us close to the possibility of a truly automatic age for all heavy industry. A single giant factory, producing annually much of the nation's needs for a given commodity—let us say airplanes, or automobiles, or any other basic machines—can be controlled and operated from a single communication-control room.

These achievements have established that "machines can think." But their creators, Dr. Vannevar Bush of the Office of Scientific Development, for example, remind us that while these "giant brains" instantaneously solve problems with which human computational ability struggle with long and awkwardly, a *human* creative mind must build into them the coded premises on which the logical processes of thought can be carried out sequentially by the machine. I cite the work of such mathematician-engineers of the Forties as Vannevar Bush and Norbert Wiener, because they are the direct continuators of the Veblen-Tolman-Jones Technical Alliance of 1919, and of the Depression social engineers. Wiener goes on record in his latest pronouncement: If the apparent "peace" of the Cold War persists, only twenty years will be required to automatize heavy industry; but if World War III comes, we shall need only five years.

But on the positive side there is not the slightest doubt that we now have at our command *all the technological makings for economic abundance.* The predictions of the Technical Alliance (1919) and of the social engineers (1933) have been more than confirmed by the actual growth of the productive and consuming capacity of the American social system and by the astounding creation of the new discipline, called "communication engineering." Moreover, it has such provocative suggestions for human learning that I shall refer to it again.

VIII

Returning then to our prior question—"How much government in the social system?"

The economic-political events of the Thirties and Forties, clarified by the scholars' researches, directed our attention more precisely to the six major factors, and their bottlenecks, which have to be reckoned with in bringing about the uninterrupted operation of the economic system:

A. *The four individualistic ones*
   (1) The banks and other investment and credit agencies,
   (2) The business structure of large and small manufacturers and merchants,
   (3) The farmers, both the six million small ones and the several thousand large farming corporations,
   (4) Organized and unorganized labor;
B. *The two social factors*
   (5) The cooperatives, and
   (6) The Government.

Of these six the Government was shown to be the single positive factor that can operate freely and effectively when all the others are stalled in conflict. To be told that brings a shudder to the spines of people who have been brought up on the notion "the less government the better." History teaches, however, that the new principle is really not new and it certainly is not to be feared. The country's experience has shown clearly that Government has increasingly been interjecting itself into the social system for more than three-quarters of a century. The record of the laws passed by the legislative, executive, and judicial representatives of the people since 1870 is clear enough. And on the whole the acts of the Government have advanced the standards of living of the people.

The scholars' studies of a high-powered industrial society in transition in the Thirties and Forties did more than point to the bottlenecks that were holding us back from full production at a high abundance level. One of the most revealing things they did was to show how the basic concepts of the American Way had been changing.[13] The law of supply and demand and *laissez faire* became outmoded, and few really believed it worked. "Freedom" as "absence of restraint" slowly gave way to "controls so designed that all have an equal opportunity for freedom." The

[13] See James K. Feibleman's *Positive Democracy* and my own *Now Is the Moment.*

long-held substance meaning of property—the Thing itself—began to give way to the functional meaning: the social use of the thing. "An expanding economy" came to mean "a far richer way of living which could be got by running the social system at full employment at abundance level, and distributing the life obtained, to the people." Notions of age changed as length of life increased. As the rate of population growth slowed down, the average age of the American people advanced toward seventy, but the old-age deadline in industry dropped from 65 to 40. Some lags in the culture persisted. College deans clung to their notion that the old-age deadline for middle-aged professors was sixty-five! The notion that such inexorable laws as the law of the business cycle govern the economic system was steadily replaced by the concept of human design and control of the economic system; men made the system and men can change it into a better one. Moreover, the problems of the people are the product of the great trends of the past, especially the recent past, and alternative solutions can be found by projecting these trends into the future. One of the most encouraging changes in orientation dealt with Property and Life. The concepts held by the blind conformists of the Genteel Tradition—that the right to property is prior to the right to life— were denied. The modern students of society have insisted that nothing is superior to the right to life. The right to life means the right to work, the right to the fullest and the best guided education, to health and recreation, to expression and free access to human knowledge, and to personal growth—in short, it means the right to the fullest possible life.

The new political economy captured other concepts, but these major ones are sufficient for our illustrative purposes. This body of great concepts, documented in two generations of popular experience and of scientific research, can now serve as the intellectual skeleton of a great program in adult, college, and school education. Here is a new outlook upon life that works under the democratic framework and consciously builds on our historic philosophy of experience. It denies every modern version of dictatorship, bravely accepts the concept of social change, and affirms that every generation shall confront its social situation as a problem and solve it by scientific study.

IX

COMMUNICATION AND THE PUBLIC MIND: THE NEW SOCIAL PSYCHOLOGY

The great concepts of full-employment-at-abundance-level were brought to life by the efforts of a hundred leaders of thought and action who crossed the frontiers of economics and politics. It was in the borderland between the two that Bellamy, Turner, Robinson, and Beard rediscovered the higher concepts of "political economy"—the union of the economic concepts of property ownership with the political concepts of freedom and control. But the integration of fields of research became much wider than that. It was inevitable that, with their great diversity of talent and interest, some among these men would discover the vital area between political economy and psychology. That happened in the explosive period after World War I. What Veblen, Baldwin, Dewey, Thomas, and Cooley had vaguely perceived in 1900, Walter Lippmann, Harold Lasswell, Gordon Allport, Gardner Murphy, Goodwin Watson, Hadley Cantril, Paul Lazarsfeld, *et al.*, documented clearly after 1920. *All the social sciences—economics, politics, sociology, anthropology—went psychological between the two wars.* Even in the earlier period, 1895–1920, so wide-ranging was the work that it was impossible to attach the old academic label "economist," "political scientist," "sociologist," "anthropologist," to any one of the pioneering students.

Their most all-inclusive, conceptual achievement was the clear grasp of the significance of *The Culture*. The first generation of anthropologists—Tyler, Bastian, Ritter, *et al.*—had perceived its significance but had not documented it. Fifty years later, Clark Wissler's *Man and Culture* (1923) and Boas' *Mind of Primitive Man* (1911) had filled in some of the gaps. Wissler seems to have been the one to have given the younger men the key spot to go to work at—a direct eye-witness study of "the community." "Anthropology," he said in *Man and Culture*, "deals with the communities of mankind, takes the community . . . as the biological and social unit, and in its studies seeks to arrive at a perspective of society by comparing and contrasting these communities." Whether or not Wissler was the impetus, the American community, of every size and type, has had a thorough going over in the past thirty years. Franklin Giddings, Columbia sociologist, had put his students at the direct, eye-witness study of American rural communities soon after 1900. The Foundations established by the great fortunes—Rockefeller, Carnegie, *et al.*—soon created "Institutes" to finance studies of rural villages, small towns, and cities of various sizes and types. The university departments of sociology trained the young students of community life, got the Foundation money, and directed the studies. By the middle Thirties the Roosevelt government was definitely contributing to the advancing community studies. Under the auspices of the Resettlement Administration, investigations of new rural communities were appraising subsistence homestead projects and FSA districts, Soil Conservation districts, Local Extension clubs, AAA districts, and tracing the changing social structure of counties in Georgia. By 1939, under governmental leadership, sociologists, anthropologists, and psychologists were investigating "the cultural, community, and social psychological factors in rural life," discovering the basic cultural patterns of land use, attitudes toward work, thrift, and other virtues, the social-economic and political organization of the community, the role of leaders, the effect of machine technology on farmers and farming, the influence of urbanization, and the factors which facilitated or offered resistance to change.

Although these early studies were exploratory, they made the students and some political officials conscious of the need of studying the community. Here was the whole culture in miniature. This was the thing to settle down and study. Here were ourselves and our children.

It was from the thirty-year chain reaction of these researches that there emerged a half-dozen detonating concepts which, taken together, *form one of the keys to our college and school curriculum structure.*

X

The key to the whole conceptual structure is *The Culture and Its Molding of Personality*. The important sub-concepts are:

Culture-pattern, first made clear by Ruth Benedict's *Patterns of Culture* (1934). A basic example is the American belief in *laissez faire*.

The Stereotype, first clarified in Lippmann's *Public Opinion* (1922).

The role of Class-membership in molding personality, and the related concepts of "Inferiority" and "Dominance-Submission."

Consent and its principles, especially Popular Understanding and the barriers between people and the event: property barriers, psychological barriers, geographic and linguistic barriers.

Communication-control (externally imposed)—Propaganda—Censorship.

No conceptual tool is more broad-based than that of "The Culture." None is more fundamental to the teacher-education program. Building on the pioneering work of the anthropologists and sociologists, scores of their students have filled in the details and clarified its meaning since 1920. The literature is "as long as the moral law." This mounting accumulation of research and discussion has finally lifted the educators' eyes out of the narrow deep ruts of separate academic phases of life and fixed them on the broad total—"the culture"; there is now no other adequately descriptive term. We also see that distinctive levels are at least threefold: first, the surface, the *material* civilization of the producing-distributing social system; second, just below the surface, the *institutions*—family, government, church, press, school, etc.; third, the deeply imbedded *psychological forces*, driving and guiding the behavior of the people—their ideas, beliefs, values, wants, fears, taboos. As Milton Herskovitz said, "We know that the ultimate reality of culture is psychological."

A convincing case was made for the most important social-psychological concept of our day—the *culture-molding process*. Insight concerning the role of the culture-patterns in the midst of which we grow up came from an astute publicist, Walter Lippmann. He perceived the nub of the culture-molding process long before the technically trained anthropologists clarified the concept of culture-patterns. World War I was hardly over when Lippmann published *Public Opinion* (1922). By it he initiated a whole generation of studies of the formation and control of the public mind, created the powerful concept of the *stereotype*, and gave a push to the study of the culture-molding process by the social psychologists. The detonating, conceptual key lay in his generalization, *"we tend to perceive that which we have picked out in the form stereotyped for us by the culture"*; more briefly, we pick out what our culture has already defined for us.

The community studies which were already under way, and the researches on social attitudes of the social psychologies soon confirmed Lippmann. The two Lynds established themselves in Muncie, Indiana, and turned out their now classic pioneer studies (1) *Middletown* in 1924–25, and (2) ten years later, under the drastically changed economic-social conditions of the great depression, *Middletown in Transition.*

But it was not until the late Thirties and the Forties that teams of trained students of the culture consciously framed their studies on the "class membership" hypothesis. Although most human societies had revealed a class structure, America throughout all its frontier generations had probably been the least given to it. In the twentieth century, under the impact of the fascist-totalitarian attack on democracy, Americans, self-conscious about democracy, had vehemently denied the prevalence of "class" in our cultural structure. America is a classless society, it was widely asserted. Although in 1930 a definitive library of studies of "class" in the American way of life was lacking, by 1950 important preliminary investigations were at hand.

The meaning of the "class" concept itself had been clarified, and now included such subconcepts as: groups of common descent and common experience, living similar modes of life, holding relatively same ideas and feelings, meeting on relatively equal terms, and feeling themselves to belong together.

All students appeared to agree on these; some, including myself, added: a definite feeling of status within one's class and with respect to the hierarchy of the classes within the society, and the feeling of "being born" into a class and taking on its attributes and passing them on to one's children.

The Lynds had indicated in their second, depression-year study that the community climate was changing in the direction of greater class-consciousness. But it was the Warner group of anthropologists (then at Harvard, now at the University of Chicago) that made its community studies on the hypothesis that America had become a class-structured society. They studied the small old seacoast city of Newburyport, Massachusetts, Negro neighborhoods in New Orleans and other southern cities, and Negro neighborhoods in Chicago. Out of some ten years of research they published the large body of illustrative documentation.[14] More recently, Hollingshead (1947) independently confirmed their findings in his useful *Elmtown's Youth*. Whether or not we do our thinking with such a rigid hierarchy of class levels as that of Warner's "Upper-uppers" to "Lower-lowers," the Teacher of Teachers can be well advised to keep the culture-molding process in the forefront of his thought. To understand a child's responses, never lose sight of the culture, and never lose sight of the culture-patterns formed by his family and neighborhood.

Meanwhile there was developing another illustration of the way in which new truth is discovered through the integration of hitherto separated fields of research: students of sociology, political science, psychology, and economics joined hands to clarify the principle of consent. This was an ancient political idea. From John Locke's famous essays, *Two Treatises on Government* and *The Conduct of the Understanding* (about 1700), through Jefferson and the Founding Fathers (around 1800) to Roosevelt's New Deal in the 1930's, the students of democratic government slowly established the idea that *Democracy would never really work well until a very large proportion of the people understood their conditions and problems.* It was not enough to ground their civil and political Rights firmly in great state Declarations and Constitutions and to implement them in the principle of the Popular Suffrage, as had been done successfully in several hundred years of political struggle. In addition to these achievements —and they were great—it was necessary for the people to understand their problems if they were to succeed in carrying on their government on the principle of the consent of the governed. That became the desideratum, the crucial criterion, of democracy. The democratic way finally could rest its case on the success of the people in studying and discussing their problems together, and in making collective decisions about them. This was the very essence of the principle of consent.

It is at this point, therefore, that the educator becomes the key man in the democracy, even though the history of democracies thus far has universally placed him on the lowest rung of the ladder of prestige.

This broad-based conception of consent through intelligent

---

[14] See Cole's use of the material in Chapter VIII of his *Educational Psychology*, "Growth and Development in the American Culture."

popular understanding, plus the role of understanding in all interpersonal human relations, slowly turned the social psychologists'
research interests to one focal point: *Communication and its control.* Lippmann had pointed to the need of studying the barriers
between the people and understanding the event, and the consequent role of propaganda and censorship. The barriers were
shown to be partly geographic (the people scattered in widely
separated regions) and partly linguistic and cultural. The people
of the world were barred off from one another by language differences but even more by subtle differences in the key concept
meanings that had been built up by the various national cultures;
witness the meanings given to "democracy" by the Foreign Ministers of the USSR and the USA!

As a consequence of still another integration of fields of study,
facts that had been isolated in the separate subjects of geography,
philosophy, economics, psychology, sociology, government, and
the new semantics came together in clear relationship. *An exciting
fusion of generalizations, when juxtaposed,* detonated new ideas.
The Bellamy-Veblen-Turner-Beard concept of *"He that owns the
things that men must have . . ."* joined hands with the social
psychologists' *"we tend to perceive that which we have picked
out in the form stereotyped for us by the culture,"* and with similar semantic notions of meaning. The new integration of these
clarified the concepts of propaganda (the distortion of the facts),
censorship (the withholding of the facts), and led to the perception of another: *"He that controls the critical agencies of communication controls the public mind."*

These brief comments on the fusion of the psychologies with
the social sciences tells the Teacher of Teachers that he can now
call to his aid a new profession of social psychologists as well as
new historians, new political economists, new sociologists. Already
they have greatly clarified the basic problems of industrial society.
Above all they have made clear that these problems are psychological. They are problems of how people feel and think, of the
propaganda and censorship by which their understandings are
controlled by those who control the mass media of communication. On a larger scale they are problems of rivalries and chauvin-
isms caused by the new nationalism arising around the modern
world, and of the perennial struggles of the great In-Groups and
Out-Groups that we still are prone to label "races."

CHAPTER IV

The Science of Behavior:
The Bio-Psychological Foundations of Education

I

A second university discipline—Bio-Psychology—was created between 1920 and 1950 as the indispensable mate for the vital study of civilization. The Creative Path along which the students of the social order were blazing new trails was widened and deepened by a broad-ranging body of imaginative students of human behavior. While the new social science concentrated on the great concepts, problems, and conditions of industrial culture, and on the explosive movements of social change that gave birth to them, the new bio-psychology centered attention on the nature and nurture of the human organism. The *joint* contribution of the two groups—the social scientists and the bio-psychologists—makes it possible today to speak of "The Science of Man." This Science of Man, therefore, embraces the personal and social study of his traits, beliefs, and behavior, as well as the economics and politics of his group life.

The building of the new Bio-Psychology provided still another example of the phenomenon of integration of fields of knowledge and research. To create an adequate Educational Psychology for teachers today one is forced to draw his material from a dozen fields of study. These embrace three major university disciplines:

1. Physiology, including endocrinology, electro-physiology, and biochemistry.
2. Social anthropology and sociology, together with concepts from the other social sciences—economics, political science, human geography.
3. Psychology, including five "Schools":
   Conditioned-response psychology

Connectionist-trial-and-error psychology

Gestalt, Dewey, and other "field" psychologies

The depth and self psychologies created out of the psycho-analysis of Freud, and psychiatry

The various personality psychologies of Stern, Allport, Murphy, and others

Here is an astonishing range of sources—from physiology at one end of the scale to anthropology at the other, with their concepts integrated with the findings of fifty years of research on five theories of psychology, some stressing the more mechanistic conditioning and trial-and-error views, others the more organic, "field" insight, problem-solving theories.

It is this total storehouse of knowledge that has finally produced the new discipline, "Bio-Psychology." From this great source an adequate Bio-Psychological Foundation of Education is now being made for the first time.

The conclusion is inescapable that *any psychology today that ignores any of these is inadequate.* It is a fact, however, that the most widely used brand in the teachers colleges today—the connectionist-trial-and-error—ignores half of them! And most of the other current brands do also.

This broad range of knowledge is a far cry from the limited one from which Weber, Fechner, von Helmholtz, and Wundt improvised the first general psychology between 1840 and 1890, and Thorndike and Judd created Educational Psychology after 1900. We must not fail, however, to credit the German innovation with being definitely physiological; witness the publication of Fechner's *Physiological Psychology* (1860), Fechner's *Elements of Psycho-Physics* (1860), von Helmholtz's *A Handbook of Physiological Optics* (1896), and Wundt's famous *Physiological Psychology* which went through six editions between 1870 and 1911. But this body emphasis was lost throughout most of the half-century during which Thorndike and Judd centered attention on ideas, skills, and paper tests, and Dewey on logical thought. It is rather astonishing to recall that although Thorndike worked with James (who was directly concerned with physiology in his early years[1]) and Judd got his doctor's degree at Leipzig with Wundt, neither one gave any material attention to body-response. Moreover, John Dewey, whose influence in the progressive education

[1] As Professor of Anatomy in the Harvard Medical School.

of teachers has been deepest, consciously and consistently devoted his life work to the "scientific method of inquiry," to "intelligence," to "thinking" of the problem-solving variety; it is rare indeed to find any discussion in Dewey of the response of the body. With the major leaders so concerned with intelligence, thinking, the brain, the neurone, it is little wonder that Educational Psychology has, throughout our times, so largely neglected the study of the response of the body. In this chapter I shall deal with this problem in some detail.

Neither did the pioneers pay attention to the social sources in founding Educational Psychology. We must constantly bear in mind that there are two foci to the teacher-education curriculum problem. There is, first, the nature of a free society, which our America aspires to be and in which our teaching is done and, second, the nature of the human organism—how it learns, grows, and develops. But neither Thorndike nor Judd, the two leading bridges between nineteenth-century psychology and the first educational psychology, paid any attention to the crucial forces and factors that were transforming the social order during their lives. I know this from my long and intimate association with the two men, as well as from their teaching, lecturing, and books. At Chicago Judd gave a course on "social forces in education" for twenty-five years; this had been stimulated by his long association with Wundt's pioneering experiments in *Volkpsychologie*. Thorndike, near the end of his professional life, published a huge tome entitled *Human Nature and the Social Order* (1940). But neither of these brilliant leaders ever permitted himself to deal with the explosive psychological factors in the social order. The vital social problems and social forces were taboo. Judd's book, *The Psychology of Social Institutions,* illustrates it perfectly. "Institutions" meant to him language, processes of exchange, methods of measuring and recording facts, etc.; there was no reference to problems of property ownership and control, war and peace, control of the public mind, and the other critical problems of our times. The younger men—Gates, McConnell, Jersild, Freeman, Pintner, *et al.,* followed the lead of Judd and Thorndike. George Hartmann and Goodwin Watson were the conspicuous exceptions among the educational psychologists, and Lawrence Cole among the general psychologists.

II

Believing that what we need at this point is a *comprehensive yardstick* for the critical study of psychology, I have designed the tentative one which appears on the opposite page. I call it a Chart for Psychology According to the "Leave-No-Stone-Un-turned" School of Thought. In a sense this has been under preparation for many years. In writing *Foundations for American Education* during the war years I was convinced that the makings of an adequate Educational Psychology could be gathered only by going to all the disciplines I have just named. The needs of the present book have driven me to make the compact synthesis.[2]

The all-embracing and organic character of the sources centers our attention first on a shibboleth of modern progressive education. This is the *Whole Child*. Let this be our cue to organizing the major concepts of our new knowledge of human nature and behavior. We shall center them around the *Human Being conceived of as a Person*.

III

These are the formative concepts of behavior that have been discovered from the interpenetration of a dozen fields of research during the past half-century. *This, therefore, is the whole of psychology on one page.* This is the vast gamut of interrelated factors that are involved in any act of response—be it skill, thinking, creative expression, or appreciation.

With this yardstick in hand we can sharpen our contrast between the Educational Psychology (Thorndike-Judd-*et al.*) of the Conforming Way and the Bio-Psychology of the Creative Path.

There are many "standard" psychologies that represent the Conforming Way but, as I have said, three dominate the field:

---

[2] I present the fuller data, in collaboration with the World Book Company, in a series of major volumes, the first of which was published in 1947— *Foundations for American Education.* The second was Lawrence E. Cole's *Educational Psychology* (1950), which he and I prepared from his *magnum opus Principles of Psychology,* publication of which we anticipate in 1952. Our colleagues in the University of Illinois—B. Othanel Smith, William O. Stanley, and J. Harlan Shores—have carried through to completion the corresponding synthesis in *Fundamentals of Curriculum Development* (1950), as has Theodore Brameld of New York University in his *Patterns of Educational Philosophy* (1950). In many points in this book I have relied on the data and interpretations of these five new volumes.

A Chart for Psychology According to the "Leave-No-Stone-Unturned" School of Thought

The Whole Person in action—a dynamic, but precarious Self—a gossamer web of five contending Selves: the Self he is, the Self he thinks he is, the Self others think he is, the Ideal Self he thinks he ought to be, the Self others think he ought to be. This is the Man, the Woman, the Child in action.

The Whole Person, developing from inherited, infinitesimal, but whole beginnings growing up in a competing-cooperating, threatening-encouraging, loving-hating-fearing world—all the factors of growth, physical, intellectual, emotional, motivational, inextricably interrelated.

A Whole Person whose life is governed by tensions—physiologically driven by his needs (tensions) for physical security, and psychologically motivated by his needs (tensions) for social security, purposes, and interests.

A Whole Person compensating, equipped by self-balancing powers (homeostasis) to compensate for internal deficits, and to protect himself against external threats, either physical or psychological.

A Whole Perceiving Person, adjusting to changing situations via body-response; adopting "sets" appropriate to his changing needs, tensions, purposes—that is, to his attitudes of anticipation of what-follows-what; the focus of the set, or attitude, being the concept.

A Whole Person, responding actively *with* patterned, *or conceptual* meaning, not "getting" meaning by some mysterious process from an unknown source—but rather creating meaning as his life style, life experience, and needs teach him to do.

The Whole Person Thinking, because of his power to delay response, to make fine discriminations in perception, to perceive patterns (configurations, "Gestalts") as relations, to use symbols in imagination, to sense and hold the direction dictated by perception and relation-seeing, to build thought models and to generalize, that is, to *respond with concepts.*

A Whole Person Creating, expressing—via the concept—what *he* sees, *his* way—but with Form.

(1) Conditioned-response—that, for example, of Hull, *et al.*, out of Pavlov; (2) Trial-and-error, originated by Thorndike and popularized for most teacher-education institutions by Gates and his colleagues; and (3) the "Field" theories: Gestalt (Insight) and Dewey (Problem-solving), the former originated by Wertheimer and developed by Köhler and Koffka; the latter originated by Dewey and interpreted by Bode, Kilpatrick, and the younger men.

Whenever educational organizations make a new report on the status of educational psychology they gather representatives of these three schools into a Committee and publish statements of the three theories.[3] *Each* of the three theories *contributes something of importance to the Teacher of Teachers.* Each one will help him build a sound theoretical foundation for the understanding of his students. But no one of these alone, nor even all of them added together, can serve him adequately.

There is another major theory that makes the Personality and the Self the organizing center. This has been developed quite independently by two groups: the first centering in the depth concepts of Freud and the psychoanalysts, the second in the work of Stern, Allport, and Murphy.

And, finally, there is the "leave-no-stone-unturned" point of view presented throughout this book.

IV

On two concepts all of these psychological points of view stand foursquare, together. First, they agree that all learning is "associative." For two hundred years most steps of psychology-building have made implicit use of the principle of association. The modern vocabulary uses the terms "conditioned" or "connectionist." Learning, as Thorndike says, is connection-forming, that is, associating. The stream of practical experience confirms it; conditioning goes on in the successive acts of everyday life.

Second, there is complete agreement on the *action concept.* Since the first works of Peirce, James, and Dewey we have increasingly had *an action psychology.* Today our better schools are becoming "activity schools." As Guthrie says: "We learn only what we have done." James put it: "Experience is ours only as we create it"; since 1900 psychologists have been saying with

[3] As in the *Forty-first Yearbook* of the National Society for the Study of Education, *The Psychology of Learning* (1942).

Judd: "We respond *with* meaning." Or, we can phrase it according to Peirce, Bridgman, or Dewey, as: Our concept of an object is "the effects which . . . have . . . practical bearings, we conceive the object to have" (Peirce). *"The concept is synonymous with the corresponding set of operations"* (Bridgman). We build meanings of objects by making practical responses to them (Dewey). To quote him: "Things gain meanings when they are used as means *to bring about consequences.*" Thus, our conceptions of learning, and our better schools, are being built on the concept of *association* and on the *principle of active response.*

V

Although here and there I think I can discern partial agreements, I can find no other single major concept on which all three standard theories, and their maverick critics, truly agree.

Consider, for example, the concept of freedom and the problem of control in behavior, including learning. Certainly this is basic to mankind's issue of democracy *vs.* totalitarianism. In a society such as the American, which treasures freedom above all things and is striving to create a new twentieth-century solution to the problem of freedom and control, it becomes the key problem for the teacher. Our way of life accepts the conception that freedom does not mean license; in an interdependent society a man can be only partly free; much of his behavior must be controlled. Whether or not our provincial private enterprisers agree, men of thought do. In a democratic society, we work toward that day when a maximum of the necessary control will be self-imposed, and only a minimum imposed by the law of the group. Yet the five-thousand-year record of Man's history in the Exploitive Tradition has failed to reveal a single culture in which individualistic Man, without social controls, did not destroy the soil, the vegetation, the forests, the minerals—and, with them, his fellow man— in his mad search for immediate profit. Painfully, and at great cost, modern man is relearning the *Principle of the Sustained Yield.* Witness the incredible inflationary destruction of civilization after World War I through failure to control the medium of exchange in country after country. Even as I write the issue confronts us in America. Will the scattered voices of the people demanding control of the money system be listened to?

It is in this cultural matrix that the teacher, as the chief guide of development and the culture-molding process, must confront the questions of freedom and control: When can the learner be freed? For what ends are controls employed? Critical, indeed, is the question: *What are the consequences for learning*, and hence for behaving, of the conditions of control set up in typical human situations? How can teachers take advantage of this knowledge in arranging the stage for learning?

A generation of scientific study confirms the generalization from popular experience, and from the progressive education trend, that an *atmosphere* of freedom, a *feeling* of being free, is conducive to effective learning and understanding. Yet the sponsors of conditioning and trial-and-error have always studied learning under conditions that denied freedom to the learner; witness the rigidities of the "conditioning-harness," the puzzle-box, and the maze. The "field" theories of learning, on the contrary, consciously provide more freedom; witness (1) the open cages, court yards, runways, etc., of Gestalt experiments; (2) Dewey's principle of "freedom to investigate," which hundreds of schools put to work after 1910; (3) the insistence on freedom of the artist and the artist-teacher, who affirm: "I must *feel* free to say what I see *my* way." Out of the experience and research of fifty years the position today is: *first*, in infancy relatively complete control must be imposed in all situations of danger, in any society, including the democratic ones; *second*, as the child develops the teacher slowly takes off the controls; *third*, the utmost care must be employed to grade the learning tasks, to make sure that the learner understands what he is doing at every step of the way.

VI

The three standard theories differ fundamentally with respect to the essence of learning, because they differ with respect to the Part-Whole Problem: This separates them on all the basic concepts: learning, integration, generalization, thinking, feeling, growth, the role of nature and nurture, personality, self, needs, motives, purposes.

The conditioning and the connectionist-trial-and-error theories are both "Part" conceptions. They depend largely on juxtaposition, on contiguity of the parts in space and in time. They visualize the parts as relatively isolated; "organism" does not really mean much to them. Their primary interest is in the brain, the cortex, and the specific neurone. (Their latest physiological ally, D. O. Hebb, slices the cortical source of action more broadly, replacing the neurone with the "cell-assembly"[4]; but his theory of behavior is still connectionism.)

Nevertheless they know that, for action, the parts must be joined together, and this, they say, is achieved by external cues. You get the clear statement of the process from Thorndike, who throughout his professional life would never qualify his conception of the additive nature of the learning process. Although he had been weaned from the old Wundtian structural view, he saw learning taking place through the forming of connections. He himself called his theory a "situation-response," or "connectionist psychology"; that is, an S-R Bond psychology. But the bonds or connections are stamped in, he said, through repetition motivated by the learner's needs, sets, rewards, and other "satisfactions." These get fixed by chance! Bits of a blundering and random activity take place that at last bring success. Thus, the crux is the "part" which is viewed as isolated, and joined only by an external forcing process. "Satisfyingness" or "annoyingness" is the chief binding force. Thorndike was so sure of his formulas for learning that he called them "laws"; for example, the "Law of Exercise" (the more frequently, recently, and vigorously a connection is exercised, the more it is stamped in, and vice versa), and the "Law of Effect," which he centered in what he constantly called "satisfaction."

That the conditioning and connectionist views are mechanistic is shown (1) by the way the experimenters set the stage for studying learning, by employing the conditioning-harness, the puzzle-box, or the maze; (2) by selecting minute abilities or skills for study because only those are controllable and measurable; and (3) by their interpretations of the behavior of the learners. Note, for example, their insistence that the center of the learner's attention is on the specific thing, not on the field—that is, the relations between the things. Note also their emphasis on the random nature of behavior and hence their interpretations of learning as trial-and-error, or success by chance. Today we question seriously the random nature of behavior. The experimental evidence shows that much of the behavior which precedes successful solution is

[4] *The Organization of Behavior.*

not random; a great deal of true but latent learning is going on
and much valuable understanding is being built up.

The field theories of the Gestalt-problem-solving groups see
these facts very differently. They fix attention on the whole
human being, on the whole situation of which he is the center,
and on his understanding and personally creative activity. They
set the stage for study as a relatively open free field. They emphasize relationships rather than things.

VII

If, along about 1930, Thorndike and the conditioning connectionists in general had permitted themselves a second look, they
could not have failed to see the impressive body of evidence in
all the sciences and arts that was finally clinching the century-
long shift in thought from mechanical to organic explanations.
Even by 1930 the concepts brought together in my Comprehensive Chart were substantially established. They all pointed to
organic, rather than to mechanical, conceptions as the key to
understanding.

Study the new psychology that is epitomized on the chart. One
concept dominates it—*The Whole.* I have accentuated it in every
paragraph of my synthesis, not only by using the word "Whole,"
but by constant reference to a half-dozen illustrative concepts.
Because of the widespread knowledge of the research and interpretive literature which document the validity of these, it is unnecessary for me to present it in detail here. Instead of writing
fifty more pages on it, I enumerate twenty examples of the validation from the entire range of the sciences and the arts; this list
will justify a laborious and critical analysis—not merely a scanned
reading:

—the physicist's concept of "the field-as-an-organization-of-forces-in-
tension"

—the biologists' concept of "integration"

—Alfred North Whitehead's "philosophy of organism"—all science
is the study of organism

—the concept of the Whole developed by the biologist-statesman,
Jan Smuts

—the basic growth conception—the inextricable *interrelatedness* of
all the phases of growth and development

—the Coghill-Lashley, *et al.*, concept of "mass-action"

—Needham's "organizing relations" as the basic principle of human development

—the Walter Cannon concept of *homeostasis,* the self-regulating behavior of the whole organism when confronted by deficits or threats

—the poet's similar concept (Walt Whitman's "O, to be Self-balanced for contingency!")

—the Wertheimer-Köhler concept of Gestalt, that is, of configuration or pattern

—Judd, *et al.*'s documentation of the concept of generalization. Lewin's psychological concept of a "field-as-an-organization-of-psychic-tensions"

—John B. Watson's concept of total body-response—"When an individual reacts . . . his whole body reacts"

—the chorus of affirmation that psychology, including the psychology of the act, is social

—the organic theme of the literature of "personality" psychology (Murphy, Allport, *et al.*)

—Gordon Allport's "functional autonomy of motives"

—the Person as the joint product of the organism and society—the union of nature and nurture, of heredity and environment

—the dynamic but precarious concept of the Self—five conflicting Selves made especially clear by Freud, the psychoanalysts and the psychiatrists

—the Alfred Adler concept of compensation, the Freudian concept of the defensive mechanisms

—the expressive artists' basic concept of "form"—the principle of organization, of unity of related parts

—the literary critics' (Waldo Frank, *et al.*) and K. Wild's concept of the organism-as-a-whole as the organ of the method of "primal awareness" (intuition)

VIII

That brings me to another thesis: *the standard psychologies in popular use in teacher education today utilize only a part of this galaxy of concepts.* Every one of them ignores indispensable key ideas. As a consequence these psychologies are lopsided, badly oriented, inadequate. They fail the Teacher of Teachers. Yet that need not be. All the makings of an adequate psychology are now available in the scholars' studies. My thesis is that the Teacher of Teachers, and *all other teachers*, must now take the comprehensive look at Man, his society, his knowing and behaving. Periodically, we must re-shuffle the cards of human knowledge. We must open the blinders that restrict our vision to a still wider arc, taking in more of the horizon. We must lift our sights to a higher orientation or, as in the case of the overconsumption of the brain and the cortex, *drop* our sights to see more clearly the role of the body-below-the-cortex in behavior. As we do these things we find hitherto unknown factors that give us newer and truer cues to understanding the living creature. It is clear that to hold firmly any one of these standard theories of behavior is to set the blinders at a narrow arc and to prevent ourselves from seeing *factors in relationship* without which we cannot get at the truth.

Looking squarely at the range, the depth, and the bulk of the total data that were available to the psychologists it is difficult, for example, to see how (even in 1930) they missed the significance of fifty years of research on the response of the body. Consider the new view of perception as an example. All of the standard psychologists worked on perception, many of them for forty years. The Gestaltist studies, for example, were primarily studies of perception; Thorndike's so-called "Laws of Effect," and hundreds of studies of attention, dealt directly with the problem of how the proper responses are selected.

Most important, it is recognized by all that the "perceptual field" is crucial in all acts of response, whether they be acts of skill, thinking, appreciation, or of the creative process. No explanations—either Gestalt or connectionist—of what the perceiver selects from the situation will make sense that relies chiefly on contiguity in space and time. Certainly the Gestalt labeling of the sudden flash of insight, as "Insight"—which creative biographies have done for two thousand years—is nothing more than labeling. It is certainly not an explanation of what takes place in the Act. But to take a wider look which will embrace all the factors of the scene requires going to the physiology of needs, tensions, drives, to experience-personality-anticipatory sets, to the psychology of life style, to the problem-solving psychology of the delayed response, to the field psychology of patterned response and closure, to seeing-relations, perhaps even to the electronics of feed-back applied to human response. Only, I say, by taking the most comprehensive look do we see that with the learner "set" to learn, the total organism—that is, the whole-acting body—selects and organizes the needed responses to fit all its physical and social needs.

I cite but a few typical, definitive researches and examples: Richter's twenty-five years of research on body deficits; his adrenalectomized rats always found the needed sodium solution, the parathyroidectomized ones always picked the calcium solution ... Cannon's life-long documentation of homeostasis—the capacity of the body to maintain a balanced state of equilibrium—and his distinguished documentation of the role of the endocrines in emotional behavior . . . The interaction of the organism and the culture as an example of cultural homeostasis, reminding us that the learner sees in each situation what the culture has taught him to see (the culture-molding process) . . . The fact that what the learner selects is profoundly influenced by his preparatory set, by the emotionalized nature of his orienting mood; these have been determined in part by his past experience as they have also built his social-psychological needs for security, and the personal, "Self" product in his unique Life-Style.

If the connectionists had really studied the revolution in modern physics with mood and mind opened wide to the meaning of the field, they would have seen its implications for their own interpretation of thinking. Witness Thorndike's own description of the generalizing processes in reading and problem-solving in arithmetic and algebra.[5] If, instead of fighting back at Köhler, *et al.*, as though they were deadly enemies, they had really opened their minds to the relational facts of pattern, revealed in the thousands of Gestalt perceptual studies, they would have rid themselves of some of the rigidities in their narrow theory and practice. They would not have found *the causes* of behavior in neurones. If they had been clear that nerve cells merely *transmit* impulses (there is no evidence that they fire the concept) they would have doubted that neurones, or cell-assemblies for that matter, "think." They would have said with the organicist—be he physiologist, or psychologist, or artist—the whole organism thinks. With Emerson, the poet, they would have pictured Man Thinking. If they had permitted themselves to consider that their concepts of belong-

[5] In such books as his *Psychology of Arithmetic* and *Psychology of Algebra,* and in his articles on reading.

ingness, wants, interests, satisfactions must be the cravings of an acting human being, they would have created a "Self," or some other concept to stand for the whole organism in action.

If the conditioners, the connectionists, and the Gestaltists, too, studying countless examples of behavior, had really opened their minds to the question: "How come? How did this man, this child, get that way?" they would have brought the modern world's concept of experience into the picture. Every scientific worker from Locke and Descartes to Peirce, James, Dewey, and most of us today, have made the role of experience central. But all the standard psychologists, including the Gestaltists, tended to overlook or to ignore it, relying on the learning conditions *in the present* to account for behavior. The Pragmatic-Experimentalist group, however, led by James, Dewey, Bode, Kilpatrick, and the Personality psychologists, the most articulate of whom have been Stern, Allport, and Murphy, all made experience—both past and present—important.

These were the primary questions asked by the mavericks of psychology. With Freud and the other psychoanalyists the key question was: "How come?" They dug into the past—if anything they went too far and paid too little attention to the present. If the standard schools of psychology could have brought themselves really to listen a bit to the researches and the logic of these newcomers, they might then have granted Freud's contention (with which most of humanity probably agrees) that childhood experience—even early childhood—plays an important formative role in all successive behavior. They might even have found, with Freud, that the sex drive is a powerful factor in behavior. They would have made much of the role of the cumulative frustrations and anxieties of life, the deep-seated effect of a sense of inferiority and the pervasive influence of psychological insecurities.

To get the full significance of these traits they might have taken the psychiatric concepts in close juxtaposition with those of the sociologist and social anthropologist, putting together such concepts as these: (1) Ours is a world of competing human beings (what family, what neighborhood, school, church, club, community is not!); (2) Human beings differ widely; (3) Every society tends to fall into a rank-order of prestige and control—as the animal psychologists phrase it, a "pecking order"—the extrovert aggressives dominate the docile submissives from infancy and childhood to old age; (4) A sense of inferiority grows, tensions arise as wishes, but the wishes are repressed. Frustrations and anxieties develop and inferiority becomes a chronic human trait.

What happens to the repressed wishes? Most psychologists have ignored them but Freud paid lifelong attention to them, insisting that they remain, pushed back out of consciousness. His hypothesis should have been considered by a really "open" theory of behavior, not shrugged off or laughed down. He created the concept of the unconscious as the behind-the-scenes, or below-the-surface, or the sub-cellar storeroom of the unwanted, not-to-be-tolerated desires. These persist and at every possible moment reassert themselves, causing defensive kinds of behavior. Adler, who left Freud, disagreeing over the role of the sex drive, created the concept of "compensation" to describe the devious routes men follow in trying to protect themselves. And the Freudians in general, recognizing the chronic human tendency toward inferiority, clarified the defense mechanisms which men invent in a competitive world in their search for security: "rationalization"; "compensation"; "projection"; "defense"; and other devices to escape the full consequences of their behavior.

The situation would have been much the same with respect to the Nature-Nurture controversy. The conventionalists' dogmatic defense of the hereditarian position would have been modified if they had listened to the findings of a long line of researches including hundreds of quantitative studies. To cite only a few conspicuous ones: Sontag's studies of the three identical triplets—Henry, John, and Fred; the case of Mabel and Mary and other studies of identical twins brought up in different environments; the case of Isabel, the deaf-mute mother's illegitimate child, brought up through years of isolation from normal family and social life; the striking case of Anna; and the much discussed Wolf-Child. The best answer we can give today to the heredity-environment question is an organic one: neither Nature nor Nurture rules completely. We recognize the joint contribution of heredity and environment in producing effective intelligence or any other fundamental trait. Equate the environments and nature seems to rule; equate the inheritance factors and the environment will tell. The organic concept carries us even further, for the integration of heredity and environment is so close (as, for example, in the case of the development of bees) that the organism can be said to "assimilate its environment." And this is also true in the human world. The physical organism obviously assimilates its "chemical environment" and the total organism assimilates its social environment by building expectancies as ways of responding in the world.

IX

But there is not much use in regretting the meandering manner in which the psychologists, followed by the teachers, put together their theories of behavior; at least not beyond the point of having made clear that no theory can be adequate that ignores any of the possible factors and sources of knowledge. Summing it all up, for the moment, then, I repeat—the full list of sources of possible clues to behavior includes at least half a dozen disciplines: all the physiologies . . . all the social psychologies of the culture . . . the three conventional psychologies—conditioned-response, connectionist-trial-and-error, and Gestalt . . . the personality and self psychologies . . . perhaps even the new knowledge of electronic communication-control.

From the comprehensive *integration* of the concepts of all these disciplines—not from their eclectic assembly—we today can build sound Bio-Psychological Foundations of Education. The *integration* of all *indispensable* concepts is the key.

CHAPTER V

The Art of Expression:
The Esthetic Foundations of Education

I

I take you next to Esthetics. This is the third great source of educational foundations. We make an important shift here. We turn from Science to Art, from the Science of Man to his Art of Living. It is important for us to be clear about this shift. While the ingredients of the scientific and of the esthetic ways of working are the same—they are the very ingredients of the act of response that we have been describing and synthesizing—the situation in which they are employed, the orientation of the worker, his goals and products, all of these are fundamentally different.

This distinction is important for another reason. Education is an art—and a technology. It is not a science. It draws its materials from the scientific and esthetic disciplines—from the science of society and the culture, the science of behavior, and the art of esthetics. These three disciplines alone are sufficient to supply curriculum and teaching with all the needed materials for the foundations of education.

Although our first Teachers of Teachers behaved as if they were unaware of it, there was as much need for esthetics in teacher education in 1900 as there was for the materials and concepts of the culture and behavior. But in 1900 there was no organized esthetics worthy of the name in the liberal arts college. Hence teacher education contained no Esthetic Foundations of Education. Such limited teaching of "the arts" as got into school and college programs was little better than superficial picturizing. Most of it was not true expression.

But at the very moment that the young men of science were pioneering—Dewey and Veblen, Robinson and Turner, Freud and Cannon—a company of their contemporaries was breaking away from the widespread habit of the architects, painters, poets, and dancers of the day of imitating the standard, classic styles of Europe. They were not only declaring their expressive independence of Europe and the past; they were also trying their wings with crude new improvisations.

Walt Whitman, the greatest inspirer of the creative revolution, in an early edition of *Leaves of Grass*, stated the essence of both the American democratic way of life and the life of a good school: "I can hear America singing," he said, "each singing what belongs to him and to none else." And Isadora Duncan, the first dancer of the twentieth-century western world, expressed it in her early essay (1906): "My art is just an effort to express the truth of my being in gesture and movement. It has taken me long years to find even one true movement." And of the American thing, she said:

When I read this poem of Whitman's, *I, too, had a Vision: the Vision of America dancing a dance that would be the worthy expression of the song Walt heard when he heard* America singing . . .[1]

I see America dancing, beautiful, strong, with one foot poised on the highest point of the Rockies, her two hands stretched out from the Atlantic to the Pacific, her fine head tossed to the sky, her forehead shining with a crown of a million stars.[2]

Twenty-six-year-old Alfred Stieglitz had come back from his photographic triumphs in Europe to launch decades of implacable warfare against the imitation and commercialism in photography, and in painting and the graphic arts. Isadora herself, mature in her seventeen years, was scandalizing the Victorians with her barelegged and corsetless dances. Louis Henry Sullivan and his argumentative young assistant, Frank Lloyd Wright, were building their new functional "American" buildings. Charles Ives, a mere boy in his twenties, was composing the first American symphony out of the folk strains of American small-town bands, while still another—Stephen Crane—was on New York's Bowery, writing *Maggie, A Girl of the Streets*. As one of the critics of the day said: "the fiddles were tuning all over America."

These were the heralds of a *new* day. In the 1890's America was beginning to speak! Before that time, with the exception of

[1] *The Art of the Dance,* p. 47. Italics mine.
[2] *Ibid.,* p. 49.

a few greats—a Thoreau and an Emerson, a Melville and a Whitman—the creative process had been debased in every medium of expression. For two hundred and fifty years we had got our language, letters, all our arts from Europe. As Emerson had said: "To be as good a scholar as Englishmen are: to have as much learning as our contemporaries, to have written a book that is read, satisfied us."

In this short book it is impossible to take space to build an adequate feeling for the full range of the creative revolution which was breaking through in every medium of expression.[3] At best I can merely illustrate it with a few examples. I shall, therefore, refer briefly to photography and the man who did more for the building of integrity of expression in the plastic arts than any other man in America—Alfred Stieglitz (1864–1947). I shall deal with the production of the American novel after 1920 and of a great literary criticism. And I shall generalize the magnificent case that can now be made for the building of a new esthetics. First, photography.

II

Photography is a bit over a hundred years old. Niepce made the first "heliograph" with the "camera obscura" in 1825 and Daguerre the first "sun picture" in 1839; this latter date is now generally accepted as the year of the invention of photography. Its century of history has moved through three major strands: The first consisted of an advancing science and technology, with emphasis on scientific principles, mechanical invention, design and construction of technical apparatus. This resulted in a breathtaking development of faster lenses and films, better lights, small efficient cameras. The second strand was primarily social photography, the record and interpretation of the life of the people. The third was creative art. Science and technology, reflecting the advancing trend of the nineteenth and early twentieth centuries, consumed the interest of most workers during the first half of this century of development. *But throughout our own transitional*

[3] Moreover I must avoid duplication of the accounts I have given in *Foundations for American Education* (1947), *Culture and Education in America* (1931), and *Now Is the Moment* (1943).

years a small body of social-scientific photographers and creative artists gave us stirring examples of true art and paved the way for the current social documentation through the camera.

Three men played the largest role in this important episode of personal American expression: Alfred Stieglitz, Edward J. Steichen, and Clarence W. White. But the greatest of these is Stieglitz.

A boy of seventeen, Stieglitz went to Berlin in 1881 to study engineering at the Polytechnic. Discovering a camera during his first year he soon made himself a world renowned master of it. He outdid his German professors in dogged insistence on perfection. He was one of the first to photograph successfully at night under electric light, to photograph in rain and snow, to capture the forces in city structures, in the moving airplane, and he was a pioneer with Steichen in color photography. At twenty-six, when he returned to America, he knew and was known to the leaders in the modern art movements of Europe.

In 1892 Alfred Stieglitz became editor of *American Amateur Photographer* and made it an organ of sincere, competent, creative expression. But more was needed—solidarity of like-minded spirits, solidarity through organization. The reactionaries in the Society of Amateur Photographers were organized, and they were opposed to the progressive ideas of Stieglitz and his fellow artists. In 1897 he reorganized the Society into the Camera Club of New York, and in the same year organized and began to edit *Camera Notes* as its organ.

Five more years passed. Again the conventionalists got into the saddle and retarded the expressive speech of Stieglitz and his friends. Once more (1902), he left the commercialists, followed by sixteen Fellows and thirty Associates, organized "Photo-Secession" and launched *Camera Work* as its periodic organ. For fifteen years, until the economic conditions incident to the World War crushed it in 1917, Stieglitz published in this organ the photographs of the greatest creative artist-photographers in the world: Edward Steichen (witness the magnificent special Steichen Supplement, April, 1906) . . . Clarence H. White (Founder and Director, 1910–1925, of the Clarence H. White School of Photography) . . . and Frederick H. Evans, to name only a few of the best. Here were also published the best critical studies of expression in the graphic and plastic arts; witness Marius de Zayas' series on modern art.

But an *organ* through which to speak and an organization to back it up were only two aspects of Stieglitz's great work. Throughout a half century of utterance he insisted on the indispensable role of Places of integrity in which true American Voices can speak. Since 1905 he maintained three successive "American Places":

First (1905–1917), the Little Galleries of the Photo-Secession, now known around the world as "291" (because of the address, 291 Fifth Avenue, New York). During the first ten years, "291" was literally the First Place to show the world's great "moderns." There, from 1908 to 1912, Stieglitz first introduced America to Cézanne, Picasso, Matisse and "the Fauves," Picabia, Braque, and Marin. He paved the way for the so-called Armory Show of 1913 and later the national publicizing of the "arrival of modern art."

Second (1925–1929), after eight years without a Place, without an Organization, without an Organ through which to speak, Stieglitz, with the help of Mitchell Kennerley, organized the Intimate Gallery. There it was that I first met Stieglitz and there I sat on the floor of his little carpeted room and looked and looked at the Marins and the O'Keeffes, the Hartleys and the Doves, and the photographs of Stieglitz and Paul Strand.

Third, from 1930 to 1947, when he died, he had his "American Place" where visitors met this man of integrity. In those three clear rooms of light and honesty, of imagination and rigorous technical competence, they listened to America speaking through the paintings and photographs of several of her greatest creative artists—John Marin, Georgia O'Keeffe, Arthur Dove, and Alfred Stieglitz. And there in that Place were stored a thousand of their paintings and his photographs, undoubtedly the most valuable art stock in our country for such a small group of artists.

So for fifty years the American graphic and plastic artist spoke through Stieglitz, through his Places, through the works of art he selected so critically to speak in the Places, through his own conversations. By the Thirties many young educators saw that the nation-wide cultivation of his concept through the colleges and schools would make America one of the most creative Places of all human history. A Golden Day of spiritual abundance—match-

ing the economic abundance our engineers would produce for us—
would be ushered in.

III

Stieglitz' life and work is a good and sufficient introduction to
the expressive revolution of our times which created the makings
of our third new discipline, esthetics. The major work was done
after 1920, but to understand it we must deal briefly with a prior
question: How does the artist work? What is it he expresses?
What is so unique about it, how is it so different from science and
the scientific method that we must have a separate Esthetic Foundation of Education? Here I shall do no more than introduce the
problem. Chapter VI will expand it more fully.

The conditions imposed upon the artist who works in any medium of expression are difficult at best, but those confronting the
photographer are rigorously so. These conditions can be made
clear by a brief comment on what the artist does in producing a
work of art. Starting with his own imagined conception—a concept, a felt-attitude, perhaps a mere urge to get something down
in objective form—the artist selects material and molds it into an
organization. The material consists of anything physical, mental,
spiritual, human or nonhuman. His working process is essentially
that of organizing forces, relating elements into a unity—not of
arranging things. The drive behind this organizing process is his
fusion of feeling, concept, and attitude. He works under the limitations of his materials and his instrument, and he works creatively
only to the extent that he understands and respects their potential
capacities. But irrespective of what the materials are, they are a
miscellany, and man works as artist by selecting those that are
useful to his purpose, molding them into an organization of unified form that expresses his feeling for order.

Returning to the photographer and his instrument, the camera:
What are his materials? They are the still and moving appur-
tenances of nature and civilization, the world of people, the
houses, communities, factories, trains, what-not, observed under
the conditions of light, color, mist, or shadow. They are the far-
flung scene of heaven and earth and the atmosphere in between.
A fusion of still and moving scenes, moment by moment these
materials put themselves together in chance arrangements. It is
impossible, therefore, to speak of nature as being organized, al-

though human beings sometimes see it so. Contrary to the popular shibboleth, nature has not created beauty. In that sense nature is not "beautiful." It is not *organized;* it is an *arrangement* of things, in an infinite number of permutations and combinations. Only under rare exceptions does man encounter natural objects which he appraises as beautiful. *Order, beauty, is man-made; it is not a function of nature,* which is subject to the laws of chance. If you doubt my generalization, organize your garden, go away and leave it for a month, then return to the anarchy into which nature has thrown it.

But man working as artist can create from the still and moving scene his own esthetic scene, rather than wait for it or search for it in the miscellaneous materials of the objective world. This is the great achievement of *creative* motion picture photography—and of the *creative* examples of modern architecture, dance, poetry, novel, theatre, industrial design—since the 1890's. The artist can organize people and things and photograph them. Or he can search for the esthetic scene in the multitudinous forms of the natural and man-made world. If he is sensitive and alert and patient, he can put himself into such strategic positions that the scene will evoke in him a deep sense of organization, and the photographic record will be an organization and hence a work of art. To do so requires great skill in seeing in an organizational way. Anybody can aim a camera at a scene, hold it still, and snap its shutter, thereby taking a picture. But only an artist can see organizationally, discover and select the strategic place for seeing, and wait for the optimum moment and capture the esthetic organization. This requires that the camera be technically acute and efficient, and that the photographer have technical control of the camera and skilled coordination in its manipulation. But only if the man is an artist will his photographic record be an organization, an evocation of the forces in the scene, of the relations between the things. Then, and then only, will it be a work of art.

IV

This is a single example of the creative revolution that, after 1890, broke through the crust of America's long worship of the arts of Europe and the past. Although only a few of the more historically minded were sensitive to it, we were then leaving the first of three stages of cultural growth through which all infant cultures pass to reach maturity. The *first* one is a long stage of transplanting the political-economic-social and esthetic practices of the mother culture (western Europe, especially Britain) on to new continents and regions. It is marked by the inevitable partial continuation of mores, ideas, beliefs, styles of the parent culture. With us in America, this was 250 years long, 1620–1870.

The *second* stage is a hectic period of rebellion against further imitation of the parent culture and the first hesitant improvisation of indigenous and original forms. With us this period was approximately from 1890 to 1920, the years during which the first teacher-education program was thrown together.

The *third* stage is marked by the slow emergence of a maturing, original, and indigenous expression of the people in every phase of the culture. While most of the expression is folk-statement—a *recording* of events and of the traits and characteristics of the people and their way of life—and a documenting of their struggles to solve their problems, here and there isolated Voices speak clearly, lyrically, and critically. A few sense the more profound cosmic depths of Man-in-the-Universe-and-in-History. With us, this is the Thirty years (1920–1950) that have already passed and that merge with those that move on and on through our twentieth century.

V

We probably should pause at this point long enough to do some careful defining of terms. You will note that in the past few pages I have been dealing with "expression" and have said little about "esthetics." You will note also that I have referred only to expressive artists, never once to professors of esthetics, or of philosophy, or of literature or "fine art." This points to a very important distinction, one, indeed, upon which my whole argument rests. It is the distinction that has been drawn throughout this book between the Conforming Way and the Creative Path.

As a student of American culture and of the way in which a new education can develop it into a higher order, I have long found my cue in the concept of expression. I define expression very simply: "I say, what I see (feel, think, intend) *my* way." It matters not whether the expression is of a political judgment on a public issue, a personal decision about an economic problem, or a statement in one of the "fine arts"; the criterion is: "Has it been said my way?" Not your way, *my way*. Not the family's way, or the Dean's way, the faculty's way, or the community's way—my way. All my expressive acts must, by definition, be mine, not copies or reflections of any standard classic way, nor of the popular way. Of course, it may turn out that my statements may show striking agreement with the statements of others; with respect to the deepest loyalties of the community and the nation this is the desired consensus. But the only essence of our treasured democratic way of life is my principle of expression: every man, woman, and child shall be obligated as well as privileged to say "I say what I think. I say what I feel." Of course, having said that, I shall then, on all matters of public interest, abide by the decision of the majority.

But not on matters of personal expression. There is a vast gamut of private interests that must be served, and that is where "esthetics" plays its biggest role. It plays it in two ways—in expression and in appreciation. The key to my theory (here I am anticipating the discussion of Chapter VI) is that the highest order of appreciation can be built only through *participation*, only through the expressive, or creative, act. Note that I make the expressive and the creative acts synonymous.

Now, who understands the creative act? Who is sensitive to the expression of another? Only he who has passed the creative act through his body. Only the expressive person. *Knowledge* about creative acts, the special stock-in-trade of the college professors of the arts, may help—a little—but the final desideratum is *expression*.

This runs counter to the conventional practice of accepting the professors of fine arts as our authorized estheticians. This latter is merely part and parcel of the wider practice in western civilization of making the Academy the official guardian of the heritage of cultivated taste and of housing the authority—generally—in the universities. Those who have become members of the Academy have traditionally been the Conformists—not the great creative artists. Those who have become the deans and directors of the arts in the colleges have, in most cases, never created anything. The issue then is between creating expressive art on the one hand, and reproducing standard styles in art, or knowing about art, on the other.

Summing up, then "esthetics," in this book means *expression and appreciation*—the latter produced, maximally, through expression. With this in mind we return to the story of America's creative revolution.

VI

My brief generalizations about the present expressive stage of American development will bring more agreement if a few of the details are filled in. To do that fully would require a larger volume. For my purposes I shall be content to illustrate what happened after 1920 in American writing, particularly in the novel and criticism. I shall make brief reference to nine of the best of its writing men—Sinclair Lewis, Sherwood Anderson, Scott Fitzgerald, Ernest Hemingway, John Roderigo Dos Passos, William Faulkner, among the novelists—and Waldo Frank, Van Wyck Brooks, and Randolph Bourne among the critics.

As we cite and scan their work, it will be helpful to bear in mind three questions:

First: Have these novels (and the corresponding paintings, buildings, dances, and theater-pieces) of America's artists been made from the actual life of America? Are they original and indigenous, or are they copies of the expression of other times, other cultures, other men?

Second: How well have they been done? How competent are they?

Third: How deep are the perceptions of the artists? Are they mere *records* of the folk-statement of the people? Superficial copies of the shape of everyday life? Documentary statement of the political-economic-social-problems? Or do they dig deep into the human character? Or, more profoundly, do they affirm man-in-all-places-and-all-times?

Some years ago, being in serious need of instruments which would help define our creative achievement, I designed a "Profile of the American Statement." It is a cross-sectional view of the creative products of America's artists arranged through descending levels from mere statements of folkways and folklore at the surface of the culture to the deeper probings into the problems and the personal characteristics of the people, and finally to the most profound cosmic and universal statements.

Summed up in scale form the five levels are:

1. Statements of folkways and folklore
2. Social documentation and problems of reconstruction, advancing sometimes into the universal or the cosmic
3. Portraits of individual character, appraisals of human relationships, and such personal expression as lyrical utterance, love songs, and descriptive idyls, some of which rise into profound "hymns of being"
4. Critical analysis of the culture, of literary portraits of it and the methods of studying it . . . broadly conceived as "criticism"
5. The foundation of the profile, consisting of concepts of universal validity . . . Man-in-the-Universe-and-History rather than men-in-this-time-and-place . . . the Great Tradition of the Person

I shall have frequent occasion to refer to this Profile.

VII

On America's time-line of the creative act, the three years that followed the Peace of Versailles were epoch-marking. A dozen writers of stature published poetry, novel, or essay at the same moment that the social scientists were synthesizing a generation's findings about industrial society. In 1919, the year that Veblen and his Technical Alliance were thinking their way through "the engineers and price system," Sherwood Anderson's *Winesburg, Ohio* told the story of "the defeated people" living "thwarted lives," in "the little frame houses" on the "often mean enough streets in American towns." And one of the writing men, Waldo Frank, got so close to the Voice of the Great Tradition in a volume of essays, *Our America,* that the critics, for once in Frank's life, did not damn it with faint praise.

The real detonation of the young writing realists was exploded in 1920, the year William Dean Howells died. Sinclair Lewis published *Main Street,* Eugene O'Neill's *Beyond the Horizon* got the Pulitzer Prize, and Scott Fitzgerald, the Princeton prodigy, published the first volume of his history of wild youth's jazz age in *This Side of Paradise.*

The year 1921 witnessed *Three Soldiers* by John Roderigo Dos Passos, a new social-documentary novelist, and the first of many later recorders of the response of the G.I.'s to two wars.

In 1922 appeared Lewis' folk-story *Babbitt,* e. e. cummings' reaction to war in *The Enormous Room,* and T. S. Eliot's long-to-be-studied-and-discussed *The Waste Land.*

This is the record of the best titles. What did they mean for the emergence of the creative act in America?

VIII

Two of the young American novelists were awarded Nobel Prizes between 1920 and 1950—Sinclair Lewis (in 1930) for his 1920–1922 books, *Main Street* and *Babbitt,* and William Faulkner (in 1950) for his great probing of the legend of Yaknapatawpha County in a dozen novels and short stories. I pause to consider these because they signalize our creative artists at the beginning of the Thirty years and measure their achievement at its close. Lewis, in 1920, recording the surface of life, was the true folk-novelist. Faulkner, in 1950, is a true Man-in-the-Universe-and-in-History. Both men made speeches accepting the award from the King of Sweden and the Swedish Academy. Lewis read a long paper disposing finally of the Genteel Tradition. Faulkner read a short one he had written in the plane flying the Atlantic, a Lincoln-like declaration of man's capacity to endure and prevail. A bit of each statement will help us to define the limits of the achievement of these artists of our time.

Lewis answered[4] the first of our three questions: "Are these statements created from our own American life?" with a definite "Yes."

I had realized in reading Balzac and Dickens that it was possible to describe French and English common people as one actually saw them. But it never occurred to me that one might without indecency write of the people of Sauk Centre, Minnesota, as one felt about them. Our fictional tradition, you see, was that all of us in midwestern villages were altogether noble and happy; that no one of us would exchange the neighborly bliss of living on Main Street for the heathen gaudiness of New York or Paris or Stockholm. But in Mr. Garland's "Main-Traveled Roads" I discovered that there was one man who believed that midwestern peasants were sometimes bewildered and hungry and vile—and heroic. And given this vision, I was released; I could write of life as living life.

To write (and dance, paint, sing, etc.) "of life as living life" *in America* has been the one significant achievement of most of the

[4] Sinclair Lewis, New York *Times,* December 13, 1930, p. 12.

artists of our half century. "I say what I see . . . my way," a thousand artists since Whitman have affirmed, and in all the mediums of expression. To create an American poem, novel, dance, play, symphony; to build an original American house, appropriate to the life to be lived in this house here and now—not a copy of a Greek house or a Georgian one, or even of a Colonial Cape Cod one. This is the theme of the Declaration of Creative Independence of the American artist. Moreover, working together in these fifty years now past these American artists have gone far toward abolishing the feeling of isolation and impotence, of "not belonging," that Lewis spoke of. The American writer, he said:[5]

. . . is oppressed by something worse than poverty—by the feeling that what he creates does not matter, that he is expected by his readers to be only a decorator or a clown . . . he has no institution, no group, to which he can turn for inspiration, whose criticism he can accept and whose praise will be precious to him.

But Lewis was speaking for the Twenties. In the Fifties, the "institution"—the group of the artists of America—is being achieved. Lewis' achievement, which got the prize for the Twenties, was the making of a good folk-statement, catching and putting down the colloquial record of the American in village, town, and city.

Against it in the Fifties stands Faulkner, the Voice of the Great Tradition of the Person. This achievement is on the most foundational level of the "Profile of the American Statement." For here the expressional artist and the documentary scientist of behavior stand on common ground—acclaiming and portraying the Person. The profoundly organic quality of the Person, rather than the surface contours of his shape, emerge from Faulkner's words:[6]

Our tragedy today is a general and universal physical fear . . . typified by our fear of being "blown up" . . . because of this, the young man or woman writing today has forgotten the problems of the human heart in conflict with itself which alone can make good writing because that is only worth writing about, worth the agony and the sweat.

He must learn them again. He must teach himself that the basis to all things is to be afraid; and, teaching himself that, forget it forever,

---

[5] Sinclair Lewis, *op. cit.*
[6] William Faulkner, *Saturday Review of Literature*, February 3, 1950.

leaving no room in his workshop for anything but the old verities of the heart . . . until he does so he labors under a curse. He writes not of love but of lust, of defeats in which nobody loses anything of value, of victories without hope and worst of all without pity or compassion. His griefs grieve on no universal bones, leaving no scars. He writes not of the heart but of the glands.

Until he learns these things he will write as though he stood among and watched the end of man. I decline to accept the end of man . . . I believe that man will not merely endure: he will prevail. He is immortal, not because he alone among creatures has an inexhaustible compassion and sacrifice and endurance. The poet's, the writer's duty is to write about these things . . . the poet's voice need not merely be the record of man, it can be one of the . . . pillars to help him endure and prevail.

Faulkner's great Yaknapatawpha saga[7] stated the "griefs that grieved on universal loves" in two hundred years of life in his Deep South. As he said of it:[8]

. . . the continuation of that record which two hundred years had not been enough to complete and another hundred would not be enough to discharge; that chronicle which was a whole land in miniature, which multiplied and compounded was the entire South.

Here is a beautiful confirmation by an artist of the scientist's concept of culture-pattern—even of the dominating patterns of the life of the people. As Cowley said of it in one of his fine "Introductions": "It is this pattern . . . that is Faulkner's real achievement." To me, it is a record of the deep myth of the people. I hasten to add that it abounds in a myriad of concrete details of their moment-by-moment utterance.

IX

Here, in Lewis and Faulkner, are the superficial beginnings and the mature closing of the creative generation. Its achievement was astonishing; hundreds of writing men and women (and painting, composing, dancing, etc., men and women in other media)

---

[7] *The Sound and the Fury* (1929); *Sartoris* (1929); *As I Lay Dying* (1930), which Valerie Bettis has choreographed in a powerful American dance; *Sanctuary* (1931); *Light in August* (1932); *Absalom, Absalom!* (1936); *The Unvanquished* (1938); *The Wild Palms* (1939); *The Hamlet* (1940); and *Go Down Moses* (1942).

[8] William Faulkner: *The Portable Faulkner,* Edited and with an Introduction by Malcolm Cowley.

made their version of the American Statement. Most of these statements were not profoundly important. But they achieved one result—they filled in the details of the folk-statement, documented the people's current problems pretty well, and sang some of the lyric songs of the people. They managed to get down into the top three levels of my "Profile of the American Statement." Their colleagues in criticism—Frank, Tate, Ransom, Cleanth Brooks, and especially Kenneth Burke—have built in the fourth one. But few of the writing men besides Faulkner sensed the profound foundational level—only Frank and, I think, Burke. And in architecture there was Wright, in the dance Martha Graham, in music Charles Ives, in the graphic arts Stieglitz and a few others.

The lesser ones recorded the average man and they disposed once and for all of the Genteel Tradition. It is as though each took the assignment of jotting down the American's "sayings and yarns travelling on grief and laughter," which Carl Sandburg permanently gathered together in *The People, Yes* (1936). These were, he said, "several stories and psalms nobody would want to laugh at . . . breaking into jig time and tap dancing nohow classical . . . the roar and whirl of street crowds, work gangs, sidewalk clamor."

Lewis was a skilled newspaper reporter and genius raconteur (and a bore, as I can testify from a score of four-hour breakfasts of brilliant repartee at Fred Howe's Sconset Tavern-on-the-Moors in 1924, with Lewis and George Middleton and Bruce Bliven, and I forget who else). Lewis certainly was of the towns that he wrote about; like Longfellow two generations earlier he could "rhyme the average man" because he was one. So he made a "folksy" record of American middle-class life, moving from one phase of it to another, recording a new type in each novel. In *Main Street* the intrigues and hopes and despairs of provincial people of the small town . . . in *Babbitt* the "boyish helplessness" of the rotarian businessman . . . in *Arrowsmith* "the stammering romance" of a medical researcher . . . in *Elmer Gantry* the rantings of a pulpiteer . . . in *Dodsworth* the loneliness of the middle-aged businessman in Paris . . . in *It Can't Happen Here* a warning to look at the possible fascist mote in our own eye . . . in *Cass Timberlane* the big lumber tycoon. Here was the folk novelist recording the commonplace. The people accepted him as they did

Mark Twain, even his "crazy" personal behavior. They merely laughed at the "God strike me dead" act that he put on in the Kansas City Church, as they laughed in Arlington, Vermont, at Norman Rockwell's *Saturday Evening Post* cover which caricatured Arlington's own gossiping natives, building up scandal through gossip. In a sense the people never would let Lewis, or Clemens, be serious.

That these were men of percept, not of concept, is shown by twenty-five years of Ernest Hemingway's writing. Always the action man, he recorded the surface violence of life—in the Michigan forests and lakes, in adolescent sports, in war and bull fights, and in gangstering. He was not interested in the forces which produced the events; only in the events themselves. He was one of the few who lacked a college education and, like most of the novelists of the time, had no connection with the roots of the culture. But the honesty of report, to which the writers gave themselves, was basic with Hemingway; he wanted to tell "the truth about his own feelings at the moment that they exist." His success showed itself in a crudely cumulating record of the brutality of the human world. To cite several violent episodes: the Indian husband who cut his throat after watching his wife undergo a Cesarean with a jackknife . . . the huddle of the refugees around a woman having her child in the mud . . . men shooting men off walls . . . men killing bulls and being gored by bulls. Someone said a Hemingway novel is a "state of perpetual war," whether it be of soldiers or bullfighters, explorers or gangsters, tired revolutionaries or strenuous athletes.

These better novelists, Hemingway perhaps in the lead, revealed one concern—the creation of a unique style. Hemingway said he wanted "a prose more intensely precise than conventional prose . . . There is a fourth and fifth dimension that can be gotten. It is much more difficult than poetry. It is prose that has never been written. But it can be written without tricks and without cheating."

There is much evidence that the artists of this period—and Hemingway, Lewis, Dos Passos, Fitzgerald, are good representatives—were sincerely disturbed about the world, resentful and angry, and confused. Witness Sherwood Anderson's desire to spit everytime anybody said "industrial civilization." But they had no cue to the factors and forces that were transforming modern society. They were utterly without conceptual understanding of the crisis in the culture. It is as though the students of the culture to whom I have referred had not lived and were not living in America. One critic-student summed them up aptly: "They worked at a major art form with a minor art vision." Since they had no access to concepts they fell back on melodrama—stories of alcoholics, human wrecks, hungry natives, Cuban revolutionaries, boozed cosmopolitans, gilt-edge snobs. Consider Hemingway's best-selling novel and the motion picture made from it, *For Whom The Bell Tolls*. It flashed up beautiful episodes of courage and feeling but it had little to do with the Spanish people and their death struggle for a free and good life in their land.

X

Another phase of the topical recording was done by the currently much-revived Scott Fitzgerald.[9] For six years, from 1920 to 1926, he produced a best-selling novel almost every year. Then he did nothing for eight years, and in the last six years of his life wrote two. Some said his record made him the historian of the "Lost Generation," as Gertrude Stein had suggested to Ernest Hemingway, that the whole group of "Sad Young Men" should be called. But that claims far too much. Fitzgerald's novels were essentially a legend he created about his own life and that of Zelda Fitzgerald and their ephemeral pals. In one way he repeated Mark Twain's success of 1880 and Jack London's of 1900: he made $40,000 a year from his best-selling novels. But he spent more than that living the experiences that went into the novels, on Long Island estates, Riviera villas, and in the Parisian play-boy world. He knew the gin age because he lived in its swirl of drunken parties and Great Gatsby tinsel, a world where women, skirts above their knees, smoked and drank at the new cocktail hour with their men.

Alfred Kazin[10] has summed up Fitzgerald's times and his achievement in a fine single paragraph:

[9] Fitzgerald, Francis Scott Key (1896–1940): *This Side of Paradise* (1920); *Flappers & Philosophers* (1920); *The Beautiful and Damned* (1921); *Tales of the Jazz Age* (1922); *The Vegetable* (1923); *The Great Gatsby* (1925); *All the Sad Young Men* (1926); *Tender Is the Night* (1934); *Taps at Reveille* (1935); *The Last Tycoon* (an unfinished novel, published with a reprint of *The Great Gatsby* and selected stories in 1941).
[10] Alfred Kazin, *On Native Grounds*, pp. 316–17.

He had announced the lost generation with *This Side of Paradise* in 1920, or at least the home guard of the international rebellion of postwar youth, and the restiveness of youth at home found an apostle in him, since he was the younger generation's first authentic novelist. Flippant, ironic, chastely sentimental, he spoke for all those who felt, as one youth wrote in 1920, that "the old generation had certainly pretty well ruined this world before passing it on to us. They give us this thing, knocked to pieces, leaky, red-hot, threatening to blow up; and then they are surprised that we don't accept it with the same attitude of pretty, decorous enthusiasm with which they received it, way back in the eighties." As the flapper supplanted the suffragette, the cake-eater the earnest young uplifter in 1913, Fitzgerald came in with the modernism that flew in on short skirts, puffed audaciously at its cigarette, evinced a frantic interest in sport and sex, in drinking prohibited liquor, and in defying the ancient traditions. In 1920 he was not so much a novelist as a new generation speaking; but it did not matter. He sounded all the fashionable new lamentations; he gave the inchoate protests of his generation a slogan, a character, a definitive tone. Like Rudolph Valentino, he became one of the supreme personalities of the new day; and when his dashingly handsome hero, Armory Blaine, having survived Princeton, the war, and one tempestuous love affair, stood out at the end of the novel as a man who had conquered all the illusions and was not waiting on a lonely road to be conquered in turn, it seemed as if a generation ambitious for a sense of tragedy had really found a tragic hero.

Like most of his literary contemporaries, Fitzgerald was not a student of his times; he was not a reformer, and in no sense a revolutionary. He was just another recorder of the life of the lost generation which he knew internally in its own terms. It was an honest and accurate appraisal of a youthful, self-publicizing fraction of the population, but it had no deep understanding. Most of it was not even great writing; it was a good pastiche of dramatic bits, sensitively patched together.

XI

A few of the novelists succeeded in digging deeper into the culture, became concerned with the artist's problem of creating a social document, as well as a folk-statement. I cite one of John Steinbeck's books, *The Grapes of Wrath,* and several of John Dos Passos', especially his epic *U.S.A.* As for Steinbeck I must content myself with one citation—one of those typical pages on which he pauses at intervals in his narrative to generalize about the problems of man.[11] This one is a beautiful counterpart of the social scientist's documentation of the great problem of I and We, of freedom and control.

One man, one family driven from the land; this rusty car creaking along the highway to the west. I lost my land, a single tractor took my land. I am alone and I am bewildered. And in the night one family camps in a ditch and another family pulls in and the tents come out. The two men squat on their hams and the women and children listen. Here is the node, you who hate change and fear revolution. Keep these two squatting men apart; make them hate, fear, suspect each other. Here is the anlage of the thing you fear. This is the zygote. For here "I lost my land" is changed; a cell is split and from its splitting grows the thing you hate—"We lost our land." The danger is here, for two men are not as lonely and perplexed as one. And from this first "we" there grows a still more dangerous thing: "I have a little food" plus "I have none." If from this problem the sum is "We have a little food," the thing is on its way, the movement has direction. Only a little multiplication now, and this land, this tractor are ours. The two men squatting in a ditch, the little fire, the side-meat stewing in a single pot, the silent stone-eyed women; behind, the children listening with their souls to words their minds do not understand. The night draws down. The baby has a cold. Here, take this blanket. It's wool. It was my mother's blanket—take it for the baby. This is the thing to bomb. This is the beginning—from "I" to "We."

But Dos Passos[12] anticipated[13] Steinbeck and the others in

[11] *The Grapes of Wrath*, p. 206.

[12] Dos Passos, John (Roderigo) (1896–): *One Man's Initiation* (1919, reprinted as *First Encounter*, 1946); *Three Soldiers* (1921); *Rosinante to the Road Again* (Book of essays) (1922); *A Pushcart at the Curb* (Verse) (1922); *Streets at Night* (1923); *Manhattan Transfer* (1925); *The Garbage Man* (Play) (1926); *Orient Express* (1927); *Airways, Inc.* (Play) (1929); *The 42nd Parallel* (1930); *Nineteen Nineteen* (1931); *In All Countries* (1934); *Three Plays* (1934); *The Big Money* (1936); *U.S.A.* (1938); *Journeys Between Wars* (1938); *Adventures of a Young Man* (1939); *The Ground We Stand On* (1941); *Number One* (1943); *State of the Nation* (1944); *Tour of Duty* (1946); *The Grand Design* (1949).

[13] Upton Sinclair, of course, anticipated them all with his original novel *The Jungle* (1906); its homiletics were successful enough in the elder Roosevelt's administration to bring about federal legislation for social reform. Then every few years came another of Sinclair's social protests—from then right up to now: *The Money Changers* (1908); *King Coal* (1917); *The Profits of Religion* (1918); *The Brass Check* (1919); *The Goose Step* (1923); *Oil* (1927); *Boston* (1928). Posterity will do better by him than his contemporaries have done.

using the novel to document the concept of the jungle[14] of our machine world. Dos Passos sees our world as a "jungle," but seems to me to show no conceptual way through it. While he has strong social interest he displays no understanding of the factors that are blocking the successful operation of the modern system. He listens to the riveting machines but fails to show what they, and the assembly line, and the vacuum tube, and the automatic factory are doing to occupational life. He states the changing conditions of I and We together and writes down some "trial sums," yet, as some critics have suggested, "I" and "We" seem to add up to nothing.

XII

For a culture to reveal a flourishing, vigorous criticism is a profound sign of creative health. This element of the creative process—criticism—is a primary function of both the man of art and the man of science. On the "Profile of the American Statement" it appears as the fourth level, next in foundational quality to the cosmic, man-in-the-universe-and-in-history level itself. I repeat, when a people have true critics laying bare, appraising their culture and the statements of their artists and philosophers about it, then one can be sure that the Creative Path is being traversed.

Has our country reached that happy stage? It has indeed. Since 1910 as profound critical statement has been made by Americans as anywhere in the world, and certainly much larger in volume and vigor. The American artist, hand in hand with his scientific compatriot, has emerged as a profound critic of both Person and Society. If this is a shocking generalization to many brought up in the Conforming Way, let them ponder the record.

Criticism, to be understood, must be conceived broadly; I conceive it to be fourfold:

> Criticism of the culture
> Criticism of *the statement* of the artist about the Person
> Criticism of *the statement* of the artist about the Culture
> Criticism of criticism

My thesis at this point is that America has been taking up her

[14] Waldo Frank's analysis of the "jungle" is infinitely more profound. I deal with it later.

stewardship of creative leadership with increasing crescendo. Although the voices have been few in number, they have been clear and they have persisted, and they have made themselves heard to varying degrees on no less than six frontiers—the social frontier, the human frontier and the esthetic, the ethical, the physical-scientific, and the educational. With respect to five of these I shall not repeat what has been said earlier or in other publications. But in the building of sound esthetic criticism the major theses of this book find convincing confirmation. I point to sample achievements.

I find the first clear sign of creative health in the heroic history of the advance guard—the "Little"—magazines. The statisticians tell us that since Margaret Fuller and Emerson edited and published *The Dial* from 1840 to 1844 (it was really "Little" for, as a consequence of the high standards set by the "Concord School of Philosophy," it had only 300 subscribers) there have been 600 of these "Little" magazines. But almost all of these have been the product of our times. Most of them have been short-lived—six months to two years—but a few persisted over a decade or even a generation.[15] Less than a hundred played a decisive part in the battle for a mature literature, but these hundred gave the young, unknown, and potentially creative American writers their only source of publication. They consistently published good work, even though it meant losing money, courting ridicule, and ignoring public taste. They have been the real advance guard, while the big publishing houses and the big quality magazines are the rear guard—conservative in taste, generally unwilling to risk on an unknown author. These latter, the tabulators say, have discovered only one-fifth of our best writers, and have done little to initiate new literary groups or movements.

It was these advance guard magazines that initiated and kept alive the conscientious revolt against the guardians of public taste. They were part and parcel of the spirit of rebellion and improvisation of the whole age. Inevitably as they threw off controls of public taste, confusion resulted, often displaying a "tangled

[15] William Reedy's famous *Mirror* lasted from 1891 to 1920; *Sewanee Review,* published by the University of the South, has the record with 50 years, 1892 to date. Harriet Monroe's *Poetry,* launched in 1912, is still going, as is *Partisan Review,* started in 1934. John Frederick's *Midland* stuck it out for seventeen years (1915–33), and Margaret Anderson's *Little Review* for fifteen (1914–29).

and delightful sense of contradiction." It is true that the group as a whole has been unschooled and frequently undisciplined. They really were thinking their new loyalties out loud, thinking their way in print, through the tangle of problems and issues of a changing civilization. It was to be expected that in the early days, that is after World War I, the spirit of Dada would get in the way of bringing about what they constantly promised—"the dawn of a new cultural synthesis." The magazines were often started to attack conventional modes of expression and to create new and unorthodox theories and practices; as for the latter, witness the abundance of their new styles of writing and their revolutionary ideas.

Most of them were short-lived and some editors deliberately planned it so; witness Gorham Munson, writing in his magazine *Secession:*

> The Director pledges his energy for at least two years to the continuance of Secession. Beyond a two-year span, observation shows, the vitality of most reviews is lowered and their contribution, accomplished, becomes repetitious and unnecessary.

Jack Lindsay and P. R. Stephensen created *The London Aphrodite* on the ground that "there has never yet been a literary periodical which has not gone dull after the first half dozen numbers." But most of the magazines died for other reasons—lack or loss of funds, lack or loss of interest, withdrawal of sustaining funds because of some shift in policy unpleasant to the backer, government prosecution or censorship, or because of internecine quarrels and misunderstandings.

But that they discovered and housed the young and unknown creatives is clear from the record. I give you a few samples:

> Julius Friend's *Double Dealer* (New Orleans) published Hemingway's two-page *Divine Gesture* (1922); six stanzas of William Faulkner's (1922) (they were pretty bad!); Jean Toomer (1922); Thornton Wilder (1922); Kenneth Fearing (1923).
>
> *The Fugitive* published Donald Davidson, Robert Penn Warren, Laura Riding, and Merrill Moore.
>
> *Blues* published James Farrell, Erskine Caldwell, and Hart Crane.
>
> Margaret Anderson's *Little Review* published James Joyce's *Ulysses* in 1918.
>
> Harriet Monroe's *Poetry* published Richard Aldington (1913); H. D.

(Hilda Doolittle) (1913); Ezra Pound (1912); Vachel Lindsay's *General William Booth Enters Into Heaven* (1913).

Masters' *Spoon River Anthology* appeared in installments in *Reedy's Mirror* (1913–14).

The Seven Arts (1916–1917), edited by Oppenheim, Brooks, and Frank, published Eugene O'Neill's first short story "Tomorrow" (1916) and crystallized in public consciousness the names of Sherwood Anderson, John Dos Passos, Eugene O'Neill, Waldo Frank, Randolph Bourne, Van Wyck Brooks, John Reed, H. L. Mencken, James Oppenheim, Louis Untermeyer, Robert Edmund Jones, and Paul Rosenfeld.[16]

XIII

But by far the most important sign of the creative health of critical feeling and thought is the achievement of the artist-students in pointing to the major split in American culture. To it can be traced the spiritual bottleneck that long stymied the expression of creative Americans and kept the educationalists in the Conforming Way. This was the dominance of the practical men over every phase of the culture and their corresponding contempt for the creative way. It was in the decade after 1915 that a new race of social critics—Van Wyck Brooks, Waldo Frank, and Randolph Bourne—became clear and articulate about this and as a consequence led a few of the educationalists into the Creative Path.

To appreciate their role, recall from Chapter 1 the sketch of the historical background of the impasse between the Practical Tradition and the Great Tradition. The key to the impasse lay in the contrasting motive powers of the two traditions. The Practical Tradition has always been driven by the single-minded motive of profit, measured in terms of Money; we have fallen into the habit of saying, therefore, that ours is a Money civilization. But the analysis cuts deeper to the Things, the Comfort, the Glory, and the Power that the money buys. So our civilization is a culture of Things; Pitirim Sorokin named it for us—*a sensate culture*. As for the glory and the power, they turned our society into a pecking order of people and of personality.

The motive power of the Great Tradition was also profit, but the profit was to be the good life for all, or at least as much of the

[16] For a clear and adequate account of their history and contribution see Hoffman, Allen, and Ulrich, *The Little Magazine*.

good life as the social system could produce and distribute. Throughout whole millennia goods were scarce and producing systems inefficient, but in our era, particularly in America, the producing system is becoming approximately efficient. Thus we stand potentially on the threshold of abundance. But the distributing system is still inhumane and inefficient because the practical men are still gripped by the motive of the Money-Thing profit for the few. Thus the practical men have long domineered over the lives of men, setting the tone of community life, establishing the standards of behavior and defining the loyalties in the press, the schools and colleges, the churches, as well as in the families. This is the Conforming Way which I have discussed at such length in this book.

As far back as recorded history can reach, the Indo-European civilization that spread from the Caspian Sea westward around the Mediterranean and out to all the continents emanated from a central constellation of ideas. Its nuclear concept was the Supreme Value of the Individual. It was a dynamic idea and became the key to the superb preambles of our major state papers. It defined the interpretation of our freedoms, concepts of work and property, of equality, of expression, and of communal relationships.

But the split between the practical men and the creative men led them to interpret The Supreme Value of the Individual and the constellation of ideas very differently. The practical men interpreted freedom as absence of restraint, which guaranteed the aggressive and the efficient ones the ownership of Things and hence control over men. Property ownership was a right secured by preemption of the Thing. Hence economic freedom—called by the French, *laissez faire* and given lip-service by all western businessmen—defined property as freedom to exploit it, that is, to own and develop it, or to withhold it from use.

As for "equality," while the practical men gave lip-service to it, it was actually defined according to the terms of Andrew Carnegie's "Gospel of Wealth": "You and I are different. I am Superior. You are Inferior. Hence I shall think for you. It is inevitable, since I am a better man than you, that I shall acquire larger accumulations of Money and Things than you. But, never fear, I accept the obligations of stewardship. My charity will be your security." This is the Patron speaking, the Lord-of-the-Manor, in

all times and climes. It was this concern for the I rather than the
We, that governed the practical men in building their social-
economic-political systems, their codes of laws and morals, their
philosophies and religions.

But the men of the Great Tradition defined the Supreme Value
of the Individual very differently. Each said to the other: "You
and I are different. But, regardless of our differences in energy
and ambition, we know, as Walt Whitman taught us to say, 'I am
a Supreme, but you are also a Supreme.' Since we know that we
must live together, we know that we must rule together." Thus,
according to the Great Tradition, the entire constellation of ideas—
freedom, equalities, work and property, and expression—have all
been redefined under the advancing recognition of the role of the
We, the communal, relationships. To energize us creatively we
need, as Frank said, [17] a dynamic *social* concept of society:

A society where, not the individual, but the potential person is the
norm of value, is one in which all intelligence is dedicated intrinsically
—one might almost say "selfishly"—to the public welfare. For the act
of social justice is in the heart of *the potential person* who knows himself *a* heart of all men and of the universe; and whose knowing—however stumbling and full of error—is action. Not the individual, not the
individual economic class or nation which is the sum of individuals,
but the person and the group of persons is the valid integer for social
justice.

Now history also records that although the Practical Men have
always controlled the fruits of the progress which they value so
highly, they did not invent its successive increments. The creators
were men of the Great Tradition, men of imagination, whose stock
in trade was concept rather than percept. They invented the
modern languages of great complexity and subtle power of meaning. They devised the concepts and instruments of precise measurement, the complex hierarchy of mathematical methods of
detecting and stating relationships. They brought about the scientific revolution from Copernicus and Galileo to Newton, Maxwell, and Einstein. They rationalized and phrased the concept and
the process of the scientific method of inquiry and work. And in
our own time it was they who created the epoch-marking conceptual researches and the great body of explosive ideas which I
have assembled in this book.

[17] Waldo Frank, *Chart for Rough Water*, p. 132.

While a share of the credit for the magnificent achievements in the modern standard of living is due to the practical men who organized and operated the producing mechanisms that the creative ideas made possible, it often fell out that greed for Things and power and prestige outran conscience and the belief in the Supreme Value of the Individual, and resulted in the exploitation of the people. But more and more, since 1870, the organizational methods of the practical men were put to work in the interest of the many, by those who share the belief that each individual really *is* a Supreme. As that happened, the Exploitive Tradition began to give way to the Great Tradition. "Populist" movements arose in each of the western countries, controls were imposed by the people upon the self-seeking practical men, and each of the concepts in the great constellation of ideas became redefined. Absence of restraint and *laissez faire* waned, freedom-as-socially-self-imposed-controls, advanced; and the substance-thing concept of property gave way to the function, or social use, meaning.

XIV

The first essays of the young social critics—Brooks, Bourne, and Frank—were aimed at the professors of the liberal arts in the colleges, who were the spokesmen of the practical men. The Masters of Capital, such as Carnegie, Rockefeller, and Stanford, had contributed most of the endowments of the private colleges. It was their Gospel of Wealth that, taken with the received tradition and animistic science of the day, dominated the climate of opinion in the colleges and universities. Whether they knew it or not, and most of them would in all sincerity have denied it, Butler and the ninety-and-nine among college and school administrators became the reflecting spokesmen of the Practical Men. It was this pervasiveness of the Practical Man's point of view in community and college that led the professors of the social sciences to shun the controversial problems and forces in the culture, and the professors of the liberal arts to regard the classics as the sole treasury of the heritage of western culture. And it was long concern with the past and its Great Books that had dominated the committees of the mass educational organizations, which, after 1890, dictated the content of the curriculum of the American high school.

The chief sign of the creative health of our country was in the continuity and crescendo of the critical writing that began with the young social critics of 1915. It was they—Waldo Frank, Van Wyck Brooks, and Randolph Bourne especially—who first discriminated clearly between the practical men and their spokesmen in the colleges and the arts, and the creative men of the Great Tradition. It was largely their pioneering that paved the way for the second generation of critical students of literature and the culture, particularly Kenneth Burke, Allen Tate, John Crowe Ransom, Cleanth Brooks, and the later I. A. Richards.

Brooks, in *America Comes of Age* (1915), fired the first gun of the attack on the spokesmen of what passed for art in America: Paul Elmer More, Irving Babbitt, Paul Shorey, George Mayberry, William Lyon Phelps, and Stuart Sherman. The theme, five years before Lewis' *Main Street*, was clear: only out of the nation's actual spiritual experiences could a great literature be made. Hence literary criticism is a social criticism; in the 1930's and the 1940's the later critics expanded the concept: "Literary criticism is biological criticism, it is emotional criticism, it is psychological criticism," Brooks's essay was the declaration of a new race of writing men, that American literature shall be made out of life *in* America. He pointed to main currents in the American mind. The first was the practical tradition to which I have referred— a "catchpenny opportunism . . . originating in the practical shifts of Puritan life . . . becoming a philosophy in Benjamin Franklin . . . passing through the American humorists . . . and resulting in the atmosphere of our contemporary business life." The other was not the rich Great Tradition with which I am concerned, for Brooks found it wanting in American life. The other was rather a "transcendental" current, originating in "the piety of the Puritans," becoming a philosophy in Jonathan Edwards, embracing the East in Emerson, producing the Genteel Tradition in the college professors of literature after 1870, and finally the aloofness of American writers from their civilization and an utterly unreal literature.

Brooks conceived the kind of expressive statement that was needed to fuse the Americans into an organic whole. Since literary criticism must be social criticism, the writing men of America must commit themselves to a "kind of socialism." He sounded a strong positive note, proclaiming that a new age in western culture has begun:[18]

[18] Van Wyck Brooks, *Letters and Leadership*, p. 53.

. . . an age of intensive cultivation, and it is the creative life that the nation calls for now. But for that how ill-equipped we are! Our literature has prepared no pathways for us, our leaders are themselves lost. We are like explorers who, in the morning of their lives, have deserted the hearthstone of the human tradition and have set out for a distant treasure that has turned to dust in their hands; but having on their way neglected to mark their track they no longer know in which direction their home lies, nor how to reach it, and so they wander in the wilderness, consumed with a double consciousness of waste and impotence.

Against this need what a travesty is our esthetic leadership! Look at "Our Leaders," the spokesmen for letters, Professors More, Babbitt, Mayberry, Shorey, Sherman, representatives of "a natural aristocracy of power." Look at "Our Awakeners," the sociologists and pragmatic philosophers of the colleges. All they have is the doctrine of "adaptation of man to his environment." Had he known Butler, Monroe, Henderson, and the professors of education of that day, he could have included them in his astute observation, for "adjustment" was precisely what they were setting up as their fundamental goals. These men, he said, are "apostles of a narrow efficiency," their philosophy is merely "rationalization of the whole spirit of American life." While they claim "that they alone apprehend reality," actually their pragmatism gives us nothing but a "method of work and an ideal of social efficiency." This pragmatism is merely a "means" philosophy. The result is, Brooks insisted, that our writers, critics, philosophers, and sociologists, who should be our real awakeners, inspire us with no driving excitement about American life. They have no "dynamic faith," and "we of the younger generation" get no help from these esthetically immature, college-trained, practical men. All that one in our predicament can do (in 1915) is to escape into an ivory tower and conform—as do the professors in the colleges and the artists.

Brooks saw that the true intellectual life can be sustained only by an "organized higher life," an "emotional" life. This can be brought about only if the poets, novelists, critics—the artists in general—become "the pathfinders of society; to them belongs the vision without which the people perish." "A race of artists, profound and sincere" is indispensable. This will bring us face to face with our own experience, for "it is exalted desires that give their validity to revolution, and exalted desires take form only in exalted souls." The pragmatism of the philosophers and the sociologists has also failed because it has tried to do the job that only a "national poetry" can do—create the great goals of life. An example? Germany, at the beginning of the nineteenth century, unified not by Bismarck and his politicians and militarists, but by Goethe the poet, who "projected in Faust a personification of spiritual energy" from the actual experience of the German people.

XV

Brooks's 1915 essay, and his *Letters and Leadership* (1918), which merely confirmed the earlier one, was a general barrage aimed at all the academicians of the Conforming Way. Randolph Bourne's *Seven Arts* essay (1917), "Twilight of Idols,"[19] centered the attack on Professor Dewey and the pragmatic philosophy upon which Bourne had been brought up in Columbia. When he won the Gilder Travelling Scholarship in 1913, and spent it meeting the creative groups in London, Paris, and other European cities, he was a devoted and admiring pragmatist. It was only after our entrance into World War I that he became disillusioned with that philosophy because of "the relative ease with which the pragmatist intellectuals, with Professor Dewey at the head, have moved out their philosophy, bag and baggage, from education to war." He said he had the feeling that he had been "left in the lurch . . . suddenly finding that a philosophy upon which I had relied to carry us through, no longer works." What was lacking in these pragmatic leaders? They were "liberal, enlightened"; they had "absorbed the secret of scientific method." What was missing? The lack was in their instrumental philosophy which could be congenial to problem-solving and technique but not to the "formulation of values and ideals." The latter had not "kept pace . . . with technical aptitude" and as a consequence the "formulation of opinion . . . in America has been left largely in the hands of professional patriots, sensational editors, archaic radicals." These pragmatists

. . . have, in short, no clear philosophy of life, except that of intelligent service, the admirable adaptation of means to ends. They are vague as to what kind of a society they want, or what kind of society

[19] Later republished in his *Untimely Papers.*

America needs, but they are equipped with all the administrative attitudes and talents necessary to attain it.[20]

The answer is clear: "If your policy as a publicist reformer is to take what you can get, you are likely to find that you get something less than you should be willing to take."

Bourne then sounded the critical note that has recurred time and again in the generation of debate over the inadequacies of a purely pragmatic philosophy. The defect of any philosophy of adaptation, even when it means adjustment to changing living experience, is that "there is no provision for thought or experience getting beyond itself." Reading these lines thirty years ago, I became convinced that this was the key to the inadequacy of the whole program of teacher education which Butler, Monroe, and the other men had saddled upon America before World War I. Actually, Bourne should have been denouncing our educational older brothers, for they were much more to be blamed than Mr. Dewey. But Bourne did anticipate a cleavage between pragmatism and poetry, between thinking and feeling, things and forces, that is crucial. It has been the nub of my appraisal throughout this book.

XVI

The Great Tradition, which created Europe and America, and its humiliation in recent centuries, is Waldo Frank's theme.[21] He defines the Great Tradition carefully:[22]

Its birth was on the Mediterranean shores. And before it spread in Europe through Rome, and through the Spaniard and the Puritan came to the Americas, it had already many forms: Egypt, Judea, Greece. Yet its essence has never changed. It is the knowledge that individual man partakes of the divine, which is his way of naming the universal and naming it good and of naming it his. It is the knowledge that his life has purpose and direction because God is in him. You can express it a hundred different ways: religiously after Ikhnaton, Moses, Jesus, Spinoza; rationally after Plato, Philo, Plotinus; theologically after Maimonides, Aquinas, Luther, Calvin; aesthetically,

---

[20] Randolph Bourne, *Untimely Papers*, p. 130.

[21] Primarily in his *Chart for Rough Water* (1940), but documented in his whole treatment of the Atlantic World: in *Our America* (1919), *Re-Discovery of America* (1929), *America Hispana* (1931). In the *American Jungle* (1937) and his novels.

[22] Waldo Frank, *Chart for Rough Water*, p. 50.

after every great master in Europe's art. There it is and it has brought dignity to individual man and a strength the Hindus never had, nor the Chinese, nor the American Indian; for all these cultures, however deep, deny the basic Great Traditior

The Great Tradition has built its life around deep concern for the Individual, but a conception of the Individual who has been transformed into the Person by the culture. This can happen to most of the individuals in the society only if the culture is appropriate to the cultivation of the Person; my earlier quote from Frank expands this. Thus the building of the Person is a process of "socialization of individuality." Frank defines[23] the Person as:

. . . the individual integrated into his Cosmos. The word is good. (It is always good to preserve for our present use words which expressed the deepest intuitions of our past. In continuity with our forefathers, there is strength; for that is life. Thus the word God is Good; and the modern who says "I believe in God" can be as radical an innovator as the first dim ancestor who said it.) The term person is good because in its Latin derivation, personna, it suggests a "speaking-through." The person, then, is the individual through whom the "Cosmos" speaks.

But our modern culture cannot cultivate true Persons because it has been attacked, in its industrial epoch, by a terrible disease: "The individual's soul, fed and grown great by its awareness of the Divine within it, believed it could dispense with the Divine." Under the drive of the exploitive forces of the modern world, it came to believe that its great power lay in the Ego, that it was served by a self-sufficient will and reason and that these could produce well-being. This, Frank says, has brought about western Man's humiliation, which we are witnessing today:[24]

Whole peoples tortured, turned loose upon a world too cowardly to receive them; thousands concentrated into camps under sadists whose task is to offend their bodies and maim their souls because they differ in statesmen whose "word" is the stale refuse of beer saloons, yet it releases whole continents into carnage; science the slave of destruction; truth the whore of propaganda; mighty nations turned into totalitarian machines for death or for desperate defense against death . . . This is the madness of the "autonomy of reason," the Sabbath of a culture of "well-being" in men who assumed they had outgrown the Great Tradition.

[23] *Ibid.,* pp. 127–128.
[24] *Ibid.,* p. 50.

Hence we confront the "Tragic Paradox" which is seen in the exploitation of the people by the system of modern capitalism, and the "pragmatist" economics and political guild socialism which is regarded as the cure for the current impasse. The socialist said: "The people, for their well-being, must own what they produce and own the tools of production . . . a practical design to abolish social injustice." But this is a tragic irony,

. . . a shallow plan because in building "socialism" the authors accepted and extolled the concept of the individual without the Divine which alone makes him whole and true. Within the socialist theory that was to overcome capitalism's injustice to man, there got embedded the view of man which had encouraged and propagated the injustice![25]

This is the Tragic Paradox. We must understand this because it accounts for the humiliation of the west. A new system must be built, one that combines freedom for *private creative* enterprise, along with the collective ownership and enjoyment of the instruments and fruits of modern living.

The real tragedy is that in the nineteenth and twentieth centuries the ablest minds of the Great Tradition, while turning their backs on the religious quality in the Great Tradition, created a new religion of their own and spread it around the world. This is the result of the scientific revolution whose magnificent social-economic-political achievements we have seen. We call this modern religion by various names—empirical rationalism, pragmatism, positivism—but all are of the same pseudo-scientific intellectual outlook. This empirical rationalism is a mere verbal religion. It is really the scientific method of inquiry which lies at the base of the great intellectual revolution of modern times. Waldo Frank and the younger exponents of the New Criticism make much of the fact that this pet way of thinking of the pragmatists excludes from their minds the possibility of any other way of knowing than that through the reports of the separate senses. They exclude the prior method of knowing, which a long line of philosophers and psychologists (Spinoza, Bergson, Croce, Whitehead) have accepted, namely, the intuitive one. Frank makes a profoundly important point:[26]

[25] *Ibid.*, p. 54.
[26] *Ibid.*, pp. 181–182.

Reality must be apprehended before the report of the senses make sense. Even as the form of a grammar must be somehow known before word sequences make sense and from this pre-rational premise, a prehension (to use Whitehead's word) must infuse the entire process of experience, qualitatively giving it life. This prehension is not transcendental in the cant meaning of supernatural or supersensory; it is simply the method of awareness of the organism as a whole. Its best name is the intuition. The whole man is the specific organ of the intuition . . . the true intuition, having the whole man as its organ, includes the reports of the senses and what is rationally induced from them. But the intuition's immediate quailty is as different from these reports as a life is different from its chemic elements.

But we are choking to death today, Frank says, because our religion of intellect—pragmatism, positivism, call it what you will—leaves out the essence of life. We appear to base reason on contingent "things," but actually on their symbols, on words. And so our "leaders" build armaments and make wars, carry on governments for personal profit, and deny the very services of the collective knowledge of mankind in building the Good Life.

As a consequence "desperate remedies" on continental scales, involving hundreds of millions of people, have been tried. In the nineteenth century there was Marxism which aimed at a collectivism produced by the laws of the machine. It was based on the scientific study of economics and history. It assumed that collectivism will naturally result in control of the system, and in enjoyment of its output, by the people. But actually under that theory the Russian communism of the Politburo has become Russian nationalism, not a true "communism" at all.

Capitalism also produced three types of fascism. The first was that of Mussolini, Italian fascism, in which the humiliation of man became an openly aggressive doctrine of the élite who have contempt for man and deliberately try to re-establish race infantilism. The second was Hitler's fascism. He was the perfect anti-Person, abhorring and degrading man, despising the Great Tradition. The third desperate remedy is in ourselves, and it is most prevalent in the *United States.* It is sheer sentimentality, a rugged individualism, which creates, *à la* Coolidge, Hoover, Al Smith, fake elegies to a fake past, and based on ignorance of the Great Tradition. The American leaders who speak of these returns to normalcy and preach isolation "really want to stay on their cosy nests, unruffled. They appeal to the Constitution because they are afraid to risk any fundamental inquiry or change which might come to their own selfish treasure." All this sentimentalism hides insincerity, falsehood, and fear behind fear, weakness behind weakness, want of love for others, and want of faith in oneself. So sentimentalism can swiftly become cruelty in forms of fascism; we see it in the Ku Klux Klan and in the un-American Committees.

XVII

This is the thesis that runs all through Frank's twenty books, his novels as well as his critical essays. It is perhaps too greatly telescoped to be clear, but I am confident I have not missed the essence. The reader will recognize my great debt to it and to Waldo Frank since the publication of his *Our America* helped to wean me from the Conforming Way.

Out of this critical prologue of Brooks, Bourne, and Frank, American criticism developed in the 1920's. Bourne died in 1919, Brooks slumped badly for ten years, never reached his 1915 peak again, and Frank was writing his novels (his *Re-Discovery* was published in 1929 and *Chart* in 1939). T. S. Eliot issued *The Sacred Wood* in 1920, one of our best personal critiques; we have had nothing critical from him since that time. I. A. Richards published (1923), with C. K. Ogden, the important scientific volume on semantics entitled *The Meaning of Meaning;* in 1924 his *Principles of Literary Criticism;* and in 1926 his *Science and Poetry.* But in the 1930's he became one of the true "poet-critics." Paralleling Richards' scientific stage came Max Eastman's even more scientific criticism—*The Literary Mind.* But my chronological chart from 1930 to 1950 is crammed full of important critical books. The "New Criticism," as John Crowe Ransom called it in his book of that name (1941) or "Modern Criticism" as Hyman names it, is of a quality "beyond all earlier criticism in our language." Thirty important books stand today as the record.[27]

XVIII

To deal critically with this record is the task of another book. Enough has been said, perhaps more than is needed, to illustrate the richness of the materials turned up in the Creative Path. From

[27] I cite them in the Appendix.

these the Teacher of Teachers can now draw the stuff for a great program. Before we close this chapter I point to two theses of my book which are confirmed by the new criticism. The first is the spectacular support that it gives to our principle of the necessary integration of fields of knowledge. Stanley Hyman, in *The Armed Vision*, reminds us that the new critics have taken their material from *all* the sciences, technologies, and arts:

Two generations of new sociology have built theories and experimental facts regarding the nature of society and the culture, social change, social conflicts, and their relation to literature.

From the bio-psychological sciences, especially from psychoanalysis, the critics carry over the study of the subconscious mind, its wishes, and "clusters" of images, the basic mechanisms of dream distortion with which they find close analogies in poetic-formation, the Jungian conception of archetypes, Dewey's brand of scientific inquiry, logic, and problem-solving, and, in some instances, the Gestalt concepts of pattern and configuration.

The physical sciences have contributed such basic theories and concepts as relativity, field, and indeterminacy.

Philosophy has been called upon for help in confronting questions of value and belief with ethical and metaphysical formulations.

Child-behavior has contributed experimental data from its laboratory investigations; the clinical psychologists provided information about pathological expressions of the mind.

The social psychologists contributed their discoveries about group behavior and social patterns.

Neurological and endocrinological physiology has supplied such concepts as homeostasis, and other physical and chemical concepts based on experimental investigation.

Anthropology has supplied theories of social behavior in different cultures; folklore, a branch of anthropology, has supplied knowledge of traditional popular rituals, tales and beliefs that underly the patterns and the themes of both folk art and sophisticated art.

XIX

The factors involved in the culture-wide split between the practical men and the men of creative thought and feeling contributed to a serious cleavage that divides our creative men. It is so basic to the development of an adequate theory that I comment briefly on it here, in anticipation of Chapter VI. Recognizing the danger in forcing differences into dichotomies, but convinced of their clarifying value, I bring this chapter to a close by mentioning another. It shows two opposing ways of looking at life and knowing, two different orientations concerning behavior. It can be captioned in various ways: Things *vs.* Forces . . . Thinking *vs.* Feeling . . . the Scientific *vs.* the Esthetic . . . Sensate Culture *vs.* Organic Culture. The critics—from Brooks, Bourne, and Frank to Tate, Ransom, and Burke—distinguish it as Pragmatism *vs.* Poetry or Intelligence *vs.* Imagination, and there is much to be said for their form.

In my *Foundations for American Education* (1947), under the caption "The Great Dichotomy," I stated the contrast as "The Thing People" *vs.* "The Force People."

The Thing People define the world in terms of substance—the thing . . . The Force People define it in terms of function—the relations between things.

The Thing People deny change . . . the Force People accept it as a fact.

The Thing People force the present into the matrix of the past . . . the Force People are oriented in the present, but interpret it as the product of the past.

The Thing People see the living creature as additive mechanism . . . the Force People as integrated organism.

In art the Thing People photographically reproduce the surface shapes and contours of things; in education they rely on memory and giving-back-on-demand . . . The Force People express the tensions, the pushes and pulls in the world, the relationships between things.

The Thing People think by comparing things with norms, and in terms of rank-order of size . . . The Force People think in terms of the study of integration of forces in an actual situation.

In every field of thought and feeling the dichotomy has split our creative men apart:

In philosophy it sets the pragmatic-instrumentalists led by Dewey, Bode, and Kilpatrick against Whitehead, Frank, and the organic realists; Charles Morris, Herbert Feigl, and the logical positivists against Pitirim Sorokin and the revelation intuitionists.

In religon it sets off Rauschenbush and the Social Gospel men, and the Higher Critics, from Niebuhr and the men of the myth.

In criticism it opposes Max Eastman, the early Richards, David

Daiches, and the "scientific" critics to Tate, Ransom, Burke, and the men of poetic imagination.

In literature it groups the folk-novelists and poets—Lewis, Hemingway, Farrell, Sandburg, Masters, Frost—and Steinbeck, Dos Passos, and the social documenters against all the symbolists from Poe to Eliot, Frank and Faulkner.

In psychology it divides the conditioners and connectionists, and even the Gestaltists, from the "Leave-No-Stone-Unturned" school.

The cleavage is defined sharply by the opposing sides. Pitirim Sorokin, speaking for the creative poets, philosophers, and sociologists, concludes that in a sensate culture science and philosophy become "a second-class sensory, utilitarian science composed of empiricism, positivism, criticism, agnosticism, skepticism, instrumentalism, operationalism." Psychology evolves into a physiology of the nervous system, religion becomes a social gospel, the educational system becomes a system of trade schools devoted to the useful arts and crafts, and to know in order to control becomes the supreme end and criterion of behavior.

Tate, Frank, and the poets agree, saying that the characteristic state of mind in educated America assumes that the only thing that is important is political organization, strategy, and a program of action. The positivist scholars assume that all experience can be organized scientifically, hence consider all expression to be "irrelevant feeling." Eastman in *The Literary Mind* (1931) says that "the modern poets"—meaning Pound, Eliot, Winters, Sitwell, Graves, Riding, Tate, Hart Crane, Cummings, Joyce, Stein—are producing a "cult" of unintelligibility. They are "free versifiers" who are "talking to themselves—in public." "All Poetry is an Act of Communication," yet the versifiers inhibit communication. Eastman says they go, by all sorts of technical devices, from free verse to free punctuation to free grammar to free etymology (referring to Cummings' use of lower-case letters, others' use of the comma, Marin's use of space on the page, etc.).

Against this the poets say: "Poetry is a thing like music, or the morning . . . for those who are sensitive enough to perceive it." Edith Sitwell says, in her *Poetry and Criticism:* "The modernist poets are bringing a new and heightened consciousness to life," and Hart Crane adds that the province of poetry is "added consciousness and increased perceptions." But the positivist temper, the poets say, has so influenced politics and education and philosophy that it is a real issue whether imaginative literature will any longer flourish or decay. Since the pragmatist-positivist is concerned with actions, he devotes himself to building "compromised programs"; this is possible because if you put three disagreeing people together they can produce a compromised program of action because their truths, their goals, their interpretations of the outcome are not important. The important thing to them is something practically actionable. But actually, rebuts the poet, nothing is of greater importance than the personal truth of each of us. *A concept cannot be compromised.*

Tate, Brooks, Frank, Sorokin go further, asserting that our sensate culture, lacking the tradition of literature and poetry, is building the foundations of a slave totalitarian society. Tate brings in the educationalists, saying that it is "but a step from the crude sociologism of the normal school to the cloistered scholarship of the graduate school." Teachers College, Columbia, he says, is the chief sinner, emphasizing adjustment to a mechanical society, and conditioning the people for the realization of a bourgeois paradise of gadgets and consumption of commodities— but not of the true fruits of the earth.

The nub of the whole controversy is the difference between the opponents over the meaning of "knowledge." The scholars do not regard literature as a form of knowledge; they regard it merely as one of many forms of political expression.

To offset this interpretation, the poets and their new critics maintain that only "through poetry and the high forms of literature" can we obtain "a complete and responsible version of our experience." They say that the use of the scientific vocabularies in the spiritual realm has created, or at any rate is the expression of, a "spiritual disorder." While Carnap and Morris and the logical positivists retort that all imaginative literature is only "amiable insanity," the poets reply that actually it provides "the only complete knowledge of man's experience." The positivists' new operational interpretation of meaning demands "an exact one-to-one relationship of language to the objects to which it refers"; in this relevance, they say, lies the meaning of all terms and propositions. Morris says in his *Foundations for the Theory of Science:* "The true meaning of the term is not its definition, it is the number of statements containing it which can be referred to empirically observed events." This is the essence of the positivistic science of semeiotics: "A concept may be regarded as a semantical rule to determine the use of characterizing signs." Roleff replies: "Morris' analysis leaves out meaning in the primary sense of meaning"; and Tate adds, "the completeness of Hamlet is not of the scientific order, nor of the experience order, it is, in short, of the mythical order." The later, more poetic, Richards agrees: "Without his mythologies man is only a cruel animal without a soul . . . a congeries of possibilities without order and aim."

XX

Years of addiction to the "leave-no-stone-unturned" school of thought swung me into the camp of the wholeness ways of looking at life and education. That led me to understand why the men of the first draft could not escape the thing-quantitative mold. I knew because I had personally fallen victim to the easy conformity, giving most of my energy from 1911, when I began my study of education at Illinois, to the somersaulting days after 1920 to educational measurement and statistics. So I know, as Dewey used to insist, "internally, in its own terms" what this pragmatic, positivistic, semantic point of view did to the first educationalists.

It led them to become mechanists, even though they gave lip-service to "generalization" and "transfer." They accepted the sensate world's assumptions and postulates. They defined the world in terms of things, viewed human beings as assemblies of parts, thought about them by comparing them with averages of groups, evaluated their capacities and performances in terms of rank-order of size, ignored the critical task of founding education upon organic concepts of the human sciences.

But years of consorting with the organicists in every area taught us to recognize that the postulates in the realms of mechanism and organism are very different. Mechanisms are assemblies of parts, marked by standardization and interchangeability, susceptible to quantity production. The concepts that "the Whole is equal to the sum of all its parts," and that there is validity in the reports of the separate senses are to be relied upon only in the world of mechanism. But in the realm of organism the whole is *not* equal to the sum of all its parts; there is always something unique left over. Hence nothing is uniform, constant; everything changes, becomes a new integration. No report of a single sense can provide enough of the organism's total reaction to produce a valid record of observation. Organisms cannot be broken up into parts with any expectation that the parts will remain constant. Hence in the world of organism we can measure only by means of instruments which will report the total behavior of the total organism at any moment.

This is the story of the Creative Path in America during the Long Armistice between the two World Wars. This can now be sharply contrasted with the Conforming Way from 1890 to 1920. Three new university disciplines have been sketched in, three great sources of knowledge about man and his society, his behavior, and his expression. From these, three equally important Foundations of Education can be, in fact are being, created: a Social Foundations, a Bio-Psychological Foundations, and an Esthetic Foundations. Around these three disciplines the entire structure of a teacher-education program can be built.

Some of my readers, competent in the historical and philosophical aspects of education, will ask: "Where is the new History and Philosophy?" To those I reply that, like the other foundations of education and the professional program in curriculum and teaching, administration, and guidance, they are to be drawn from these three university disciplines A sociology, a psychology, and an esthetics, each of which is drawn from adequate sources, will supply the basic materials needed for education. But to make that affirmation convincing, a prior step must be taken—the building of a new theory. To that task we turn to Chapter VI.

Part III

Frontiers of Theory and Practice

CHAPTER VI

Frontiers of Theory in Teacher Education

I

Enough is known. If the wealth of creative thought can be gathered and organized, teachers will command sufficient wisdom to guide the youth of the world. The School of Tomorrow can be brought to life today.

But we, the Teachers of Teachers, stand silent, unable to organize our wisdom and command the motive power to put it to work.

Enough is known of our culture to design the content of a great teacher education.

But the Teachers of Teachers are bogged down in bewildered inertia among its glorious miscellany of materials.

Enough is known of man, his knowing and his behavior, to organize our teaching.

Yet the Teachers of Teachers seem unable to grope their way to more than a fraction of the known knowledge.

Enough expressive experience has been lived to guarantee a high order of esthetics.

Yet we have no esthetics in teacher education.

Enough is known of the first principles of conduct to solve the problem of freedom and control.

But the Teachers of Teachers still lack the rudiments of a theory of life and education.

The missing key is motive power. The Teacher of Teachers must recover the Magic Mirror in which he sees, not what he is, but what he could be. He must lift himself out of the deep rut of the Conforming Way onto the broad highway of the Creative Path. That is the need as we move out onto frontiers of theory, for difficult tasks of imagination are demanded of us. It is a conception of wisdom, organized and focused, that we must now command.

The cue is in the building of a great theory. (Some prefer the term "philosophy," but to get the job done I think "theory" will serve better.) To focus these scattered fragments of man's knowl-

149

edge in a great design of teacher education the prior task is to develop a dynamic and comprehensive theory. Only so can we organize our wisdom and provide the motive power to put it to work.

Every engineer knows that before he can build a bridge, a dam, a power plant, an engine, he must design it—in imagination. To do that he must assemble and organize the irreducible body of facts upon which the design is based. But before he can create the design he must build a sound theory in imagination.

Every physical scientist today knows only too well the part played by theory in turning the first scientific revolution into the second: witness the three-hundred-year failure of the Galilean-Newtonian mechanical theory, turned into the startling success of the electromagnetic field theory of Maxwell, Einstein, Bohr, *et al.*

Every artist knows that before he can build his house, his poem, his dance, or his symphony, paint his canvas or revitalize his Valley, he must design it and his design will be the expression of his deeply felt theory of the creative act.

So the educator must know that before he can build the life and program of a good school, he must design it, and that his design will be the inevitable product of his theory of life and education.

II

The prior difficulty today is with the sources. They are not only voluminous, scattered, and remote; they are alien to the tradition of philosophy building in which the Teachers of Teachers have been brought up. Most theorizing, done by persons called "Professors of the Philosophy of Education," has been done without regard to the *current* knowledge of the society and the culture, human behavior, or esthetics. It is an eclectic and additive process. All new theories are built up from earlier, *classic*, theories such as those called "Idealism" or "Realism," that have little or nothing to do with our industrial civilization. If our teacher education is to be appropriate to our times and to our critical needs today, it must be built from *our* social order, *our* bio-psychology of behavior, and *our* esthetics. So my statement of sources is not a devious task; it is direct and simple. It evolves naturally out of the studies and findings of Chapter V.

The *foundational sources* of the theory lie in man's most valid knowledge, as organized in the disciplines of the scholars, the artists, the philosophers, and the religionists. This will sound acceptable to the conventional philosopher of education—*until we begin to specify the disciplines.* Then he will, I think, gather up his skirts and move away a bit. Anyhow we must specify that we mean the new "disciplines" that have been built in the Creative Path, not the old archaic ones of the Conforming Way which still dominate the college curriculum. By "man's valid knowledge" we mean Man's knowledge of our mid-twentieth-century society and culture—its traits, characteristics, problems, and issues; man's knowledge of our people's behavior, caught in a period of drastic stresses and strains, revealed in our best bio-psychological, psychiatric, and social knowledge; man's knowledge of our expressive artists working in every creative medium today.

But the sources are historical as well as contemporary. We depend very much indeed on man's knowledge of history.

> The history of his changing society and culture
> The history of thought and feeling
> The history of the consequent philosophic and religious interpretations

But this is the *New History*—as Robinson and all of the creatives have called it since his first work. The history of *our* present society, *our* thought, *our* best philosophizing; not the old history that ignored all of the social order, half the data of psychology, all of esthetics.

It is these new and vital sources to which we must go. They are indeed the very ones we have partly gathered and organized in this book: not fully, but sufficiently to provide adequate illustrations for the preface to my theory. I say preface advisedly, for a complete exposition of such a theory would require a major book. When fully gathered and organized, the materials from these sources will constitute the Foundations of Education: Social, Bio-psychological, Esthetic, Historical, and Philosophical-Religious. They will be based on three contributory theories:

> A theory of Society and the Culture, which will be the key to the social Foundations of Education
> A theory of Behavior, which will be the key to the Bio-psychological Foundations of Education.
> A theory of Esthetics, which will be the key to the Esthetic (Expressional and Appreciational) Foundations of Education

These must all be designed by the Teacher of Teachers, and the program of the Teachers College built upon them, definitely in the light of the needs of teaching in American schools. The process will be a never-ending one, for the dominating theme of modern life is change. Year by year the culture changes bringing important shifts in social conditions, altering the trends, projecting new problems, and reshaping the issues. Year by year the scholars' researches throw up new concepts, revising their interpretations of old ones. So our theory of culture, behavior, esthetics, and education varies with all these changes, being constantly rebuilt on the most current validated knowledge.

This is the total over-all problem and my proposed order of work emerges from it. I begin with two prefaces to a Theory of a Science of Man: first, a theory of society and culture; second, a theory of behavior.

III

I. A Preface to a Theory of the Science of Society and Culture

The theory of education springs from a prior question: "What is education for?" The answer is produced, in the long run, in the matrix of the culture. The ultimates, the great allegiances, are born of the people's way of life, that is, of the culture. Occasional men rise above them, but the deepest loyalties of most men are stereotyped in them by the climate of opinion, beliefs, and values of the people. The design of education, therefore, must start with a theory of man living in society, and molded by his culture. Hence *it starts with the great concepts which are the keys to the life of that culture.*

These concepts are precipitated by the history of thought. Of all the foundations of education, *the history of ideas is prior and fundamental in building a theory of education.* I do not mean by this statement the customary eclectic assembly of ideas from idealism, realism, pragmatism, and other classical interpretations of knowing. This conventional method of developing a philosophy of education is essentially static and unprogressive, and causes an ever-lengthening lag between the culture and the theory. Quite to the contrary to that method, the method I suggest will take out the lag. Instead of finding the First Principles in the classic statements of the past, we shall build the theory directly from the scholars' knowledge of the universe, the culture, and of man's behavior.

Philosophers of society have devoted much speculative energy in the past century to the building of theories of societal development. As the speed of industrialization increased after mid-nineteenth century, many of these, published in voluminous form, received widespread discussion. I name four as typical of the range. One provided the motive power for the Russian revolution of 1917. No one of them, in my judgment, fits our needs.

First: Social Darwinism, much discussed in the latter nineteenth century, extensively developed by Herbert Spencer. This was an elaborate carrying over of the principles of evolution to the theory of the origin and growth of human societies. Long ago this theory dropped out of the center of discussion.

Second: Dialectical Materialism: Karl Marx's theory that modern industrial methods of owning, producing, and distributing goods bring about the formation and struggle of opposed social classes—primarily the owners *vs.* the workers. As industrialization advances, these become irreconcilable enemies in a struggle embracing more and more of the peoples of the world. Marx, a student of Hegel, was influenced to build his theory around the latter's theory that the dialectical back-and-forth interaction of thesis and anti-thesis results in a new and better synthesis. Each synthesis, taken as a new thesis gives rise to a new anti-thesis, the ensuing conflict producing another new synthesis, which in turn becomes a new thesis, which in turn produces a new anti-thesis, and so on, and on. Out of this dialectical process applied to great populations, Marx and his followers around the world foresee the eventual success of a "Communist" society as the last and permanent "synthesis." An enormous library of discussion has been written in a score of languages about this theory, and the rise and fall of governments around the world is the practical exhibit of its earth-shaking effects. But I am convinced it does not fit twentieth-century American conditions and needs.

Third: The Cyclic Theory of Oswald Spengler: According to Spengler, the history of civilization is a cyclic record of the birth, infancy, adolescence, maturity, and decline of one civilization after another. There are many causes but the chief one is that as they mature, they lose their roots in the agrarian, or soil, base. This wordy and academic speculation has had little impact in America, no impact at all on social theorists and technologists with whom I am congenial.

Fourth: Pareto's Theory of the "Circulation" of Groups of Élite Rulers: The rise and fall of societies is measured by the type of "élite" that rises to rule. The opponents are always of two sharply contrasted types: (1) the "fox" type—materialistic, exploitive, and scheming; (2) the "lion" type—idealists of integrity. I found Pareto's four dull tomes largely a waste of time and effort.

These four social theories illustrate the range of academic discussion of the past three generations. All have always seemed to me—even the Marxian, which has gripped the political leaders of hundreds of millions of people—to be unrealistic in the face of the myriad facts developed in thirty years of study of our culture.

IV

The cue to the theory that does make sense in a society caught in a cultural revolution is the concept of social lag, first made clear by William F. Ogburn. This has been dealt with at length in Chapter III. It goes to the causal heart of social change—the lag of institutions and psychological and moral factors behind creative science, technological invention, and production.

Succinctly outlined, the steps in the cultural lag are:

A prolonged period of creative scientific thought brings about novel technological inventions.

The productive material culture changes very quickly.

The institutions—family, government, corporate way of life, and the like—lag behind, changing, but more slowly than the economic machinery.

Moral codes and the psychological and moral factors—values, beliefs, definitions of basic concepts, fundamental concerns of the people, the climate of opinion—lag still further behind, indeed change very slowly. Among them, however, the lag varies greatly. Those that are directly connected with economic ownership and control (recall, for example, the swift change from an employment old-age deadline of sixty-five to a young middle-age deadline of forty) change with distressing rapidity, while others—such as the concept and mood of *laissez faire*—resist alteration.

As these things happen a basic tug of war ensues between the struggling forces of I and We. This defines the resources and obstacles in the culture in which the moral-ethical problem of our times must be grasped and stated. Succinctly restated, we have:

> Moral codes lagging behind social practices, the latter producing a new social order and new problems; the people continue to deal with these by means of old and outmoded ideas. This perpetuation of old culture-patterns and ontology stands as an obstacle in the way of creating a new ethics.

Here, then, is the cue to a theory of our society that makes sense: great social trends out of step: economic productivity . . . the creative processes of government . . . the understanding and capacity of the people for organized action—all those out of gear. The supreme criterion of peace and abundance is that these trends shall be brought into step with one another.

Thus, in building a theory for our times, the history of ideas is the cue to our first step. As Comte said a century ago: "Ideas rule the world or throw it into chaos." It is the key ideas, or concepts, of the scholars' knowledge that will constitute the structural outline of our theory. So I begin there.

V

The Key Concepts of Theory Are the Product of the Modern Hierarchy of Revolutions

The study of the scholars' multiplying studies leaves no doubt that we are living today in the matrix of a hierarchy of revolutions which are now in the sixth century of uninterrupted development.

I. The *first and most basic one is the Intellectual Revolution* which began in the late fifteenth century. This has now moved through two conspicuous phases, in a sense through two intellectual revolutions:

The first, the mechanical or Newtonian era, covered approximately the period from the 1500's to the 1800's A.D. Newton died in 1727, but physical science was "Newtonian" until the later nineteenth century. This stage was marked by the great shift in thought from the doctrine of Authority to the doctrine of Experience.

The second, 1830's–1950's, the organic interpretation of man in the universe which, especially after 1900, ushered in a new electrochemical age, marked the great shift in thought from mechanical to organic explanations.

II. The *second stage* in the emergence of the hierarchy of revolutions of modern times *is the Technological Revolution*. This, like the scientific revolution which gave birth to it, moved, in something over three centuries, through two phases. The First Technological Revolution, starting in the late sixteenth century, created the crude structure of Western industrial society in the 1800's. The Second Technological Revolution, lagging behind its intellectual progenitor, emerged in the first half of the twentieth century as the technically efficient age of today. This is primarily the age of World Wars, and of World Depressions.

III. The *third stage is the Social Revolution,* the revolution in institutions. This was produced conspicuously by the Technological Revolution, but more fundamentally by the prior intellectual shifts in thought. It has already altered social institutions to such an extent that the change is recognized even by the man on the street. Moreover, because of the lag of popular understanding, and of codes of behavior behind the changing institutions, it is important to study whether we have already entered into a new, or *second,* Social Revolution.

Briefly put, this is what I mean by saying that we live in a hierarchy of revolutions which, taken together, constitute the cultural revolution that has been sweeping over the earth for not less than five hundred years.

Our prior task, therefore, is to make ourselves competent students of the great shift in thought in modern times and of the technological and social changes that it has already brought about. We do that through the study of the lives and works of the frontiersmen of thought. Thus we build on the cumulative knowledge that man has gleaned from the study of his developing life on the earth and in the universe. *This is the only way we use the so-called* "great books," but it is an important way. These help to build an understanding of the outstanding concepts which are keys to explaining the universe and man in the culture.

Moreover, it is these concepts, organized and clarified, that constitute the intellectual skeleton of both the theory and the program of education, including the education of teachers. To explore the key concepts is, therefore, of prior importance.

VI

I suggest that there are three ways in which the teacher of

teachers can conceive these basic concepts and their use in designing both the theory and the program of education.

I. The First Way of Conceiving the Key Concepts: The Super-primary Concepts

Study of the history of ideas suggests that the modern sciences and arts rest, foundationally, upon a fairly compact body of super-primary concepts. I have in mind, and suggest as examples, seven explosive ones:

The first is Energy as a field of force. Put differently it is "the field"—an organization-of-forces-in-tension. In the physical sciences this is the concept of the electromagnetic field successfully stated in the equational form in three generations of mathematical work by Maxwell, Einstein, *et al.*

The second is Cultural Change. This concept has revealed itself, especially since 1900, as the clear cue to our social and personal problems. Cultural change accelerated in every phase of the culture so devastatingly that already we can describe it as *cultural revolution.* It has affected the production and distribution of goods and services . . . the life on farm and in village, town, and city . . . family, government, schools, press, church, and all institutions . . . basic ideas, beliefs and values, loyalties and objects of allegiance, thought and feeling. We shall now be well advised to *teach the expectancy of accelerated change.*

The third is Experience. This is the first of two primary concepts which mark the modern shift in thought and underlie the bio-psychological sciences. In our day it has got itself stated as the concept of *"action"* by the psychologists, biologists, and the technologists in education. In the past half-century it has also revealed itself in the human arts and sciences as the concept of *"movement."* It is becoming increasingly clear that the experience-action-movement concept is indispensable to the psychology of meaning as well as to the understanding of the creative, or expressive, act.

The fourth is "Integration." This is now revealed in the new physical science concept of the field-as-an-organization-of-forces-in-tension. This is expressed in the bio-psychological sciences as organism, in the social sciences as organization. For a generation students of education have increasingly founded their treatment of behavior and of curriculum and teaching upon it.

The fifth is Growth, or Development. The grasp of this concept in the bio-psychological sciences, and in later years in educational technology, is the product of three generations of study and criticism of the *doctrine of evolution.* The growth concept is now the accepted basis of the new educational psychology and of its application in curriculum development and teaching in the schools.

The sixth is the Culture and its Molding of Personality. While a newcomer in the galaxy of educational ideas, its validity as a super-primary concept has been established by fifty years of accumulating researches in social anthropology. It is true that it is applicable only in the human sciences and arts; nevertheless it must not be neglected as a super-primary concept in the building of both theory and program in education.

The Seventh is Expression. This points to the universal human capacity for, and the tendency toward, the creative act. The next novel step to be taken by the designers of educational theory and the builders of curriculum is to recognize and provide for the creative act as a prior element in the educative process.

II. The Second Way of Conceiving the Key Concepts: As Products of the Great Shift in Thought

Those seven super-primary concepts, which are so broad that they appear as intellectual foundations of all of the modern sciences and arts, can be expanded and defined more clearly if we break the shift in thought into its two major components:

First, the shift from the doctrine of Authority to the doctrine of Experience.

Second, the shift from Mechanism to Organism—in every realm of thought and inquiry: physical, biological, psychological, social, esthetic, ethical; that is, from mechanical to organic explanations, from things to energy-force-relations.

The close study of the history of ideas reveals seven basic concepts which restate the foregoing super-primary concepts in their respective areas. Two of them relate to, and clarify, the shift from the doctrine of Authority to the doctrine of Experience; the other five similarly clarify the shift from mechanical to organic explanations. All have played an important part in the reconstruction of education during the past half-century. Hence I organize them with special reference to their use in the development of a theory and program for education.

1. FROM AUTHORITY TO EXPERIENCE. This shift in thought reveals two basic ideas:

First, the shift from concern for the Individual to concern for the Group. In modern times this precipitated the increasing discussion of freedom and control—in the family, in community and national government, in the schools, and in the expression of the creative person. The problem is revealed most sharply when stated as the survival of the Individual—his protection from the undue encroachment of the Group—a matter of critical importance today.

Second, the corresponding shift from the defeatist view of the compulsions of nature to the emphasis upon the molding role of the environment. This is the Nature-Nurture problem. Its recognition has been revealed in our times in the increasing emphasis upon the social. In psychology the Self is seen as social; indeed all psychology is regarded as social psychology. The doctrine of social use has been increasingly relied on in education, and the function concept ("Of what social use is it?") pervades all of the sciences and arts.

2. FIVE CONCEPTS WHICH CLARIFY THE SHIFT FROM MECHANISM TO ORGANISM. *First,* the shift from Things to Forces—the relations between things. This becomes clear as we see the changing nature of the two technological revolutions. The First, or Newtonian, Revolution, was marked by the inadequate connecting-rod idea of energy as motion produced by the impact of things lying in a line of direction. The Second Technological Revolution was founded upon the concept of the field as an organization-of-forces-in-tension. This shift from "Thing" to "Force" has been revealed in our times in the expressional arts, in the bio-psychological sciences, as well as in the physical sciences. Thus we have a restatement of the principle of the field as the basic source of energy; this underpins all the sciences and arts.

Second, the shift from Statics to Dynamics in the study of society and the culture as well as in the study of the physical universe; that is, from a fixed conception of society to a dynamic view of accelerating cultural change (witness the contrast between the constancy of Victorian concepts and the shifting objects of allegiance of the twentieth century).

Third, from Passive Conformity to Active Expression, as revealed in the psychology and esthetics of behavior as well as in social-economic-political changes in the culture. The passive has given way to the active in education, in biology and psychology. We know, we learn, only what we do, what we have done. Experience is ours only as we live it. Here is the action concept in every phase of life—economic, political, social, esthetic; this is the cultural change from the age of impression to the age of expression. This is the Experience concept put to work.

Fourth, from Substance (Structure) to Function, affecting the interpretation of all the sciences and the arts. In economic life this is the shift from the belief in the priority of individual pre-emption, ownership ("possession is nine-tenths of the law"), to the idea of social use, the good-of-the-greater-group. In philosophy it is the shift from the Nominalism of particulars to a new Realism of generals; in the arts of expression, from producing a likeness to expressing the artist's feeling for the inner forces of life. We re-state here the prior question asked in appraising every phase of the culture. In considering the reconstruction of the social system we ask: "What is a social system for?" In the art world: "What kind of life is to be lived in this house?" "What human purpose is to be served by this esthetic object?" "What is this line to do?"—either in a painting, in a poem, or in a musical composition. This is the prior function question.

Fifth, from Part to Whole. This has been clarified by the discussion of the Part-Whole controversy of our time which shifts the emphasis from analysis to integration. In the new physics this is the concept of the field-as-the-organization-of-forces-in-tension. This field concept appears in the biological and psychological sciences variously labeled as organism, or integration, or organization. In education the shift in thought reveals itself in the increasing attention to the concept of integration. This is true in the study of learning, thinking, expression, the interrelatedness of growth and development, in curriculum reconstruction, and in the development of an adequate teaching method.

In spite of the shift, we note, however, the persistence of the mechanical point of view even to the present day: in physics still by unanswered questions of the relation of quanta to relativity and field. In the human sciences it is shown in the long search for a single control of behavior, for the homunculus—"the little man" in the brain cap, or in the endocrines. Its latest revelation is the current hypothesis of the students of communication-control that, "the neurone pattern is equivalent to the behavior pattern."

III. The Third Way of Conceiving the Great Concepts

With special reference to the Social Foundations of Education, and recognizing that I am merely restating those ideas which have been gathered in Chapter III, I suggest that there are ten "institutional" concepts which describe an important trend in the organization of society and the culture. Without interpretation, I merely enumerate those:

—From competition to cooperation
—From free-action to control
—From decentralization to centralization
—From individual planning and responsibility to group planning and responsibility
—From diversity to standarization
—From disintegration to integration
—From inequality to equality
—From possession of things to functional status in society
—From the medieval method of deduction from philosophical givens to the modern scientific method of direct observation and interpretation

This, in briefest form, is an *illustrative* outline of key concepts for a teacher's theory of society and behavior. I italicize *illustrative* because it is admittedly incomplete, especially in the physical and natural sciences.

It is these dozen super-primary concepts that are the open sesame to a theory that will really serve us. Study them carefully, recalling the manner in which they have recurred in section after section of this book: witness "field-as-an-organization-of-forces-intension" . . . organism (and the shift from mechanism to organism) . . . integration . . . Wholeness (and the shift from Part to Whole) . . . the shift from Things to Forces . . . the interrelatedness of Growth (the organic, or integration idea again) . . . the Culture (Wholeness again) and the culture-molding process . . . the shift from I to We, the Group emphasis . . . but these all accentuate the *environmental*, and the shift from the hereditarian view . . . Note the manner in which several coalesce around the *Action Concept:* the very shift from Things (static) to Forces (dynamics), from Passive Conformity to Active Expression (the key to the great expressive age in the arts of man), and the shift from Substance (Things again) to Function (dynamic use). And a careful analysis of the ten shifts in institutional concepts shows the recurrence again and again of these same expressive ideas.

These, then, taken with my comprehensive chart for psychology (Chapter IV), will serve as adequate illustrations of a broad conceptual foundation for our total theory—including the theory of society and culture, the theory of behavior, and the theory of esthetics. Granted this is the basic structure we have only to note some further illustrative details concerning each theory.

VII

Fundamental to any discussion of a theory of our social order and its progressive reconstruction are the basic postulates that we make with respect to it. These can be clearly organized:

—Postulates with respect to the nature of our times on the historical curve of modern cultural change, and the acceleration, prediction, and control of social change

—Postulates concerning the nature of our industrial-democratic society, its economic-political factors

—Postulates concerning the culture-molding process, the structure of the society in groups and classes, the dominant beliefs and values, the characteristic culture-patterns, and the theory of culture

From my earlier studies, which have been synthesized in Chapter III, I present these briefly.

This theory of society postulates, *first,* that for more than a half-century we have been living in a period of tremendous transition between two stages of industrial-democratic culture. It is a period of more drastic, world-wide cultural change and social tension than has hitherto been revealed in modern Euro-American history. Its transitional nature is established by the fact that three great social trends—economic productivity, social control through government, and popular understanding—have separated one from another by such vast gaps that they not only have produced the critical social problems of today, but have now made it possible for us to grasp the significance of social change and alternative solutions for the problems.

Our theory postulates, *second,* that a description of society, documented from the scholars' studies, can now be built into the curriculum of school and college. The key to this description lies in the economic-political characteristics of our industrial-democratic society. First and foremost, it is a large-scale system of limitless power, in which basic commodities are produced by corporate-owned, power-driven machine factories of increasing technical efficiency. The power until recently has been molecular, based on natural fuels (coal, oil, moving water), the resources of which are fixed and limited in amount, and the supply of which is exhaustible within a short time. Atomic fission, now successfully completed, revolutionizes the power phase of the productive system by making unlimited resources available.

But it will also require such vast financial support, and carries such dangers of monopoly and destruction, as to make it seem certain that in our time strong national control will have to be imposed on power production. It is possible that *within the lifetime of my younger readers it will have to be world-controlled.* Because of the technological and social revolutions of modern times all industrializing nations have moved swiftly into a trend toward public control of the production of basic quantity goods and services.

Third, our theory postulates also that we now confront a problem of *uninterrupted full-employment-at-abundance-level, which is novel in the history of man.* The American industrial system is rapidly reaching such high producing efficiency that there seems little likelihood that the accelerating technological displacement of workers can be offset by predictable gains in new kinds of employment *in the mechanized industries.* It is inconceivable to me that the second industrial revolution, in the midst of which we now are, will *not* increase the imposing of government control on private enterprise. The history of the business cycle during the past three generations lends little support to the view that competitive free enterprise alone can provide full employment of

American labor *on a standard of living commensurate with our natural and human resources.* Already the facts of social trend have clearly documented the conclusion that the American social system is a Mixed Economy—part private, part public; part decentralized, and part centralized. We may as well face it—the trends are in the direction of more, rather than less, centralization and public control.

Fourth, in spite of the advance of public control, the economic system is still primarily privately owned and administered. In every stage of its development it has prospered only by continuous expansion, and to live under the private enterprise system, this expansion must be guaranteed. Can private enterprise do this *alone?* We do not know. I personally doubt it.

The answer, *fifth,* must postulate that ours is a pecuniary social order, resting on money and price. Everything needed for full production and employment is available in the United States now, except the money. The possession of money is crucial. The stability of the system rests upon the stability of the units of money, price, and of wages and the interrelationships of these with profits. One nub of the problem is, therefore, the fitting of prices, wages, and profits into a sound and designed unified plan. Social experience in America has not yet determined the respective roles of private enterprise, government, and cooperatives in this process. But that *we need creative work on the money system,* is clear.

Sixth, will the voluntary investment of private savings, or private creation of credit (debt), hold the growth of our private enterprise system (which can continue to exist only by uninterrupted expansion) at the needed rate to provide full production and employment? We do not know; the history of the system has not yet clearly demonstrated the answer. Neither do we know to what extent government—so-called "deficit"—financing can and should be employed, although recent history suggests its continued use. Neither has history established the danger level of the public and private debt incurred by the system and its relation to national wealth and annual national income.

Seventh, history has established clearly the crucial role of some Buyer, such as the government, periodically giving large-scale orders for continuous production. During the Great Depression the Federal government was the largest-scale buyer of goods and services. During World War II it bought approximately half the goods and services produced and there was continuous and full employment at the highest standard of living in our history. Today we are putting 20 per cent of our national income (seventy to eighty billion dollars) into the heavy industry of armament. As I said earlier, *this is the governor of the economic machine, it has been built by the creation of a large-scale and accelerating national debt.* For the moment we are secure.

Eighth, we must begin now to work at the occupational problem. This will be the most difficult mass creative problem of the next twenty-five years. It is my theory—and I am certain that the scientific students and the electronics engineers agree—that we must invent new and exciting occupations for tens of millions of persons that will be displaced by the complete automatization of heavy industry in the next twenty-five years. I repeat, if the governor of the economic machine fails to rise and fall with the social-economic pressures, we shall either *solve the key occupational problem of an automatic heavy industry,* or we shall face economic collapse and political revolution. The study of the curves of social trend convinces me that that day is not many years ahead—perhaps fifteen, perhaps twenty-five. Hence we must *alert the Teachers of Teachers to get ready now to help create the new occupations.* The new generation of American youth must be prepared now to take part in them and their continuous improvement.

VIII

These are the chief economic postulates for a theory of society and the culture. Their real significance is bound up with corresponding and inextricably interrelated political postulates. The first is, as Turner expressed it sixty years ago, "economic power carries political power"; history has taught us to add: changing economic conditions change political conditions and problems. In exploring this fusion of economic and political concepts we must bear in mind that our time is a period of ordeal for the believers in the democratic method. After hundreds of years of increasingly successful democratic life, the western world has been living for a generation in a terrifying interregnum of totalitarian dictatorship. It has been marked by four successive examples: *first,* Italian fascism; *second,* the rule of the Japanese War Party and by Chiang Kai-shek and the other Chinese war lords; *third,*

Hitler's nazism; and now, *fourth,* the totalitarian nationalism of the Russian Politburo. Having become World Economic Power No. 1, America is now accepted as the leader in the struggle to defeat, permanently, this concept of dictatorship as illustrated in the USSR Politburo and its allies and satellites in China and eastern Europe. There is no other national leader on the earth today. Our theory must also postulate that, at the moment of taking up the burden of world leadership, America, more than any other industrializing nation, must face great issues of domestic economy. It alone stands on the threshold of bringing forth, in some form of cooperative commonwealth, a civilization of magnificent economic abundance, democratic behavior, and integrity of expression. But it too faces internal strains of potentially catastrophic proportions.

We are strong enough to lead the world toward some form of democratic, Mixed Economy, but are we wise enough? We shall soon see for the testing moment is now. Our measure is being taken. The test is whether enough of the American people can grasp the established fact that, in company with other industrializing peoples, we have been living for several centuries, and shall continue to live far into the future, in the midst of a hierarchy of world-wide revolutions. It is this fact of a revolution in ideas, mood, and outlook as well as in social institutions, that sets the framework of our theory of education. Our prospective teachers must be persuaded that their chief obligation is to help bring a vast minority of our people quickly to the point of saying: "This *is* a time of deep social transforma'ion. Our times *are* different from those of our fathers and we must be willing to think differently and consciously to govern differently, if we are to build a decent world for our children." The people's acceptance of this point of view will be facilitated by seeing clearly both the giant potentialities in our culture and the dangers that menace it.

They must see that we confront drastic choices: abundance *vs.* catastrophe . . . democracy *vs.* the slave state. Of our many harassing problems two are central to all, and they must be understood if the nature of our times and our educational needs are to be grasped:

Problem No. 1: Full Production and Full Employment, at a High Standard of Living While Preserving Democracy.

Problem No. 2: World Peace through American-Russian Cooperation.

The consensus among the students of modern industrial culture is that these two problems are inextricably bound up together. It is a basic postulate of my theory, therefore, that the problem of world peace cannot be solved except as the problems of production and employment are successfully met in the major industrializing countries. I postulate also that the efficient operation of the economic system cannot be brought about except through *the wise application of continuous planning and of cooperative democratic control,* on a scale that this nation has never succeeded in attaining in the past.

This means that our theory has taken a position, and it has chosen the democratic one, on the second drastic choice before our people: "How shall the setting up of planned controls be done?" The issue is clear: it is totalitarianism *vs.* democracy, some form of cooperative planning and law-making. We hardly need to remind ourselves that these two methods of national social development are in actual operation in the two great competing cultures of the world today. The cleavage between the USSR and its five satellites, and the fifty-two other nations which are marked by more or less democratic ideals and processes, is sharp and clear. There is at stake one of the greatest decisions of world history and it can all be summed up by this sharp contrast—totalitarianism *vs.* democracy.

IX

From the sketch we have already made of the bold facets of the theory of economic and political society emerges the third critical aspect—the understanding of the people. This takes us to the social-psychological problem of consent. Our theory of society and the culture postulates that there are three principles of consent. The first two—the guarantee of the rights of the people in written charters of liberty, and the creation of the suffrage—are on the way toward solution.

But it is the third principle of consent that takes us to a critical phase of our theory of society and culture for teachers. Since the people must understand their conditions and problems, one of the two chief educational tasks of our times is the swift, nation-wide building of adult education. It will not be easy for there are serious pitfalls in the way of popular understanding. There are barriers of physical geography, of racial and regional diversity of population, and serious linguistic barriers because the printed word, or the radioed oral word—the chief vehicle of common understanding—has made communication bafflingly indirect.

Most serious of all, there are property barriers between the people and their understanding of the events that mold their lives, and these have brought about a monopoly of the facts by those who own the great mass agencies of communication—the press, the radio, the newsreel, the television, the public platform, and the forum. Thus the ancient problem of monopoly has raised its ugly head again—this time in the strategic area of communication. If the people, for example, are to understand the baffling problem of full production and full employment, they must know just such strategic generalizations as we have stated in the past few pages. But the danger is that he who controls the agencies of communication will also control the public mind; that he will determine the stereotyped meanings and concepts that grip the public mind, either by withholding the facts through censorship, or by distorting the facts through propaganda.

Moreover, there are psychological barriers which would exist even if the people controlled the mass agencies of communication. It is clear now that if the people are to understand the facts, the facts must be organized in meaningful form. Only the scholars in our modern world give any sign of being able to organize the vast welter of economic, political, social, anthropological, biological, and psychological facts. To guarantee public understanding, the facts must come to the people so related and organized that the crucial factors of a given problem can be grasped. Here is a herculean task for the competent and unbiased student.

X

Finally, our social theory is built around another of the super-primary concepts—the culture and its molding of human personality. The theory sharply distinguishes the society, the grouping of the people, from the culture, their way of life. I postulate all that has been said about the American way throughout this book, and must not repeat it here. But as for the culture-molding process, I say again it is crucial to the work of the Teachers of Teachers.

All of the scholars agree on its significance in our lives. The concept sums up the subtle give-and-take by which the climate of opinion and the common ideas, beliefs, and values of the community build in every individual the basic attitudes and beliefs which direct his conduct. The process is twofold: action and reaction, egocentric culture exerting pressures, molding and labeling . . . the egocentric individual either adjusting to, or defending himself against, or making over, the culture. Out of a generation of scholarly study of the culture-molding process we postulate another central concept for our theory: the *Stereotype*. As Lippmann summed it up thirty years ago: "We tend to perceive that which we have picked out in the forms stereotyped for us by the culture." This is the Law of the Stereotype.

The implications for our theory of social education are clear: *the teacher is the strategic guide of the culture-molding process.* We know that the concept of growth and development is central to our theory of behavior, and hence of curriculum and teaching. The question of who guides this culture-molding process becomes of extreme importance. Particularly is this so in a democratic society in which the people believe that every individual shall not only have an opportunity to rise to the highest stature of which he is innately capable, but *shall also be guided in reaching it.* It is the conscious anticipation of desirable kinds of growth that distinguishes the school from any other social enterprise, and makes the teacher the strategic guide of the culture-molding process. The teachers, even more than most parents—because of the latter's limited educational insight—are responsible for anticipating the living of young people. They must see to it that not only the facts, the conditions, and the problems of society are passed on to the younger generation, but also the central ideas, beliefs, and values of the people. To do this the teacher, as the only competent agent, must be constantly on hand selecting the important elements in the culture, interpreting them as adequately as possible, and building understanding among the children and the youth. Thus the teacher must not only pass *on* the culture, he must in addition *pass* on the culture.

XI

Finally, the building of a social theory serves its great purpose as the foundation of curriculum development. It is a basic postulate that the curriculum must be designed from the very life of the American people. To do that successfully in our changing world the teacher must become a competent student of that culture. *This is a requirement that has never been met in the history of education in any country.* Yet we know, at this mid-century point of reorientation, that if the teacher is to design the life and program of the school from the American way of life, he must know his America—its modes of living, its achievements and efficiencies, its liabilities as well as its assets. There is no short cut to that knowledge; there is only the rigorous study of American culture itself. The curriculum designer must become a student of the new sociology, economics, government, and art as well as the psychology and pedagogy of childhood and youth. If it be objected that this is too large an order, then it can only be replied that if it proves to be too large, we shall fail in building an adequate teacher education in our times. Such a failure would mean that modern peoples are not yet competent to solve democratically the problems of technically efficient industrial society. We cannot—we dare not—permit such a failure.

Putting the problem another way, there are two great tasks before us on the creative path in education:

> *The first:* to get our Society into the School and the School into the Society. This is the Social Problem. Our outline of the teacher's social theory is now before us.
>
> *The second:* to get the Whole Child into our awareness and hence into the School, and the School into the Whole Child. To deal with this problem successfully we need a new bio-psychological theory *based on our total knowledge and integrated with our social theory.*

Brief though it is, this is my preface to the theory of society and culture for the teacher. This is one-half of the twofold problem of a theory of the Science of Man. To complete it we need a theory of human behavior.

XII

II. A PREFACE TO A THEORY OF BEHAVIOR: THE NATURE OF THE ACT OF HUMAN RESPONSE

We can take off from a well-worn shibboleth of the new education: "The Whole Child." As we do so let us keep the compre hensive chart of the Whole Person (Chapter IV) before us. It will supply all the major concepts that have contributed to our study of the Whole Child. For twenty-five years teachers have given lip-service to the idea, but most of them have not really known what it means. Some have grasped the psychologists' related term—"organism-as-a-whole." Some have dimly sensed that a mysterious thing called "field theory" has something to do with it. But most of us in education and psychology (and also, Hebb says, in physiology) are not at all sure of our ground. Today, because of the present state of our ignorance, *we still lack an adequate program of education, principally because we lack an adequate theory of behavior.*

I shall follow the tradition developed by Dewey and others fifty years ago of centering analysis on the nature of the act of human response. There are four such acts, and four corresponding "life situations," that can be distinguished with sufficient clearness to help the teacher:

—acts of skill
—acts of thinking
—acts of expression . . . creative acts
—acts of appreciation

I pick only the second and third for illustrative study.

XIII

Consider the great unknowns: *What takes place* in the act of thought? *What takes place* in the creative act? What is going on while Cézanne stands fifteen minutes, in intense concentration, holding a blob of paint on his brush, appraising the juxtaposition of lines, planes, colors, masses, textures on his canvas? What does he see of the organic relation between them and his imagined conception, the alterations of relationships that would be produced by laying the blob at various places? This is the creative act. Is it "thinking"? Does its control reside in the brain, in the reports of the separate senses? It is still a very debatable issue.

Are other forces at work? Where? Is it this nebulous thing called "feeling"? Where is its control? In the brain? Or in other parts of the body? What is its "organ"? We do not know, and there is little interest or discussion of it. Nevertheless, we shall make the act of thought, and the creative act, clear to young people in schools only as we ourselves clear up what takes place within these acts.

It really seems incredible that eighty years after Peirce, Wright, and the Metaphysical Club we are in such confusion. Seventy years after the integrating generalization of Mach, Ehrenfelds, and Dilthey that "the whole is not equal to the sum of all its parts" —we still do not know. Sixty years after James's great psychology of "feeling" and "seeing relations" . . . fifty-five years after Dewey's "Reflex-Arc" article . . . forty years after Wertheimer's and Köhler's documentation of the role of pattern and "closure" in bringing "the flash of insight," neo-connectionism still dares us to be "general."

And all these have come only in recent times, following centuries of accumulating confirmation of the role of "the flash of insight," in the autobiographies of creative minds. These men have all *labeled* the uniqueness of the act of creative thought. Glimpses of its nature emerge from Dewey's 1910 analysis of the "Complete Act of Thought." More light is thrown on it by those who sympathetically use the Gestalt experiments—witness Lawrence Cole's recent splendid interpretation. But no one has *explained* it sufficiently to build a theory and practice of education upon it.

XIV

Most of us, however, act as if we knew what does take place. The progressive drift of thought is toward organism-as-a-whole interpretations; witness the steady accretion to the adherents of "field" theories. The vocabulary of scientists as well as artists abounds in such terms as organization, whole, pattern, relation-between-the-parts. In longer terms, we have acclaimed the great organic shift in thought in modern times. We have said with the new physicists that "mechanism is dead!" Out with all S-R Bond connectionisms, or conditioned-response psychologies. "Mechanism is dead in the human sciences, and in the art of education!" Out with the specific and in with the general!

Yet, in every one of these sciences, as experience and scientific knowledge accumulate to demand a place in our theory and our practice, the specific keeps bobbing up!

Even though "mechanism is dead in physics," Einstein is struggling to get quanta and field-relativity into a single unity.

Warren McCullough, Arturo Rosenblueth, and Norbert Weiner have recently posed a one-to-one correspondence between the neurone-pattern and the behavior-pattern.

D. O. Hebb, after years of laboratory experiment and armchair integration of the findings in the no-man's land between electro-physiology and the psychologies, comes forth with a "new" conception of "cell-assemblies, diffuse structure in the cortex, and diencephalon which are capable of acting as closed systems." This "series of events" is, he says emphatically, "the thought process" . . . the very prototype of attention, set, attitude, expectancy. But, although this makes a momentary kind of sense, *no matter how thick you slice it, it is still connectionism.*

While we now know in spite of Cannon's forty years of research on glandular secretions, that the *thalamus does not control emotional behavior,* we also know that it plays a significant part in it.

While we know that "reading" does not consist of word knowledge, we know also that specific word knowledge is indispensable to intelligent reading.

And after confronting the Part-Whole problem for fifty years we know that no practicing on the Part will give us mastery of the Whole. Nevertheless, without specific study of that bothersome Part—those intricate measures in the piano composition, or the one-step combinations in four-place column addition—no mastery of the Whole is possible.

Again and again we are warned that our deepest theoretical problems cannot be solved on an either-or basis. Neither field theory nor connectionism is the total answer. In spite of the drift toward field-organic theories, neo-connectionisms constantly rise to defy us.

We still do not really understand our key concepts. Why?

XV

The chief factor is that our frontier workers are still centering their attention on the cortex and *not on enough phases* of the functioning of the organism to give us an adequate picture of the whole child in action. We are not studying the whole child! Both the researchers and the teachers have made the great shift in thought from authoritarianism to experience, and in the twentieth century the teachers created the first examples of the experience-centered schools. This was a great achievement.

But our frontiersmen have failed to make the second great shift —that from mechanism to organism—and really to put into practice the concept of organism-as-a-whole. We in education seem to be unable to break the habit of doing all our studying of behavior in terms of ideas, thinking, the brain, intellect. Our myopic worship of the brain is frightening. To cite a single example, from Darwin's *Emotions in Animals and Men,* to Cannon's latest *Bodily Changes,* the seventy-five-year-long search of the endocrine physiologists for the control of the emotions was primarily a search for the homunculus—the little man who rules behavior from the skullbox. And the total result? Failure to find him! Yet the society— still giving lip-service to the whole child—slices off the cortex, hands it to the teachers and says: "Educate it! But keep hands off the body": A real concern for thinking, for intellect, and a vast contempt for the nebulous concept of feeling—which is regarded as outside the scientific pale. And even our beloved brothers in experimentalism have fallen into the same trap. And the result for us—the teachers—is fuzzy theories, *on those rare occasions when we hold any,* and a general state of bafflement.

The reason for the persistence of such lopsided explanations of behavior is not far to seek. It lies in the very nature of the culture and the academic climate of opinion in which our brilliant leaders grew up. A Veblen, interested in 1900 in the molding of America's creative minds of the coming fifty years, would have predicted that this would happen. It was in the cultural cards that schools would teach facts and skills, and that psychology would wallow in the connections of the brain and ignore the rest of the body. The signal achievement of the western Europeans in building the modern languages, the higher mathematics, and the scientific method of inquiry was alone enough to guarantee it. For centuries western society had engaged in an orgy of competitive individualism and its creative minds had—with only a few mutant-like exceptions—given themselves to precise measurement and technological invention. Its lesser minds had committed themselves all-out to the production of things and their corollary emoluments.

In such a quantitative-minded culture the *only accepted way of knowing* was through the minutely controlled reports of the *sep-*

arate senses—especially the sense organs in the head. Under the halo of the achievements of science and an incredibly efficient technology, both psychology and philosophy were doomed to become emphatically intellectual. In one university the scientific method of inquiry became such an "open universe" that its devotees are today unwilling to let their minds conclude what the facts of life conclude. They leave their minds open at both ends, instead of closed at one end, to make it possible for a few ideas to jell.

XVI

But against this popular separate sense interpretation, four groups in the sciences and arts stood out. A small brigade of heretical artist-teachers said that by the "Whole-Child" they meant just that—the Whole Child, not his head alone, nor his brain. Heretical young psychologists said: "The causes of behavior do not reside in the neurone, they reside in psychic tensions." "The thalamus does not control the emotions," said the physiologists, "the autonomic system plays as significant, if not a greater part." And the expressive artists of the great Age of Expression found the key to tensed movement on the canvas in what I am now convinced is *the tensile sense of the moving body*.

How it happened that the geniuses of our Expressive Age threw off the grip of the thing-quantitative mold is beyond my ken. But they did and after 1900 an indefeasible cleavage arose to divide the great honor role on which we inscribe the preferred names.

Nothing illustrates our confusion, nothing reveals our lack of an adequate theory better than the cleavage that I described in Chapter III, between pragmatism and poetry, between science and art, between thinking and feeling. *And the pity of it is that it is unnecessary.* Each has a part of the truth; neither one has all of it. Whether or not the mere integration of the truth that now resides in the two will be sufficient for our theoretical purposes I am not yet convinced. But that each one is lopsided is clear. The former stresses the brain and the reports of the traditional senses, the latter stresses the rest of the body and what it alternately confuses, sometimes calling it emotion, other times, feeling. The former has built a too-perfect, too-rigidly intellectual theory based on a clear documentation of the reports of the separate organs of sense, while the latter lacks any clear conception of organs, and does not perceive the basic facts of its physiology. Dominated by the view that basically the nature of the human act is always the same, *irrespective of situation,* the devotees of the scientific method still insist that the act of problem-solving cannot be distinguished from the creative or appreciative acts. Those who bring evidence in support of the clear distinction are quite often disposed of, without benefit of logic, and with the horrendous epithet—"you dualist!"

We need, above all, to drop our sights below the brain and take in the whole body, the whole situation, and the whole experience. (In fact it might be a good idea to have a limited moratorium—shall we say a 50 per cent moratorium?—on the brain.) I am confident that in the years ahead the dialectic of the group process of those of us who include the feeling-as-body-tension orientation, as well as some form of neo-connectionism, will produce such an adequate working theory. It will not be a compromise between pragmatism and poetry, for a concept cannot be compromised; only a strategy, a program of action can be compromised. We shall produce a new concept, a higher product of the two.

XVII

Every human act—skill, problem-solving, and the creative or appreciative acts—every act has two clearly marked-out phases, not one. There are two foci—not a single center. And they are concurrent—not in sequence.

I shall call them the Feeling-focus and the Thinking-focus: a kind of broadcasting, to-whom-it-may-concern phase, and a specific cell-assembly phase; a shotgun and a rifle bullet phase.

Let us dispose of the much-discussed specific one quickly. I find, in every "set," a rifle-pointing kind of perception—the use of particular numbers, words, musical notes, blobs of paint, turns of the wrist and hand, muscle-units, gestures of the face—that is very well described by Hebb's "cell-assembly in the cortex . . . a diffuse structure . . . capable of acting briefly as a closed system, delivering facilitation to other such systems and usually having a specific motor facilitation." A switchboard conception of the cortex is undoubtedly indispensable if we are to account fully for the connection of such specific stimuli and behavior. I agree that no human act can be specifically directed, that no general, broadcasting, organism-as-a-whole response can become an efficient act, without the operation of something on the order of the cell-assembly.

But there is no proof that the cause of behavior—the prior event —lies in the cortex. Moreover, the attempt to establish priority between the general and specific phases of behavior is probably not important; no harm will be done by assuming they are concurrent. Both are important, both may contribute to the firing process that explodes the concept.

XVIII

It is with the second phase—the reverberatory, organic, diffuse phase of the act, and consequently of behavior—that I deal at some length. From a dozen creative paths, other than that of stimulus-response psychology, emerge new makings for a theory of its action. That there is such a phase even Thorndike connectionists recognize by using such labels as set, attention, attitude, interest, wants, and belonging. A newer term that takes us straight to my own theory is expectancy, or anticipation-of-what-follows-what.

For twenty-five years I have been studying its documentation by scientists and artists who have worked independently on widely separated frontiers.

First: from the scientists:

—From the study of Lewin's group experiments in field theory and topological psychology

—From forty years of playing with Lipps's empathy idea

—From mulling over the futile seventy-five-year search for the control of emotions in some homunculus in the skull cap, and the failure of 10,000 lobotomy studies to locate him. As Cole has said, in a brilliant unpublished Appendix to one of his books, "the more intensively we study the functioning of organisms, . . . the more we are inclined to abandon the entire notion. Whether we study the brain waves of a man solving a problem in mental arithmetic, or the chemical changes occurring in the nerves of a frog's leg, we never discover anything that looks like a mental event. Nerves do not 'think.' They merely transmit impulses . . . No one ever caught a nerve cell—or a 'cell-assembly'—thinking, or learning, or imagining"

—From the mounting evidence that the outflow of the autonomic system is the key to the complex responses, to the frustrations, inferiorities, and anxieties caused by social threats to our security

—From the study of the sex drive, the hunger drive, and other primary physiological needs of the organism

—From the proof of the control of behavior *via* the alternation of chemical-deficit-states in animals and men; witness the salt-hunger of Richter's adrenalectomized rats, the calcium-hunger of those who had been parathyroidectomized

—From the studies of what the incredible new electronic computing machines cannot do—namely, create premises and build them into themselves. They can "think"—solve any problem which humans can codify—but, says Vannevar Bush, *they cannot create*

—From the accumulating psychiatric and group process evidence of the control of behavior by the dialectic of human experience in interpersonal relations.

—From the attempt to use the electronic engineers' concept of the "feed-back"—astoundingly successful in the control of intricate machine processes in war and heavy industry—as a provocative supplement to my concept of tensed-body movement in the study of human learning and the creative act

Second: from the artists:

For twenty-five years the supreme role of tensions in poetry, the good prose page, musical composition, the creative dance or other theater piece, in expressive painting and sculpture has accumulated in my documented records. Hence, I share the view of the poets and their brothers, the modern critics, who maintain that through the tensed body responses of expressive art, music, poetry, and the high forms of literature we obtain a uniquely complete and responsible version of our experience. It is one which no scientific semiotic can possibly give us, even though every statement of it, as Morris says, "can be referred to empirically observed events." (I ask you—in parenthesis—which would you give up, if you could keep only one of these two: the thirty-year product from the Ogden-Richards-Morris-Korzybski-Carnap study of "semantical rules," or the thirty-year feeling product known as "Shakespeare." The latter is recognized the world over as one of the few complete statements of man's experience. Actually, if we put the former in its true place—as problem-solving thought—we can keep both—and undoubtedly shall.)

XIX

There are other voluminous sources that provide an impressive body of experience and evidence for the importance of the general matrix in which all specific phases of the act are fired. Take the data on the behavior of primitive men. I am confident that if our philosopher-psychologists had been practicing anthropological students of primitive man or if they had paid attention to the expressive artists of their own time, our lopsided emphasis upon the verbal and the higher central nervous system would not have occurred. For we know now that before the rise of the perfect languages and the scientific method of thought, the body was accepted as the indispensable instrument through which man could understand, communicate, and express himself. The body, conspicuously in the dance, expressed the primal awareness of the organism-acting-as-a-whole. In the words of Havelock Ellis, one of the great students of the arts of man: "The art of dancing stands at the source of all the arts that express themselves first in the human person." Livingstone, the African explorer, reported that when one Bantu met another from a remote Bantu division, he asked first: "What do you dance?"—not, "Where do you come from, what is your tribe, or clan?" Ellis adds: "What a man danced —that was his tribe, his social customs, his religion." That is, the gesture of the total body, not the verbal description *via* the larynx, was the fundamental instrument of expression and communication of the group culture. The nature peoples of the world, unhampered by rhetoric, have always danced their culture time-beat; they dance it today, not only with their legs and torso, but with their arms, fingers, knees, and toes.

I must not delay here to outline the steps by which man first cultivated this understanding of the prior role of the body, in early sophisticated societies, then lost it in our own. Suffice it to say that the last several thousand years of history may well have been an intermediate stage in that long decline of interest in the body in expression and communication, as linguistics slowly gripped the attention of man.

XX

This brief reference to the great role of the body in the expression and communication of all nature peoples, and even of the sophisticated agrarian peoples, is confirmed by the studies in modern times of a wide-ranging group of philosophers, psychologists, and students of esthetics, semantics, and the history of cultures. These have long insisted that knowing consists of two phases:

> *First, and always prior:* the primal awareness of the organism-as-a-whole—the Self.
> *Second:* its more precise sense-perceptual and verbal "documentation."

Their evidence comes from many epochs in history and areas of living. I can merely point to these, not document them in detail. Witness, first, the record of the works of art, in prescientific world's creative history, that history has pronounced great: the Parthenon, the Gothic cathedrals, the Iliad, the books of Confucius, the Divine Comedy, the Shakespearean sonnets and plays, the world's great State Papers and principles of government. These were all works of profound organization—created by the total human organism as a sensitive instrument for design, during seventy generations of history before the advent of the scientific method.

There is also the affirmation of the modern philosophers from Spinoza to Bergson, Croce, to Jung, and Whitehead. As Miss Wild, bringing together several centuries of work in her illuminating study *Intuition,* sums up[1] their position:

> Primal awareness has a place in perception, conception . . . and what is common to all knowing . . . the mental act by which the conclusion is understood . . . is in itself immediate; it is the spark from heaven, it is the flash of lightning that makes clear what has only been partially understood.

The autobiographical writings of creative men—philosophers, scientists, mathematicians, poets, musicians, artists in all media—confirm this ever-present role of organic awareness both in new intellectual discoveries and in creative statement. From Plato and Archimedes to Galileo, from Newton, Mozart, Poincaré and Peirce, to Waldo Frank, the novelist and critic of today, the autobiographers agree on the presence and the indispensable role of the intuitive act.

[1] K. W. Wild, *Intuition.*

Within the schools themselves, including the great Laboratory School of John Dewey, the literature of the creative act refers to the "intuitive flashes of insight" which artist-teachers find revealed in the expressive work of young people. Mayhew and Edwards, collaborating with Dewey, say:[2]

> There are occasional flashes of insight, like those of the laboratory worker, in which he intuitively knows how to do what he wants to do or what he should choose, although he cannot explain why. [They add that] It was a fundamental principle of the school to await the dawning of those directive insights, to trust their arrival, and to provide the conditions that foster their awakening.

This is a bare sample of the vast body of testimony that is available from philosophers, scientists, artists, and students of education but it must suffice. *Again and again our studies lead to the conclusion that the act of knowing consists of two phases, not one;* first, the primal awareness of the organism-acting-as-a-whole; second, the documentation of this awareness through the separate senses, with specification and verification through the use of words. Teachers must become alert to them both, distinguish them carefully, and use them in education.

XXI

We turn now to what I think is the most critical step in my theory of behavior. I am not unaware that it is the spot where I walk much more alone than I have thus far.

To get both the general and the specific phases of the act into my theory and make them coordinate in importance, each must be dealt with in terms of its sense organ. No behavior without a mediating organ! Our theories to date rest upon the accumulation of information acquired *via* the traditional sense organs—sight, hearing, touch, taste, and smell, and other recently added ones, such as temperature, pain, and equilibrium. These, it seems to me, must be accompanied by the conception of a hypothetical organ that can account for the explosive general matrix—set, attitude, grasping the problem, poised attention, expectancy, anticipation-of-what-follows-what.

For some students, the concept of kinesthesis, covering the sensation of strain in muscles, tendons, and joints will perhaps be

[2] Katherine Mayhew, and Anna Edwards, *The Dewey School*, p. 423.

sufficient. I have long considered it and have found it very useful. But it is too static, as also, to me, is Kurt Lewin's topological psychology; both are too positional. This is true indeed of topological mathematics, which is suggestive and certainly is fun as its devotees insist, and I agree, reading the limericks that they have written about it. But to me its pictorial diagrams describe potential energy while we are seeking a concept that will carry the connotation of kinetic energy.

I have, therefore, found it necessary to *postulate a dynamic movement sense*, which is general throughout the organism and which will stand for the total tensing adjustment of the body. Somewhere in that tension there is the firing contact that sets off the act. I use *tension* in the dynamic positive sense, not in the negative sense of frustration, anxiety, and fears. I use it in the push-and-pull, attraction-repulsion, field-force-energy sense of the newer physical sciences. There seems to me to be no need to distinguish tensions in the human field—calling them in quotes "psychic tensions"—from those in the realm of the physical universe or of our own planet. I would have us in psychology and education do our theorizing about the tensional forces operating in the interpersonal relations of people, in the same terms as the most convincing theorizing in the physical sciences. The chief difficulty is that we do not know enough bio-physics. Is it fantastic to assume that the same theory that produced Mr. Einstein's $e = mc^2$ may explain the explosion of energy in the pushes and pulls, attractions and repulsions, between lovers, wife and husband, child and parent, child and teacher, rival office-seeking politicians, gang leaders, and even between the deputy foreign ministers of the USSR and the USA? The resulting behaviors we know only too well. The causes of face-to-face behavior lie hidden in baffling complexes. But, that energy is released in every act— that we know, and in some curious unknown way it produces acts of love or hate, friendly cooperation or bitter enmity, creative and imaginative expression, or dogged prejudice.

For years I have stumbled about in this morass, trying one lead after another. I fear I shall continue the process during the next twenty-five years. But I have always come back to this over-all concept of the *tensile sense of the body*. It is, I am convinced, an important key to the creative act and the critical step in the act of thought; it is possible that it may prove to be the crucial one.

But it must have a name—a conceptual label, as clear and direct as "thinking."

XXII

I give it no new name. I call it Feeling. But one important caution! It is to be sharply distinguished from emotion, which is primarily the product of the endocrines in the blood stream; witness the red-face of anger and the stimulation of the heartbeat due to the increase of adrenalin in the blood stream, and the release of glycogen stored in the liver; or the traditional dry mouth of fright of the novice in public speaking, due to the inhibition of salivary gland action. Paraphrasing Stein: The artist paints his picture *via* feeling but may destroy it *via* emotion—because of his anger, or despair.

My conception of feeling-as-body-tension has respectable historical support from students in the human sciences and the arts. Theodore Lipps, the German psychologist, commenting sixty years ago upon the response of human beings in their reaction to buildings, says that the individual understands a building, or any part of it, only by responding to it, by "feeling himself into" it; Lipps called his theory *einfühling*, generally translated as empathy. One can perceive a column which holds up parts of a building only as his body vicariously exercises the function of the column.

The concept can be generalized in the psychology of meaning. We are aware of objects only as we can make appropriate movements with respect to them. Looking at, perceiving, grasping the meaning of any object means an actual tensing of the muscles, as we enter into relationship with the field. The inner tensions, the stresses, are felt in the shoulders, the torso, the mouth and face, and other parts of the body. This incipient response of the body— this feeling-as-body-tension—consists of an intricate integration of inner movements. These constitute the instrument by which we respond to qualities in the outside world. We judge weight, length, breadth, depth, and the resistance of materials through this *tensile sense*. We recognize shapes, forces, distances, and respond to the powerful explosive gestures of the face, with tensed body-movement. These incipient movements, felt in the body, make it possible to understand the fragile nature of an eggshell, the cylindrical quality of a column, the compressive strength of a foundation stone, the tensile power of the cables of the suspension bridge.

According to distinguished critics of the arts, body-response is central both in expression and appreciation. John Martin says: "If we are to get any pleasure or profit from a dancer's perform-ance, we cannot merely watch his patterns with our eyes, but must actually participate vicariously in his movements." We do it with "a sixth sense," that is, "a muscle sense . . . embedded in the tissues of the muscles and in the joints."

Precisely the same conclusion comes from the world's greatest painters. John Marin, asked to explain the apparently chaotic masses of color and line, which seems to depict nothing realistic in the life of the city, says he is not trying to reproduce the objects in the city. On the contrary, he is trying to express the moving tensions—the pushes and pulls in the life of the great city. He says:[3]

I see great forces at work; the large buildings and the small build-ings; the warring of the great and the small; the influence of one mass on another greater or smaller mass. Feelings are aroused which give me the desire to express the reaction of these pull forces, those influ-ences which play with one another; great masses pulling smaller masses, each subject in some degree to the other's power.

These are but a few of the many revealing examples of the role of the tensile sense as the artist attempts *to depict tensed body-movement* on his canvas, in order *to produce movement* in the observer. Movement has, indeed, been the primary, subtle, con-cept in expressional painting since Cézanne—as it was with the greats of earlier epochs. It was revealed in Duchamp's experi-mental painting called "Nude Descending the Staircase," ridi-culed at the Armory Show in 1913 by the newspaper boys, who renamed it "Explosion in a Shingle Factory" and jeered: "Prob-lem—find the nude!" There was no nude and no staircase. Nat-urally! Because Duchamp was trying, not too successfully, it is true, to paint "descent"—that is, movement itself.

XXIII

This brings us to the problem of seeing relations—and of the concept. The perception of relations is indeed the nub of the

[3] John Marin, *Letters of John Marin*, p. 2 of text.

perceptual process in thought, in mathematics, problem-solving thinking, Gestalt explanations, and in creative art. James was on the trail of it years ago, writing his great *Psychology,* when he referred to the inner-movements within the body as "felt-relations." "So surely as relations between objects exist," he said, "so surely do feelings exist to which these relations are known." Our very language is built that way. He points to the relational words— prepositions and conjunctions: "We ought to say a feeling of *and,* a feeling of *if,* a feeling of *but,* quite as readily as we say a feeling of blue or a feeling of cold." Most relations are feelings. "The perception of space is interpreted in terms of 'feelings of motion.' " A "line is a relation; feel it and you feel the relation." His analysis of a comparison and discrimination is made in terms of "felt differences" . . . "feelings of movement in joints."

Thus, in my theory of the act, *the tensed body acts as a sounding board, responding to the world as feeling.* Knowledge of a thing becomes a feeling of its relations. The felt-relations of the body are central in every human response.

The felt-relations are central, granted, but what touches off the flash of insight? The concept. The "cue" concept, magnetizing the "field" of readiness or attitude "explodes" the meaning. The concept may be either straight body adjustment or, in any verbal situation (face-to-face, reading, or literate-memory), it may be organized in *words.* In the latter situations we respond with word meaning, verbal concepts. These also are generalizations. Moreover, to use the social psychologist's language, they are stereotyped responses—those which we have been taught by experience, by our needs, by our personal life style, to expect.

As I see the act, the organism, responding as a whole, adopts a general attitude, or set, that is appropriate to the meaning with which it is responding. In Thorndike's terms this is a "readiness" to respond, in the Gestaltists', a structuring of the field; in Lewin's, the field of meaning. This is the first stage of thinking which Dewey described as "the felt difficulty." Entering into the attitude or set is the complex total resultant of the individual's drives, needs, tensions, his earlier experience in the culture, and his total life style. The set is his expectancy that his act will be followed by certain behaviors in other persons.

This general response is focused by the verbal response. This is not specific. It, too, is a generalization. *It is the concept. I con-*

ceive of it as exploding, or firing, or touching off the response in a
way that we describe as meaningful, as an act of understanding.
It is the concept that makes the reports of the senses make sense.
The verbal, or symbolic, aspect of it is the product of long, cumulative learning experiences in childhood and youth; in learning to
live with, behave in, and control the social world by means of
words. Between the age of one and two the child passes through
the stage of integrating specific word-symbols with general body-
response to objects, human beings, ideas, to everything in the
environment.

It is this twofold organic process that is called conceptualizing
or generalizing. We know now that from the years of infancy,
when the capacity to verbalize begins to develop, every act of
human response becomes an *act of generalizing*. These generalizations range from fairly specific meanings which we call percepts
to broader ones, which we call concepts. There is no sharp distinction between the two. We define a percept in general terms
as "that organization of the perceptual field which is made by the
perceiver"; note that its very terms—"organization" and "field"—
are general.

The fact that percepts and concepts are on a continuum is
applied in curriculum development by the utmost care in grading
the concreteness and abstractness of situations through which
percepts and concepts are learned. Consider, for example, how
the concept "modern transportation" is built through accumulating experiences in dealing with a long list of concrete percepts
such as wagon, cart, truck, car, automobile, locomotive, bus, airplane, train, railroad. If the course of study has been well arranged, and carefully graduated in difficulty and complexity,
young people should come to the problems of democracy in the
senior high school equipped to think promptly with concepts as
broad, for example, as "the dependence of the people of the cities
on uninterrupted and efficient power transportation."

A similar graduated program of experiences will be needed
if teachers are successfully to develop the growing mastery over
percepts and graded concepts so that youth can deal clearly with
such an abstract concept as "a large-scale industrial system of
limitless power must be nationally controlled." The cumulating
school experience must result in a steadily maturing hierarchy of
concepts, such as the following: "Natural power from wind, mov-

ing water, animal muscles . . . Mechanical power from steam engine, gasoline engine, electric generator, etc. . . . Molecular power, based on such natural fuels as coal, oil, moving water, their supply of resources fixed and limited, exhaustible within a short time . . . Atomic fission (with a vast array of other meanings upon which its understanding is based), now completed, revolutionizes the problem of power, requires gigantic financial endowments, and carries such dangers of destruction as to make it possible, perhaps probable, that the production of atomic power must be nationally centralized and controlled, perhaps world-controlled.

The previous pages of this book abound in examples of the role of the concept. Perhaps the clearest one, certainly the most compact one, is the bringing together of a score of key concepts on one page of my comprehensive chart for psychology. As I said immediately following it, "These are the formative concepts that have been discovered from the interpenetration of a dozen fields of research during the past half century" . . . and then added: "This, therefore, is the *whole of psychology!*" To the extent that my concepts are sound, it is the whole. For each concept *is the key* to a body of meaning needed for understanding. In the psychological theories of the future, the key concept will be central.

A second example comes from the twenty years in which I was engaged in building the social science course of study, Man and His Changing Society. There I learned from the hard knocks of curriculum-designing that it was only a graded hierarchy of concepts that would provide the needed organizing principle. The total scope of the material was staggering—nothing less than the range of civilizations, past and present, American and around the world, and episodes describing them varying in abstractions from the learning of the primary school to that of youth in the high school. It was the study of modern industrial peoples in action— man making and doing, producing food, shelter, and clothing, transporting and communicating, buying and selling, moving about and governing . . . man meditating and contemplating, creating and appreciating with esthetic materials . . . man's institutions, languages, use of science and art . . . his "psychology"— ideas, beliefs, values, what he wants most and fears most. The content covered, in short, the total cultures of the world.

What would reduce this inchoate mass to some semblance of order? The answer came at long last—the Key Concept. We used it for thirty years; it has never been proved to be unsound. The curriculum maker uses it as his cue to organization of materials, the classroom teacher as his cue to organizing his teaching.

XXIV

This notion of the cue concept as the organizing factor of meaning illumines another central idea of the sciences and the arts, and hence of the theory of knowing and of teacher education. This is Integration. The word is from the Latin integratus, meaning made whole. Its meaning has been worn thin by our shibboleth phrases—"whole child," the educationalist's "integrated program," "integrated curriculum," the psychoanalyst's "integrated personality." It is indeed a synonym for wholeness. Integrative is the exact opposite of additive; mechanisms are additions—assemblies of parts—but organisms are integrations, fusions of parts. Once more we find ourselves with the Part-Whole, with the Thing-Force problem.

We need the concept of integration constantly, yet are stymied from achieving a perfect picture of it. While physical theory has, in the second intellectual revolution, moved away from all mechanical explanations (as Henry Margenau constantly exclaims, "Mechanism, in physics, is dead!") toward organic, or integrative theories—and theory in the biological, psychological, and social sciences, with it—we are still left with the picture of Mr. Einstein struggling to get quanta and field-relativity into a true unity. We still lack the complete concept of integration, if you like. Hence, I suggest that we agree to use it as a synonym for that degree of wholeness which implies the completest imaginable interpenetration of parts. If a visual physical image is desired to clinch it, think of two steel rails being welded under the intense heat of a workman's acetylene torch (or whatever the current fuel is) into a continuous rail. The parts of the welded joint are more interpenetrated—integrated—than the parts of the two rails. The joint is stronger than any other section.

In this book we have employed the concept in other ways; for example in the integration of fields of research, thereby finding new concepts and new understanding. The new disciplines have all been the result of it: the new political economy, as the integration of related economic and political concepts . . . the new social psychology, as the integration of the social sciences and psychology . . . the striking development of an integrated bio-psychology, illustrated in my comprehensive chart . . . the development of industrial design after 1920, bringing the Bauhaus Group together in Germany and, after Hitler scattered them, here with the native Americans—Bel Geddes, Loewy, Dreyfus, *et al.*, fusing the techniques of engineers, abstract painters, psychologists, manufacturers, artists in other media, students of public taste . . . the emergence of the new literary criticism since 1920, drawing its materials from a vast range of sources—psychoanalysis, Gestalt psychology, the data of laboratory and clinical behavior, social psychology's discoveries of group behavior and social patterns, neurological and endocrinological physiology, the social sciences, folklore, physical and biological sciences, philosophy, religion, and mysticism. A current frontier and exciting example is the development of the Cybernetics group, studying control and communication in the animal and the machine. Its personnel integrated the concepts of mathematicians and physicists, physiologists, neuro-anatomists and nerve physiologists, electronics engineers, social psychologists, anthropologists, students of social-economic organization, and designers of precise machine construction. Finally in my own bailiwick there is the building of the new integrated programs in Foundations of Education which draw on *all* the disciplines!

XXV

Integration is, in short, the conceptual key to general or foundational education, and to the common learnings of men. The experiments with many varieties of General Education produced disorganization long before it brought order into the curriculum. The chief reason was, as Dr. Kenneth Benne of Illinois reminded us in one of our recent roundtables, that our usual practice has been "to rush in and integrate—materials, fields, subjects, professors, without an intellectual analysis of the process of integration." I agree, adding, *without a conceptual analysis.* For more than a generation, educationalists in company with psychologists and creative workers in the physical, natural, and social sciences and the arts have found it to be the key concept—integration itself the clear integrating principle for their changing and accumulating materials. The mathematical-physical scientists sought and found in their "field-relativity" concepts the principles that would open the path to the true source of energy. Stimulated by the concept, their colleagues in the human sciences are now searching for similar organizing concepts that will clarify the behavior, development, and learning of the human being.

Within the field of education the search is for the cue to learning and teaching, and for the organization of the complex bodies of new curriculum materials. We are finding it in our recent roundtables, in the *basic role of integration through concepts.* We distinguish two problems: *first,* the logical problem itself—that is, the theoretical problem of integration through concepts in producing learning and understanding; *second,* the practical problem of how integration of curriculum materials is brought about. The emphasis is on psychological integration, integration within the individual. The role of purpose is stressed; "Integration within a person, with a purpose . . . whether we're going 'fishing' or something else." Real integration can come about only as persons, driven by human purposes, work at solving problems with the unique but related conceptual meanings contributed from their special disciplines.

The logical problem of the meaning of integration centers attention on the concept, conceptual analysis, and synthesis, and through the person's use of concepts. My friend Dr. James Umstattd illustrated it from the University of Texas curriculum experience. In one seminar they developed a conceptual synthesis through the integration of materials, but without the necessary integration in persons—that is, in competent students in the various sciences. It was unsuccessful. But in another seminar the chief source of integration was the interaction of professors in the sciences—professors who were competent in handling the key concepts, and much greater success was attained.

Hence the tendency is to focus curriculum-building upon the situation, the problem, for there is the nub of integration. In education we are concerned in developing understanding. Understanding of what? Of problems—either the personal problems of the individual or the social problems of the group. Furthermore, understanding is developed in the run of the people for the purpose of making policies. The root of policy-making is the ability of the group to make choices. "Choice is the nub of social policy making," says Dr. Benne of Illinois. "Action by itself is nothing; we must define what we mean by action. Action is precipitated by the necessity of choosing between alternative programs and strategies when the group is confronted by a problem." Thus the social problem is the nub, and we shall clear up the meaning of integration only as we discuss it on the policy-making level, on the level of choice.

Thus our discussion of theory focuses on the study of the problem on the conceptual level; the key concept is the cue to getting the related ideas together. This is the approach of the Foundation for Integrated Education (Messrs. Kunz, Margenau, Mather, Montagu, and others); "to synthesize fundamental concepts in which we find consistency." The cue to the task is "the situation." Dr. B. Othanel Smith of Illinois puts it: "We believe that if we go at a problem conceptually, we cannot help but involve ourselves situationally"; and added—"The problem approach which does not work at the conceptual level cannot produce clear understanding; it does not overcome the muddle-headedness of the man who lacks a consistency of ideas."

XXVI

Finally there is the task of putting the theory of integration-through-concepts to work in curriculum, learning, and teaching. That takes us to the practical problem of integration through the skeleton materials of the organized courses and areas of instruction—the syllabi and basic readings. The Illinois Social Foundations Group, leaders in our most vigorous educational theory, insists—and my practice has long agreed—that integration comes about through the fusion of materials organized around a problem and a choice situation. The choice situation compels you to look around in the disciplines to see what material you can use. In General Education this means the scholarly disciplines in the sciences and the arts. Within the Foundations of Education it means the sociology, psychology, philosophy, esthetics, and history of education and comparative education. Experience has taught us to agree with Dr. John Brubacher, that "there are two ways of looking at the integration of materials: the subject-centered way and the problem-centered way. Neither is completely satisfactory"; he implies that both should be used.

There is a real need for exploring the integrative role of the concepts of the separate subjects, the historic disciplines. Drs. Benne and Smith suggest that each of them—history, philosophy, sociology, etc., may have a unique method that will bring about the necessary degree of integration. Hence we should study the concepts and methods of these scholarly disciplines, in the foundations of education, as well as in the basic sciences. This is not only for the purpose of integrating those concepts from various sciences which are inescapably related, and whose fusion is necessary for understanding; it is also to find any unique concepts and methods that can be properly used only in their indigenous forms. It is indeed probable that each of the scholarly disciplines has evolved unique and indispensable methods for describing and analyzing human problems. At our present stage of employing the meaning of integration we may lose clarity and miss the truth by too quickly blurring the lines between the disciplines.

This completes, for the moment at least, analysis of what takes place in the act, as the nub of the theory of behavior. It also rounds out the theory of a Science of Man for American industrial society. We turn now to the third and last phase of the basic theory of teacher education, that is, to esthetics and the creative act.

XXVII

III. A PREFACE TO A THEORY OF ESTHETICS

Fortunately, much of the spade work for a theory of esthetics has already been done in stating the social and psychological theories. I shall ask my reader to assume that all the major concepts that have been developed in the preceding chapters apply to man-working-as-expressive-person, as well as man-working-as-skilled-technician or as problem-solving thinker. First, then, since part of what I shall say will be controversial, several basic assumptions:

Let it be agreed *first,* that this theory of esthetics is for the education of *all men,* not merely for the professional artist. I assume that every human being has some creative, or expressive capacity; I use the terms "creative" and "expressive" interchangeably. Because our next cultural problem in industrial civilization is to prepare most of our youth for a craft and creative work, for life outside of the mechanical industries, the building of an esthetic theory is a prior educational step. Hence my theory assumes that every child shall have both the opportunity and the guidance to develop creatively to his maximum ability. The goal of esthetic education is every-man-working-as-expressive-artist. If I use the phrase "Man-as-Artist" I shall mean therefore, all men, not a few specially endowed ones.

Second, we must not assume, of course, that all men are equal in sensitivity and creativeness. The law of individual differences applies to expressive acts as well as to acts of skill and thought. In making an expressive act, a man implies not only: "I say, what I see, my way" but also "I say it, to the best of my ability, *with form.*" It is especially with the addendum "with form" that I am concerned. There are vast differences in expressive capacity, in any population—in or out of college. Human beings are distributed over a vast scale of creative and appreciate sensitivity, in the same manner that they range from I.Q.'s of 200 (genius) to I.Q.'s of 50 (moronity) or less. When measured against the rate of the talented ones most of our people seem pretty mediocre—even dull and insensitive. But, when the potentialities in the general population are compared with the present product of a rigidly mechanized school that has never had an esthetics in its theory or program, the prospect is encouraging.

Third, I assume also that the expressive, or creative, act takes place with any material or activity within the purview of human experience. It is not restricted to the traditional fine arts, although it includes all of the conventional ones of course. But in addition to these man expresses himself in his personal relations with people, in his use of tools, in carrying on any phase of his normal life as a member of a social organization, and in and out of school and college.

Let it be agreed also that all that has been said about the conditioning of men by the culture applies here. At this point I urge my reader to turn back to page 95, Chapter IV, and re-examine the chart of my "Leave-No-Stone-Unturned" theory of behavior. The chart would, actually, have been equally appropriate here, for the ingredients of the creative act are the same as the ingredients of any other act, be it skill or problem-solving thought. Man-as-Artist creates as a whole person, as an integration of contending selves, driven by needs, tensions, purposes, equipped with self-balancing abilities, and capable of adjusting *via* body-response to the peculiarities of a situation. His attitudes of expectancy are the product of his personal experience and life style. In the creative act, as in problem-solving thought, he has the capacity to delay responses, to make fine discriminations in perception, to perceive patterns as relations, to use symbols in imagination, and to respond actively with conceptual meanings. Moreover, I assume that the creative act like the act of thought, is composed of the two phases—the broadcasting, to-whom-it-may-concern phase which I call the feeling focus of the act, and the specific cell-assembly, or rifle-bullet phase, which I call the thinking focus. In short, Man-as-Artist is a Whole Person creating, *via* his attitudes and concepts, what he feels, his way, and with unswerving determination to make his statement with a maximum of organized form. I repeat, the ingredient of the acts of Man-Creating are the same as the ingredients of his acts as Man-Thinking.

XXVIII

But there the likeness ends, and that brings me to an issue of long-standing controversy. Students of the creative act, who hold the theory stated here, maintain that there is a significant difference between the act of problem-solving thinking and the expressive act. Dewey and his followers deny this, maintaining that they are merely different aspects of "the *act*."[4]

The key to the theoretical issue lies in the Self's organization of the ingredients of the act, and this is determined by the nature of the situation. The ingredients are the same in the two acts, but their organization is different because they are used in totally different situations. What makes the organization different? What is the individual's goal, his objective? What is he after in the two situations? What determines that? *His supreme need at the moment.* In Dewey's act of problem-solving thought the individual seeks the specific answer to a problem, the definite factors of which are prescribed by his external environment. In my creative act the uniqueness of personal internal environment, personal

---

[4] I find that words written about this problem twenty years ago fit our conditions today; viz.—a paragraph disapproving "the current tendency to apply the word 'creative' to any kind of active, vigorous learning; lectures by professors of education subsume under the caption 'creative' the most obvious kinds of repetitive learning, mastery of skills, and acquiring of information. Nothing but confusion can come from such a careless use of meanings and vocabulary." *Culture and Education in America,* pp. 364–365.

experience or life style, while involved in the act of thought, cannot alter the product of the act—namely, the single organization of factors that will produce the answer. Given for example, the conditions of an equation such as $C = \pi D$, there can be only one correct value of π—namely, 3.14159, to the decimal place desired. Any human being working with any values of C and D, must arrive at the same value of π, which is called a constant. Or, consider the popular parlor game known as "The Riddle of the Three Containers." There are three containers holding three, five, and eight quarts respectively. The first two are empty, the third is filled with water. The problem is to divide the liquid into two equal parts without using any facilities other than the three containers. There is one most efficient solution to the problem. It consists of the most efficient minimum of back and forth pourings.

But my act of expression, a personal statement, is unique. In a creative situation there is no single answer which can be duplicated by another person. In fact no creative situation ever duplicates another. In the act of expression my goal is "to say . . . what *I* see . . . *my* way . . . with form"; to express what I feel there is of life in the excerpt of it which is before me; to make a personal statement which will objectify my imagined conception. The key then is in the meaning of the concept expression.

I define expression as *my personal statement of my imagined conception;* in more commonplace terms: I say, what I feel, my way. What I feel in a given expressional situation is contributed to by the same ingredients of experience, life style, personal philosophy, attitudes, etc., as in the problem-solving situation, but my special need for objectifying the *imagined conception* is the distinguishing factor. In the process of imagining, the Self sets in a special bodily adjustment and conceptual organization. This is the nub of the feeling phase of "I say what I feel." It amounts to "I state what I perceive, *in imagination.*"

XXIX

Perhaps I can make the distinction between expression and thought clearer by an example which will involve both acts. I take one from a cumulative personal experience I have had in designing and building my Woodstock house over a period of twenty years. The very fact that I have never had an architect on the place, acting myself instead as owner-designer, also illustrates my deeply rooted esthetic theory. First, to give the needed setting, I quote what I said about it some years ago in my essay, *Now Is the Moment.*[5]

The owner-designer builds his House and cultivates his scene— a room at a time . . . whenever he has grown to another room. A house indigenous to the land and the local culture; built by local labor from the stone, sand, and gravel of the Man's own hillside . . . property-dividing walls torn down, the field rock brought to the plateau, lovingly appraised and chosen stone by stone . . . the local soils and native trees, birches—white and black, maples, oaks, moved onto the gravelly rock plateau and sheltering foliage nursed around the expanding House. Like his mentor, Louis Sullivan, "necessity, not tradition" compels every increment of design and construction; the necessity the Man felt organically by the slow accretion of living on the land. Out of no worship of either familial or classic styles, but out of long months of looking and absorbing, come sensitized intuitions . . . organic awareness of true functionality, in terms of the needs of life . . . and these he builds.

The ever-present task, before he builds and step by step as he builds, *is design—form imagined, to fit the needs of the life to be lived there.* But if the design of the man's House is to be truly organic— not to be merely a mosaic of isolated and non-functioning bits—one organism, the owner-designer, must experience it—for only he can be truly sensitive to the life to be lived in it.

The nub of the statement is "The ever-present task . . . as he builds, is *design—form imagined,* to fit the needs of the life to be lived there." No human being other than the owner-designer can possibly know "the needs of the life to be lived there"; no other architect—no matter how skilled, imaginative, or sensitive. This house is my statement, the objectification of my feeling for the life to be lived on this plateau, within this space, in relation to this valley, in relation to this terrain, vegetation, forest texture and contour.

Let us study one excerpt from this cumulative twenty-year building operation that will illustrate the distinction between the two acts we are studying—thought and expression. At one stage, a big roofed-over outdoor living room was integrated into the north side of the house where it looks out upon eleven little mountains

[5] Harold Rugg, *Now Is the Moment.* New York: Duell, Sloan and Pearce, 1943.

across the cultivated valley. This was a delicate operation, for the house was then composed of seven large rooms, spread out on three slightly differing levels, with seven different roof lines, and roof slants, four of which are in view from an enclosing low front wall. Here is a beautiful case of complex uniqueness of situation, and of a problem that is both technological and esthetic.

The esthetic task was partly defined by certain problem-solving situations. The maximum size of the terrace was prescribed in advance, partly by the remaining space of the plateau and partly by the position of the house. The determination of *minimum* sizes of stone columns and the cross-timber supporting the porch roof, also the hidden rafters supporting it and tying it into the slanting roof of the living room—all these were straight problem-solving situations. These answers are found in the standardized facts of handbooks (actually my friend Ishmael Rose, the craftsman-builder, knew these from his trade experience).

But the final determination of materials, dimensions, slant of terrace roof, organization of lines and planes, total fusion of the whole terrace living room with the house—all of that was a complex series of expressive or creative acts. The whole design operation, lasting many months, was an esthetic experience. Take any phase of it—let us say, the determination of the dimensions of the timber cross beam and of the two square stone columns which supported it. This was "form imagined," achieved through myriad feeling-as-body-response experiences—long looking and absorbing —sitting on the wall enclosing the outside lawn. Everything about the terrace had to "feel right" with the organization of house and plateau and forested mountain land behind it. But it also had to "feel right" for the family life that was to be lived there.

There is a delicate organic process and product, the cumulative resultant of many improvisations and readjustments. These were total body reactions, thoroughly tensional (I use the term positively, not in the sense of frustration), including many revisions of visual-feeling perception. The perception of relations was focal; for example, my imagined feeling for the relation between various sizes of stone column (16-inch, 18-inch, 20-inch, 22-inch, 24-inch) and the total size and organization of porch and house. A 20-inch column was finally chosen from all the imagined ones because it felt right in the total scene. An old barn timber, 8 x 10 inches, and 28 feet long was finally chosen as the cross beam. The

fitting of shallow-slanting porch roof into the more steeply slanting house roof was a particularly delicate organic feeling operation. These problems of design were all achieved through endless
improvisations, first statements, followed immediately by revised
second, third, fourth . . . to nth statements. Each of these was a
twofold response, both shot-gun, to-whom-it-may-concern phase,
and rifle-pointing phase. Each was both general and specific, a
total response of the organism-as-a-whole. Each was a continuously revised succession of "imagined conceptions." Each *was my
statement, objectifying what I felt my way.*

But each revision revealed the role of the addendum with form
—*that* I insist is the key to the whole definition of the creative, or
expressive act. "I say, what I feel, my way—with form," is the expressive principle. The concept of form is not a will-of-the-wisp,
personal matter. On the contrary, the cumulative experience of
men working creatively has built a consensus of criteria for it.
My esthetic theory embraces three such principles:

 —The principle of organization
 —The principle of economy
 —The principle of functionality

I was governed by all three in designing my house. The first—
organization—has been thoroughly illustrated in the foregoing
pages. Nothing would satisfy the owner-designer but that the felt-
relation of terrace-to-house-to-plateau-to-mountain-behind-and-
to-valley-in-front, should be a unity. The only organ that could
produce it was his total feeling organism. The prescription of organization required endless revisions until the best one was
achieved. It was his personal organization, as Whitman sang it—
"what belonged to him, and to none else." Given this particular
artist's problem, no other human being could possibly achieve
this particular organization—except by chance alone. This illustrates the clear difference between expression and problem-
solving thinking—the uniquely personal creative process and the
uniquely personal product.

The principle of economy was illustrated constantly in the
design of the roof slant—all these illustrated Louis Danz's fine
definition of the principle of economy: "that organization to which
nothing can be added, and from which nothing can be taken
away."

Finally, there is the principle of functionality, Louis Sullivan's great contribution to our understanding of the expressive act. That required the owner-designer to ask the prior questions: "What kind of life is to be lived in this designed space?" To ask of each part: "What is this for? What is its function? What is this to do?" It is this function question that forced me to decline to let any architect, other than myself, design my house.

XXX

One more contrast will, I think, clinch still further the distinction I am drawing between the creative act and the act of thought. This is the distinction between representative and expressive art. Cézanne, Matisse, Picasso, Marin, among the modern painters; Martha Graham the dancer; Eugene O'Neill the playwright; Faulkner the novelist; Ives the composer—all of these are called expressional artists. They all strive to state by means of some material, depending on their chosen medium, what they feel, their respective ways.

But there are thousands of mediocre painters, writers, musicians who are no more than representationalists. They are not creative artists; according to my theory of esthetics, they do not even deserve the name "artist." Why? Because they merely copy the external shape of things. They re-present things; they reproduce the contours of things. They make their pictures look like the things. A good likeness is their criterion of excellence. If that is their ruling obsession they had far better use a camera for its reproduction would be much superior to their best efforts.

Such painters are Thing or Noun painters, whereas expressive artists are Force or Verb painters. Thing or Noun painters paint the static shape of things; Force or Verb painters paint the relations between things. We see how consistently the three aspects of my theory—social, psychological, and esthetic—hold together in related unity. The details of the theory illustrate the organic, or wholeness, principle. Note the emphasis on the energy-force concept—that is, the field conceived as an organization of tensions. I call these men Verb painters because they paint movement; recall the Marin quotation: "I see great forces at work [in the city]; great movements . . . Feelings are aroused which give me the desire to express the reaction of these pull forces." He is painting his imagined conception of the life of the city, not the rec-

tangle gridiron plan of the streets, the verticalness of the buildings. He, an organized Self, is not reproducing the physical
dimensions of anything.

The difference between thinking and expression is also revealed
in the differences in body-adjustment, or set, or anticipatory attitude, in the two kinds of situation. In problem-solving the organism is set to look for the right answer that is prescribed by the
externally determined factors. What Dewey calls "recognizing
the problem" is the physical adoption of the appropriate set. Not
until this is achieved can the one correct relationship be perceived.

But in the expressive act there is no known-in-advance unity of
relations to which the appropriate adjustment can be made. That
is achieved at long last only as the Man-as-Artist gropes his way
through one statement after another, his physical sets changing
as his urge to say something gets down in objective form. With
each successive act he alters the statement (painting, poem, or
composition) to fit the body-tensions which appraise the extent
to which it says what he feels. What he feels is his imagined form,
his imagined conception; this is the norm against which his advancing statement is measured. What he feels changes, too, with
each new increment of statement. The alternating flux of perception, conception, body-adjustment, and statement is the creative
process. Thus, quite opposite to the known-in-advance fixity of the
goal in the case of problem-solving thinking, or of the representative art, is the unknown, ever-shifting goal of the expressive artist.
This explains the true artist's feeling of unwillingness ever to
regard his statement as finished. But the thinker knows when he
is finished; it is when he gets approximately the answer that any
other person could get from the same data.

XXXI

Still seeking the answer to the question: Just what is it that
takes place in the creative act?—I have been intrigued by Norbert
Wiener's suggestion that the "feed-back" may provide an important cue to "learning." If it does it also provides a cue to the creative process. Feed-back is the homely, self-defining term employed in current work on communication-control in machines.
It refers both to the mechanism and to the process which controls
the pointing or calibrating of such "machines" as anti-aircraft
guns, elevators, the switching apparatus of telephone exchanges,

and high-speed electrical computing machines. It is, says Wiener,[6] "control of a machine on the basis of its *actual* performance rather than its *expected* performance." "It involves sensory members . . . which are actuated by motor members and perform the function of *tell-tales* or monitors— that is, of elements which indicate a performance." Feed-back is an element which has been built, let us say, into an anti-aircraft gun, which must be correctly aimed at the point on the trajectory of the airplane where the gun's missile will pass through the plane. Under ideal conditions—including, for example, warm weather (when the gun swings in response to command)—the mathematics of this self-pointing process is complex enough. But under abnormal conditions (when the gun's grease is frozen or mixed with sand) "and the gun is slow to answer the orders given to it," an element is built into the gun which "reads the lag of the gun behind the position it should have according to the orders given to it," and which uses the difference "to give the gun an extra push." If this is too hard and the gun swings too far, the feed-back will pull it back, perhaps too far the other way. A series of oscillations follows—as in the automatic elevator adjusted by feed-back to come to rest exactly at floor level, at which point and moment both doors can and do open. The mechanism controlled by "input of stored data," as well as new message, must be synchronized with "the output behavior" of the elevator and the doors.

Wiener suggests that something very similar to this occurs in human behavior: witness the unstable automobile driver's wobbly control of the wheel in moving traffic, or the human adjustment of body-response in any physical act—for example, the process of picking up a glass of water. That something on that order happens in the act of problem-solving thinking I am satisfied. Certainly the feed-back element, built into the stored data of organized human experience (memory) is an enormously intricate fusion of cortical call-assembly, of tensile dynamics in the musculature, of release of endocrine secretions in the circulating blood stream, the overt as well as incipient movements in eyes, head, arms, hands, torso.

The nub of the complex process is the organism's attempt *to perceive* (partly visual, partly muscular response, I think) *the relations* of parts that will produce the felt (imagined) organiza-

---

[6] Norbert Wiener, *The Human Use of Human Beings,* p. 12.

tion. In problem-solving this reaching, adjusting process acts in true feed-back manner, reflected in the cut-and-try oscillations of percept, and of more general concept adjustment. Some phases of it can be seen in the creative process of the painter (or writer, dancer, musician)—the improvising of a first statement . . . its comparison (a total body-response) with the imagined conception . . . the putting down of the new bit of color or shifting of line, mass, or texture . . . its bodily appraisal, again with a *new* imagined conception as the norm . . . and so on . . . and . . . on . . . oscillations of adjustment (sets, or attitudes, of anticipation) coming to a more stable rest along *a line of direction*. This line of direction appears in the expressive painting, poem, play, design of the house—in all creative acts.

It makes a good deal of sense to carry over Wiener's language —in discussing the feed-back behavior of the machine—to the human creative act; for example—"Behavior is scanned for its result and the success or failure of this result modifies the future behavior" . . . "Feed-back is the control of a system by reinserting into a system the results of its performance." And his direct suggestion for human learning: "If the information which proceeds backward from the performance is able to change the method and pattern of performance, we have a process which may well be called learning."

Turning around on my own creative processes as quickly as possible (trying to study them at the moment of doing them!), I find, in my own acts of writing, a good deal of confirmation for a role of feed-back in it. I put down a hunch, write notes, a tentative sentence statement. It is now part of the stored experience, changing the previous storage of concepts. Its juxtaposition with a new imagined conception produces another statement, which acts in turn to push further in one direction or another. This is a total process, the union of the specific call-assembly and the general broadcasting phases. This is the feeling-for-relationship, the tensile sense expressed in the incipient movements of the body. This is prehensile awareness. This is the first, "I know." This is the true form of cut-and-try-and-appraise; it is not the *random* "trial and error" of the Thorndikians.

XXXII

The theory of the act, stated in the preceding chapter, and of the creative act just stated, prescribe the educative conditions which we set up in the school. Needs, tensional states, revealed in urges and restless movements, are central to the whole process, and the self-balancing principle is constantly at work. The principle of freedom receives here its supreme implementation; the expressive man must feel free to say what he feels, his way. This reminds us that the creative act is squelched, is in fact forbidden, in all authoritarian societies. Thus we reiterate that in the American democratic social order constant provision for the expressive process in school and college is a desideratum of a good education. What a tragedy, therefore, that it is denied in ninety-odd per cent of the schools and colleges of America today!

Among the needs to be satisfied is the need for security, the release of fears. In a society marked by the Conforming Way and the rank-order concept of widespread inferiority, this becomes of deep concern. One of the teacher's primary tasks is to build attitudes of confidence. Constantly he must imply to his students: "You are not inferior. You are, as Whitman said, Supreme. You, as a Person, have a statement to make, and you have some ability to make it." And there are many known techniques of doing it; these the Teacher of Teachers must teach.

One step is to teach the importance of improvising the first statement. No second statement without a first one preceding it. Say something, put anything down, improvise! This is the first step. It is indispensable because once it is made, it becomes the norm against which the imagined conception can be revised. Each revised imagined conception becomes, in its turn, the new norm for the next statement and so, on . . . and . . . on.

Then there is the question of technical mastery. When shall knowledge of skill in using technique be taught? The conventional teaching of the arts in the regimented school puts it first. In the schools generally grammar precedes such creative writing as there is, and that is little enough. "Perspective" precedes expressive painting. When would our theory provide it? When a learner needs it, and knows that he needs it. When he strikes a consciously felt need for it. Then, and in general only then, does the teacher teach technique. Moreover, on any specific occasion he teaches only that amount of technique that the learner needs for the stage of learning and growth to which he has arrived. Some anticipation of learning needs is wise, of course; judiciously employed it may save time and effort in development and avoid frustration.

One fundamental attitude must be the constant by-product of expressive learning—namely, the art of criticism, of self-discipline. We must cultivate in our youth the "divine discontent" which is every artist's prevailing mood. But it must be a discontent based on high standards of statement-making. It is said that Matisse worked three years on one portrait, requiring one hundred sittings. This is the never-satisfied perfectionist, applying ruthlessly the check-rein of self-discipline.

XXXIII

This must conclude my prefatory note on a threefold theory of society, behavior, and esthetics. While far from complete these three will serve as illustrations of what the theory of teacher education might now become. This shows what I mean, when I say enough is known of our society and culture to design the content of a great teacher education. Enough is known of man's behavior, of the act of human response, to design a good working theory of curriculum and teaching. Enough is known of expressive experience to guarantee a high order of esthetics.

We need no longer stand silent, bogged down in a morass of materials. We can command the motive power to organize our wisdom and to put it to work. For we grasp the rudiments of a theory. It is threefold. The theory of society and the culture will provide the key to an adequate Social Foundations of Education. The theory of behavior will give the open sesame to the Bio-psychological Foundations of Education. Finally, its theory of esthetics will guide the building of an Esthetic Foundations of Education.

CHAPTER VII

Frontiers of Practice in Teacher Education

I

There were three groups of malcontents who stepped over the traces of the Conforming Way just after World War I. One group created the three disciplines of the Science and Art of Man, a second put them to work in general education, and a third applied them in teacher education. The latter's work did not lag much behind; some of it went on concurrently through the Twenties, Thirties, and Forties. The Creative Path was being blazed through the inert mass of formal school and college education.

As a consequence, we do not start from scratch. That is the heartening theme of my final chapters. I have known this for a good many years but recently have had fresh occasion to be clear about it. World War II had kept me long from my colleagues in education. My need was great to talk to them face to face, to find out where we stood, to pool our theories and our practices. Another sabbatical made that possible—a 14,000-mile, coast-to-coast automobile trip, stopping at 35 universities and colleges for one-to three-day roundtables. The talk at each stop was exciting; fifteen to thirty peers, long separated, were together again. Adding up the meetings, over a thousand teachers of teachers took part, from ninety institutions. It is a small fraction of the thousand teacher-education institutions in America, less than a tenth, yet a fair sample. The State University of each state on our route was visited with its College of Education, and at least one State Teachers College was always included.

I found out much of what my colleagues are thinking about our world and about ourselves. They found out what was on my mind. It is an important process, this art of disciplined conversation, the most important one in the self-education of teachers. The teachers of teachers should practice it often.

II

I was deeply stirred by what I saw and heard in a few college centers—in state colleges such as the small one at Troy, Alabama, and the rapidly mushrooming one at San Francisco, and in that rare Social Foundations Group of Smith, Benne, Stanley, and their confrères at Illinois. In these I found the devotion to the problem of rethinking and reconstructing education, and the burning enthusiasm and dynamic spirit which had characterized the best of the child-centered schools in their youthful days immediately after World War I. I confess I came back to our own Teachers College with a deep nostalgia for the exciting months of the Depression Thirties when my colleagues foregathered in Main Hall around Heard Kilpatrick and created the *Social Frontier*, and the John Dewey Society, and the new Division I of the College— Social and Philosophical Foundations of Education. The spirit and the unity are both gone from our center now, but much of it has come alive again in Illinois and Florida, in Troy and San Francisco and Cheney and Drake and Wayne and a dozen other places. And that is good. That is exactly as it should be.

I found in these groups more than optimistic fervor. Pervading them is a mood of research and inquiry, of criticism and appraisal, which promises much for the continuous development of the work. And I found quite generally on this sabbatical jaunt, in places where there is not quite enough self-starting apparatus, a real interest in doing something important about teacher education, provided some group leads out in advance. The very fact that more than a thousand professors assembled from some ninety institutions for these little roundtables, in many instances traveling long distances, was impressive evidence of the widespread feeling for the need to rethink and rebuild. In the course of my trip I became convinced that, given the leadership of a few persons to organize them, such dynamic roundtables could be assembled now in a hundred regional centers in the United States. Most important of all, the interest was not confined to our colleagues in the departments of education. One of the most heartening facts was the presence, in many of these roundtables, of deans and professors of the sciences and the arts and, in quite a number of institutions, of the president himself.

I repeat, we do not start from scratch. In a dozen centers a new generation of young men and women is working vigorously at creative reconstruction.

III

The findings of the sabbatical trip were confirmed by other developments since World War II. A vigorous young leadership had taken over in the National Society of College Teachers of Education which was provided by some of the very persons I found on my visits. This society,[1] formed fifty years ago by the Thirty who made the first program of teacher education, has kept somewhat freer from the conforming influences of the standardized machinery of the national mass organizations. A really new generation of leaders[2] assembled in 1946, in the strategic moment that the postwar years provided for men of thought to take thought together. Committees were set up for all the Foundations and some of the major professional tasks of education, and scores of regional meetings were held in a dozen states. Colleagues in the professional study of education met with Gordon Hullfish at Ohio State University from a half-dozen nearby colleges; groups from Michigan colleges met with Eggertsen and Soderquist at Wayne; at Drake they assembled from Iowa colleges to meet with Macomber and Hagman; from three other nearby states they came to confer with C. B. Smith and Ralph Lyons at Tuscaloosa; at Livingston, Alabama, another Ohio group met with Painter at Akron University, still others with Lewis, Hines, and Hay at Florida; and there were meetings at still other centers. The theme was: Before we can build a new world, we must design one; but first we must pause a moment to look backward and forward, to appraise our passage and chart our course.

We not only discovered ourselves, we discovered that our time

---

[1] The early presidents were Charles De Garmo, James E. Russell, Paul H. Hanus, Charles H. Judd, M. V. O'Shea, W. W. Charters, L. D. Coffman. Although it is a little startling to find him in that company, John Dewey was their president twice in the early years.

[2] Such persons as B. Othanel Smith (president in 1948); Kenneth Benne, and W. O. Stanley of the University of Illinois; Theodore Brameld of New York University; John Brubacher of Yale; Claude Eggertsen of Michigan; James G. Umstattd of Texas (president in 1950); C. B. Smith of Troy, Alabama; Freeman Butts and Bruce Raup of Teachers College; W. H. Burton of Harvard; Frank S. Freeman of Cornell; S. E. T. Lund of California; Obed Williamson of Cheney, Washington; Anna D. Halberg of Wilson Teachers College, Washington, D. C., to name only a few.

was favored above all others for the development of the Creative Path. We became convinced that as one of the great self-conscious professions we can now gather and appraise our new knowledge, and build a Consensus together. We can create the needed university disciplines—the Foundations of Education—now.

IV

From whatever angle our problem has been approached the conviction grows that the next major step is to build into our programs a central body of material and activities dealing with society and the culture. My book has made very clear that the lack of Social Foundations has been the gaping breach in our armor. The analysis of the crisis in human affairs makes clear that to fill that gap constitutes the chief task of statesmanship in education. A chorus of agreement comes from various parts of the country. The new graduate programs that have been developing for the past fifteen years are an indication of it. The building of general education rests upon it, and the reconstruction of the curriculum of the school and college waits upon it. There can be no doubt, the spot to go to work is the Social Foundations—the cooperative study of American and world civilization in mid-twentieth century.

V

For not having to start from scratch today we can give thanks to a company of our vigorous peers of the Twenties and Thirties. Had their earlier first statement not been made, the second ones that are being made today would themselves have been merely crude, first improvisations.

There were two earlier movements—one in the liberal arts colleges and one in the teachers colleges. The former started the breaking up of the traditional domination of the classical college curriculum; the latter filled the long gap in the social program of teacher education. The two together created a new conception of education for all the children of all the people. Its theme today is General Education and it is centered in the higher schools of the nation.

The birth struggle took place in the same university center—in Mr. Butler's Columbia, and Mr. Russell's Teachers College—where for twenty years the founding fathers of teacher education worked within the framework of the practical men. The first event, in the Twenties, was the creating of the well-known integrated Columbia freshman course, "Introduction to Contemporary Civilization,"[3] generally called "CC." The other one, in the Thirties, was the Teachers College Discussion Group that gathered around Dr. Kilpatrick and became the nucleus of the sixty Fellows of the John Dewey Society for the Study of Education and Culture. It was this Teachers College Group that created the *Social Frontier* and produced (1934 to date) the first example of an integrated course in the Educational Foundations[4]—"Education 200F."

As I look back now to the day after the Armistice, November 12, 1918, when John Coss and I were reminiscing in Washington about what the war had done to us, and talking about what we were going to do after the war, I am still rather amazed that the thing could have happened in Columbia and Teachers College. But it did. While a few other colleges tentatively tried out new "survey" courses in the social studies, Columbia's "CC" experiment was established and continued uninterrupted from the fall of 1919 to now.[5] My own work in building a new over-all portrait of industrial society and of getting it into five thousand American schools after 1919 was always encouraged by the College and the University. It was the American Legion hierarchy that drove the books out of the schools in 1940.[6] But the Columbia-Teachers

[3] See *A College Program in Action*, by The Committee on Plans, of Columbia College, the undergraduate men's college of Columbia University. Published in 1946 under the editorship of former Dean Harry J. Carman, it is an account of the first twenty-six years of the Columbia experiment in "general education." We should be reminded that it was also in Columbia and at the very same moment that John Erskine built his "Honors in Great Books" course that trained Mortimer Adler, Scott Buchanan, and Richard McKeon, who later caused such academic stir and public furor with their retrogression to perennial Neo-Scholasticism at St. Johns College and the University of Chicago.

[4] This was the two-semester course required of all graduate students. Education 200Fa is "Education in the American Culture"; Education 200Fb, "Education as Personal Development." Started in 1934, this has now been studied by a total registration of probably more than 25,000 students.

[5] I myself came to Teachers College and its Lincoln School in the same year of 1919 and set up its Social Science Research Group, which (1920–1928) produced the Social Science Pamphlets that were used experimentally in 375 public schools scattered over thirty-eight states.

[6] See my *That Men May Understand* (1941), especially Chapters IX–XI; also my *Building a Science of Society for the Schools. A New Social Science Program—Man and His Changing Society* (1934).

College administrations, although constantly harassed by the patrioteers in the Thirties, never faltered in their determination to house these two attempts to make scientific studies of society and apply the results in college and school. I have always wondered why, for in other cases their record is not so clear. Perhaps they took the Cattell-Dana-Robinson-Beard case (1917) as a signpost of trend.

VI

I turn to the liberal arts developments in General Education first for a very important reason. They were created entirely on the initiative of professors of history, philosophy, economics, government, and sociology. The education professors never had anything to do with them. Rarely, if ever, in fact were they invited to collaborate with the liberal arts men on similar undertakings dealing with education. This is important to bear in mind, in relation to the later building of Foundations of Education. In Chapter II, in dealing at some length with the problem of control and design, it was made very clear that a college program can be designed adequately only by those who have control. It was also made clear that the professors of education have not had, and do not now have, control over their curriculum in teacher education. The key to control still lies in the departments of the sciences and arts. Hence the changes that have been and are now being made in college curricula bear directly on our problem.

John Coss came back to Columbia from war work in 1919 and did what he said he was going to do: "help make an orientation course that would really introduce the Columbia College men to contemporary civilization." He was one of several who came away from the war experience determined to try to make it impossible for another generation of youth to pass through school and college, and be called to fight another war, without knowing what it was all about. He worked at it for years as Chairman of the faculty which developed the "CC" course, and died in the midst of it. Dean Harry Carman said in 1946, in making a twenty-six year report[7] of its working, that it was

. . . the beginning of a quiet and gradual revolution in undergraduate instruction throughout the United States. Although a number of colleges are still weighing the idea of requiring introductory courses

[7] Harry Carman (Ed.), *A College Program in Action,* p. 22.

so planned as to acquaint the student with the framework of Western culture, yet the dissemination of the idea has been very wide; and its use as a basic formula by many of our most important colleges and universities in the present re-examination of curricula is evidence of the depth to which it has influenced higher education in this country.

I can attest from long association with the various ramifications of the General Education movement in both the schools and the colleges that this is not an exaggerated appraisal of what happened. Such revolution as took place in the college curriculum was certainly slow, quiet and gradual. Very few colleges followed Columbia's lead in building a general orientation course in the social sciences throughout the Twenties, although some tentative beginnings were made. But by the Thirties the economic and social changes had begun to affect the colleges markedly, and before World War II began many of them had started to make changes in their rigid academic programs.

VII

One can see from Dean Carman's (1946) statement of the aim and content of the Columbia CC course, that it was not a very revolutionary change from the content and aim of the classical historical courses.

Columbia had organized and developed three basic courses. In order of their appearance chronologically they are Contemporary Civilization, (1919) the Humanities, (1937) and the Sciences (1934). The college assumes that it is not its business to turn out specialists in a narrow field. We are interested in liberalization rather than in specialization. We have proceeded on the basis that while we are interested in guiding students into particular channels our special function is to help them see life broadly and as a whole. In other words, we believe that every student who graduates from college should have a working understanding of the institutions which make up our economic, political, and intellectual habits and attitudes. We function in a changing world; but there are certain values, the results of the experiences of a Western civilization, which constitute our heritage. In a very real sense, these values are fixed and proper understanding of them forms the whole man.

There were three significant things about it. First, it was the first major and long-time experiment in getting several liberal arts departments to cooperate in building an integrated course; in spite of their troubles they succeeded very well indeed. Second, within the historic and classical framework they dealt with our industrial civilization and got at the nature of the factors and forces that brought it about. Third, although seventeen years were required to do it, the other two major divisions of the Columbia College—the arts and the natural sciences—were finally persuaded to join in the development of the General Education movement.

VIII

Dr. Withers, who knew it in its earliest days, appraised it as a mixture of the traditional scholastic approach and the social problems or issues approach, stressing awareness of cultural heritage *via* Great Books (Erskine was developing his Honors in Great Books course at Columbia at the moment) heavily historical and philosophical (witness John Randall's fine *Making of the Modern Mind,* which was used in the course), but giving some time to basic maladjustments in our society such as poverty, crime, unemployment, war, etc. However, it is representative of scores of such courses organized as a part of the General Education movement and gathering momentum in the Thirties.

Certainly much more was happening throughout the country than the making over of a few college courses. Long-standing interests among college men were shifting. Long-time trends of new education were coming alive. Cultural forces, especially those affecting the population, were compelling changes in the curriculum of both high school and college. The years which brought unemployment to 15,000,000 people also precipitated what came to be called "The Youth Problem," and new experiments in higher education. It was as though all the tentative beginnings of the formative years had come to a focus in the Great Depression.

The question: "How many and which youth, sixteen to twenty years of age, should be given some kind of 'higher' education?" was not a problem fifty years ago. Higher education, it was fairly agreed upon, was for a small selected group of children of the more well-to-do and professional classes; half of the young people were at work by the age of sixteen. But, by the beginning of the depression years the tightening up of the labor market, caused by the increases in technological efficiency in industry, had made it increasingly difficult for young people to find a place in gainful occupations. For most of them this meant staying on longer in school. This was encouraged by a concurrent change in the attitude of more and more of the financially less well-to-do parents, who urged their children to stay on through high school, and in many cases through college, primarily to better themselves economically and professionally.

During the Twenties and Thirties the holding power of the school was increased by the compulsory laws of the states which advanced the age of leaving school. This had important effects upon the abilities and interests of the high school and college populations. As increasingly larger percentages of youth remained in school, administrators reported that the "general level of verbal intelligence" seemed to be dropping. Larger percentages of youth were failing to pass the traditional high school courses, and the results of the standard test scores and of individual Binets showed that the average I.Q. for the junior and senior years had dropped from above 115 (in 1920) to below 110 by the middle 1930's. Some people even questioned whether the general mental level of the population was declining.

But as these drastic changes occurred in the population the traditional liberal arts curriculum, fastened on the high schools by the professors of mathematics, languages, and the sciences in the 1890's and 1900's, changed almost not at all. A few progressive secondary schools tried to alleviate the situation by diversifying their academic curriculums, introducing courses with vocational emphases, providing opportunities for creative outlets, and organizing the curriculum in new ways. Even up to World War II, however, it was still evident that half of the high school population really could not profit from the curriculum of the school. In 1934 Dr. Malcolm MacLean, Director of the new General College at Minnesota, spoke very bluntly:

Out of the evil materials of depression, out of the mixed good and evil of expanding technology and invention, out of social, economic, and political lags has been built an immense but temporary dam (the American higher educational system). Against it the unexpended energies of youth are pounding, backing up month by month. It is my judgment that, unless useful power channels are cut quickly to by-pass the flood, the dam will go out . . . General education may be a protective, useful, power channel by-pass. . . .

It is obvious that, for these new masses of students, the forerunners of whom have been coming to us since the war and since improved machinery has increasingly curtailed job outlets, we must have new types of education. *It is certain that our standard patterns. . . . will not do for the great majority, may not even be perfectly designed in themselves to answer the needs of changing society.*[8]

The colleges still dominated the high school program, although many had liberalized their entrance requirements, introducing scholastic aptitude tests and broader types of comprehensive examinations, such as that in English Composition, to give the student an opportunity to show his ability to organize material and to express himself. In spite of all this, the seven liberal arts, with their emphasis on mathematics and linguistics and other abstractions, continued their stranglehold on the education of our youth. From thirty years of close participation in, and study of, the trends I blame most of this on the indifference and even downright opposition of Harvard and the older eastern liberal arts institutions. The too-much-discussed-and-quoted Harvard Report (1945) was really a middle-of-the-road, twenty-five years late, and begrudging acceptance of the facts of social and educational change.

IX

In contrast to such behavior was that of the three hundred colleges that cooperated with the so-called "Thirty Schools" (actually twenty-nine) of the Progressive Education's "Eight-Year Study" (1936–1941). This was unquestionably one of the most important studies of the relation between the high school and the college in our educational history. It was carried on by the Commission on the Relation between School and College and financed by very large grants from the Carnegie and Rockefeller Foundations. The standard fifteen-unit entrance requirements of the colleges were temporarily suspended and the high schools were permitted to rebuild their curriculum and guidance programs without the ancient academic hurdles. The progress throughout the entire college course of 1475 pairs of students—each experimental student from the thirty schools matched by a control student from a conventional subject school—was closely observed, measured, and recorded. Dean Hawkes of Columbia and a committee of college

[8] In Gray, W. S. (editor), *General Education. Its Nature, Scope, and Essential Elements,* pp. 119–120.

presidents and deans, who had been profoundly skeptical of the study at its beginning, said of it at the end:

... the students from the schools whose pattern of program differed most from the conventional were very distinctly superior to those from the more conventional type of school.

I should add, that in extra-curricular interests non-athletic in character, the graduates of the thirty schools were markedly more alert than their comparison group ...

It looks as if the stimulus and the initiative which the less conventional approach to secondary school education affords sends on to college better human material than we have obtained in the past.[9]

My own summing up[10] of the results of the Eight-Year Study, based upon membership on the Commission and close examination of the records, was:

Matched person for person, the graduates of the progressive schools were more competent, more creative, more alert and intelligent after four years of the new type of high school education than their mates in the conventional schools. They won more academic honors; they had more intellectual skill and information; they were more systematic and objective in their thinking, knew more about the meaning of life and education, and had a deeper and more active intellectual curiosity. They were markedly more concerned about the life of their own community and the crucial affairs of the world outside. They had more resourcefulness. They won more honors in student organizations, athletic teams, music, the theatre, the dance, and the other creative arts. When left to their own resources, they initiated more important and stimulating nonacademic activities.

The five-volume report, published in 1943, was one of the most important educational reports in the history of American education. Tragically, no attention was paid to it. If one desired to obtain a hearing from the people who control education, no worse moment could have been chosen for its publication than 1943, in the midst of the grave uncertainties of World War II. The developments during the postwar years have been distressing indeed. The directors of most of the thirty schools have either retired or moved on to other positions. Many of the staffs have changed schools and the newcomers carry on the old academic tradition.

[9] Aikin, Wilford M., *The Story of the Eight-Year Study*, p. 118.
[10] Harold Rugg, *Foundations for American Education*, p. 600.

My own study of eighteen of the progressive schools in 1944 was confirmed by the much more complete (1951) study of Professor Frederick L. Redefer,[11] for many years the Director of the Progressive Education Association, and now Professor of Education, in New York University. Both of these studies showed that positive achievements of the Eight-Year Study have gone almost unnoticed by the high schools and the colleges. It was indeed a tragic denouement.

X

Meanwhile, the General Education movement did gather some momentum in the first two years of the liberal arts college. By the middle Thirties the experiments in forming the new types of General College—those at Minnesota and Chicago were very important—the rapid development of junior colleges, and the emergence of a dozen new-type private colleges, all indicated that the General Education conception was taking hold of the imaginations of those who were doing something about a new secondary education. This movement for the reconstruction of education for the ages sixteen to twenty had had early, but unlistened-to, forerunners long before 1900. As early as 1875 imaginative college presidents, such as W. H. Folwell of the University of Minnesota, had advocated joining the freshman and sophomore years of the college to the junior and senior years of the high school, thereby creating a new American college. The NEA's Economy of Time in Education Committee, which served in recurring periods before and after 1900, agreed with the contention that the period of "general education" was too long and that the weak spot was the last two years of the high school and the first two years of the college. Eliot of Harvard, in his famous 1888 speech before the NEA on "Economy of Time in American Education," had supported the plan. Progressive college administrators such as Harper of Chicago and Jordan of Stanford were by that time organizing the first two years of the college as "junior colleges." After World War I, the number of these increased rapidly. By 1927 it was 325, by 1937, 528; by 1950 well over 600, with nearly 300,000 in attendance; 45 per cent of these latter are public institutions.

By the depression years progressive experiments had also de-

[11] Unpublished doctoral study at Teachers College, Columbia, *The Eight-Year Study, Eight Years After.*

veloped in several private colleges, conspicuous among them being Bennington, Vermont; Sarah Lawrence in Bronxville, New York; Antioch (Horace Mann's college of the 1850's) in Yellow Springs, Ohio; Bard at Annandale-on-Hudson, New York; Black Mountain, North Carolina; Mills near Oakland, California; Stephens in Columbia, Missouri. And New College had an all-too-short but conspicuously productive life as the experimental undergraduate college of our own graduate Teachers College. Perhaps the best example of the new response to the need for a modern four-year General College was that which was developed in Pasadena, California, after 1928 under the leadership of the Superintendent of Schools, Dr. John A. Sexson and the Principal, Dr. John W. Harbeson. This was a unique public institution, developed over a quarter of a century as the top four years of a fourteen-year school system. Here at last the American conception of education, from infancy to adulthood, for all the children of all the people, was becoming an actuality.

Thus the question of what education should be, for youth between the ages of sixteen and twenty, had become the center of real concern. A few administrators of higher schools had begun to confront the realities of our times. Certainly some recognized that this was a time of world-wide crisis in human affairs, a period of widespread insecurity caused by the strains and conflicts of a society changing with startling speed. It was a time marked by a prolonged and dangerous tangent of authoritarianism and totalitarianism from the mainline of western democratic advance, an incredible revival of barbarism, in which moral degeneration had indeed reached a new low under the fascist dictators. And it was a day of widespread confusion among intellectual leaders. Some among these administrators (I am thinking of such men as our beloved Jesse Newlon) saw that ours can become a new day marked by creative activity; in spite of the tragic fact of a million teachers bogged down in a deep sea of inertia, there was great potential leadership among many.

The brave and vigorous leaders saw these were the realities. But what kind of higher education would fit the needs? *How can we educate a generation of strong and intelligent young men and women, competent to cope with the novel problems of our times? How to develop young men and women of integrity, of strong moral fiber, and of tough spirit, who will work for and fight for*

the abundant and democratic way of life? Some among the liberal
arts college men, I say, saw the problem realistically. Malcolm
MacLean, Director of Minnesota's experimental General College
in the Thirties, did, I am sure. Listen to his affirmation of the
uselessness of the old education and the vision of the new:[12]

I have talked with many graduates who, looking back, can see
only five or six courses in four years of college that have been of value
enough to warrant the time and energy spent upon them. That they
do remember these as of value arises, I believe, from the fact that
they were taught by great teachers whose vision was wider than their
specialties. Their real education begins afterward when, with a consuming curiosity, with thousands of bottled-up unanswered questions
buzzing for an answer, they turn their eyes on the contemporary
world, their world. They believe that they should have had a general
education rather than the fragments of specialties plus the one long
specialty that most get.

Our concept of general education (at the General College at
Minnesota) is designed to make young people at home in their
complex modern world rather than to give them an analytical, minute,
and complete picture of the intricacies of one phase of it; to give
them the chance to make themselves supple and adaptable to change
rather than rigidly prepared for single occupation; to enlarge their
vision to see the wholeness of human life instead of leading them
deep into microscopy, and to let them acquire a sense of values in
the many phases of adult living outside the strictly vocational.

Some of the liberal arts men have caught the conception of the
whole man guiding the creative resolution, but none has put it
better in a few lines than Louis Wirth in describing the aims of
the Undergraduate College at Chicago:[13]

We believe that a general education should deal educationally with
the whole person—or, as the recent report of our curriculum committee put it, with men and women as knowers, actors, and appreci-
ators. When we say, then, that the object of a general education
is to aid the student in seeing the world whole, we are not merely
uttering an empty rhetorical phrase. We mean that we are aiming to
present the world and man's knowledge of it as nearly as a unity as
the best of present-day scholarship allows us. To this end we want
our students to be acquainted with the best that has been produced

[12] Malcolm MacLean, in W. S. Gray, *op. cit.*, p. 121.
[13] *Ibid.*, pp. 31–32.

in the past and in the present and to be able to think independently and clearly about it . . .

Their introductory course in the social sciences has one major theme:

. . . the social, economic, political, and cultural consequences incident to the industrial revolution, which apparently transformed human life more profoundly than any other similar event in modern history.

Their material is organized

. . . into an ordered view of an epoch in human history which exhibits in a strategic way the fundamental bases of human existence and of social change.

XI

But few of the leaders in the liberal arts colleges were as forthright as those at Minnesota, Chicago, and Columbia. Many to this moment still cling to their traditional conceptions of a "humane" liberal education and shield their medieval curriculum—now called by some "humanities"—from too close examination. Their newest statements of objectives *are not from the direct study of our times;* instead, with Mortimer Adler, they define a good education "in terms of what is good for men at any time and place because they are men." And some, too many in my judgment, go the whole way with him and the Neo-Scholastics and call for "a synthesis of faith, reason, religion, and philosophy, *supernatural and natural knowledge* [*which*] *is necessary for a unified culture*" (my italics).

But most of the die-hards fall back, with Howard Mumford Jones of Harvard, on beautiful statements of the "liberally educated man," such as Thomas Huxley's famous sentence:[14]

That man, I think, has had a liberal education who has been so trained in youth that his body is the ready servant of his will, and does with ease and pleasure all the work that, as a mechanism, it is capable of; whose intellect is a clear, cold, logic machine, with all its parts of equal strength, and in smooth working order; ready, like a steam engine, to be turned to any kind of work, and spin the gossamers as well as forge the anchors of the mind; whose mind is

[14] Clarissa Rinaker, Ed., *Readings from Huxley,* pp. 139–140.

stored with a knowledge of the great and fundamental truths of nature and of the laws of her operations; one who, no stunted ascetic, is full of life and fire, but whose passions are trained to come to heel by a vigorous will, the servant of a tender conscience; who has learned to love all beauty, whether of nature or of art, to hate all vileness, and to respect others as himself.

It *is* a beautiful statement. Who would not accept it as a broad-based platform for the teacher to stand on, in any college, at any time? But these fine words could not get implemented in a program of curriculum and teaching that is fit for our times. Such definitions are quoted by those who give lip-service to general education for all men while in their hearts they still distinguish between *common education* for the masses, which some frankly call "hand education," and *special* or "head" education for the élite.[14a] They have never really opened their minds to the possibility that the profound intellectual concepts of the new biophysics, or of the social sciences that account for the current social system, can build Mr. Huxley's "cold logic machine," or his "clear intellect," just as well as Cicero, or Horace, or Tacitus. It does not occur to them that enthusiasm can be engendered in the adventure of our current human tasks, in building the abundant life today, that it can and will build a human being "full of life and fire, but whose passions are trained to come to heel, by a vigorous will." And they cannot imagine that personally creative expression by our students, aided by an education in discriminating criticism of *modern* literary works, can develop "the love of all beauty." They doggedly assert that only the Great Books of the past can do these things! I fear there is not much understanding of the new sociology, biology, and psychology of learning in these stuffy scholars of the "humane" arts. Shades of Messrs. More, Babbitt, Shorey, and Mayberry—fifty years after their passing! Let them really try their mentalities, *as learners*, on the hierarchy of ideas we have brought together as the basic materials of the new disciplines.

Fortunately, this breed of die-hard humanists is dying off. Many of the young generation taking their place are truly concerned

[14a] See the various discussions of the Neo-Scholastics (Perennialists, is the name they prefer), especially their official statement, *Liberal Education,* by Mark Van Doren, or the writings of either Mortimer J. Adler or R. M. Hutchins, the latter formerly of Chicago, now with the Ford Foundation.

with building a general education for the seven million in the high schools and the two million in the colleges comparable to the courses at Chicago, Minnesota, Michigan State, Illinois, or Columbia. Even the very belated Harvard Report[15] defines general education as "that part of a student's whole education which looks first of all to his life as a responsible human being and a citizen." Their aim at last seems to be to reach all the people; a liberal education, formerly meant only for the élite, is now that which "helps to make free men," and General Education is shown to be the only way to the "free society."[16] And I do not find anything about "hand education" for the people, or "head education" for the "better classes."

XII

As I write I have before me descriptions of some thirty General Education college programs, representing a fairly equal number of public and private institutions, universities, and liberal arts colleges. I must not deal with their details further for the center of our interest is in the *new teacher education.* Perhaps enough has been said to picture the general college milieu in which we are now rebuilding that teacher education. That it has changed much in the past twenty years is clear, and also that a considerable body of experiments in the social and natural sciences, and in the arts, is under way. But before leaving this phase of the problem I should like to pass on to my readers an illustrative and tentative appraisal of the social science trend, by which I have recently been helped. It is an analysis of eight major types of "CC" courses now in use in American undergraduate colleges, made by Dr. William Withers.[17] These are practically all instances in which the college requires the course of all students for two, three, or four semesters. Some of these (marked "S" below) are merely "survey" courses, assemblies of materials from history, economics, government, sociology, philosophy, etc. Others are truer integrations (marked "I").

[15] Harvard Committee on General Objectives of a General Education, *General Education in a Free Society.*

[16] The best single description, by the college men themselves, of the new general education courses in the social sciences is to be found in Earl J. McGrath's *Social Science in General Education.* Dubuque, Iowa: W. C. Brown Co., 1948.

[17] Chairman of the Department of Contemporary Civilization of Queens College, New York City.

1. *The formal subject-matter approach* (S)
   This type offers segments of history, economics, sociology, and political science organized in much the same manner as introductory courses in these fields but with only the "rudiments" provided and with a certain social breadth in that an attempt is made to relate the various subject matters to each other a little. (Examples: Dartmouth, Colgate)

2. *The scholastic approach* (S or I depending upon the way it is done)
   This type of course stresses intellectual history, great movements, great books, awareness of the cultural heritage of western civilization. It is heavily historical and philosophical. (Examples: Columbia, Harvard, St. Johns, Wesleyan)

3. *The American civilization approach* (S or I depending on the methods and organization)
   This type centers the content around American development and American issues. Where the rest of the world is brought in it is in terms of *our* relation to the world. (Examples: Amherst, part of the Chicago course, Stephens)

4. *The social problems or issues approach* (I or S depending upon the organization)
   Few colleges organize their entire courses around social problems, but a number devote half or more of the time to consideration of basic maladjustments such as poverty, crime, unemployment, war, etc. Syracuse organizes its program largely around various aspects of the problem of citizenship. (Examples: Syracuse, Arizona, Teachers College, Columbia)

5. *The individual orientation approach* (The individual in the culture) (I)
   This type usually begins with an analysis of the growth of personality and then proceeds to segments on culture and personality. It then considers broad social issues as they are faced by the individual such as freedom and authority, security and insecurity, cooperation and competition, rights and responsibilities, justice and arbitrariness. (Examples: Colorado State Teachers, Brooklyn)

6. *The individual problem approach* (I)
   This type aims at marshalling the social sciences to promote "effective living." It begins with the psychology of "personality" and proceeds to the role of the family, marriage, sex, parenthood, personality adjustment, economic security, freedom of the "individual," the role of government and its relation to the individual, the role of prejudice. It ends with a broad consideration of how the individual can improve his relationship to society. (Example: Michigan State College)

7. *The social sciences approach* (I)
   This type lays stress on social science analysis. The object is training in analysis rather than content. The content may consist of comparative study of cultures, the theories of social change, selected social problems, and problems of social action. (Examples: part of the Chicago course, Iowa, part of the Minnesota course)
8. *The social values approach* (I)
   The main purpose of this type is to assist the student in arriving at a sound social philosophy. The content is usually comparative. Ancient cultures; American democracy, its history and assumptions; Soviet Russia, Great Britain, and China may be studied in sequence. At the end there is a segment devoted to the reexamination of American civilization. (Example: City College, New York)

XIII

These are the new approaches in a single broad field—the social sciences—and this is the flux of study and trial of new things that is going on in the colleges. As we turn to the parallel developments in teacher education we can be encouraged by what seems to be a fact—namely, that the Teacher of Teachers can count on a liberal arts curriculum reorganization of considerable scope. Certainly, in place of a dozen separate college subjects, there is much experimentation under way with three general orientation courses in the freshman and sophomore years:

First, the study of contemporary civilization and its historical development—man and his society and culture; traditionally, the social sciences.

Second, the study of man and his behavior and development; traditionally, the natural sciences.

Third, the study of the arts of man—the humanities—man and his expression; traditionally, literature, music, graphic and plastic arts, theatre, etc.

These *look* like our hoped-for "foundations" of education—Social, Bio-psychological, and Esthetic; at least they are steps in that direction. But the caution I stated earlier will bear repetition: these experiments in course reorganization are being done, in almost all places, by the liberal arts people themselves, *without any reference to, or collaboration with, the professors of education who are trying to develop unified programs in the social and bio-psychological foundations.* That is of such importance that I shall make much of it a little later.

XIV

To put the Teacher of Teachers in the full perspective of all this and to capitalize on the crucially important technique of the group process that was the basis of the revolutionary steps, I must take you back to Columbia's Teachers College again, and to 1920. The colleagues who in the Thirties composed the Social Frontier Group had not yet assembled there. There were only Heard Kilpatrick and I. He had taken over Philosophy of Education and was making it into a very different thing from Butler's (or MacVannel's) fairly archaic "Principles of Education." Kilpatrick had begun to move out toward his project method (1918) idea. Ten years later he was making a social philosophy of education, one for a "changing civilization," as I was beginning to title my books. I was giving most of my time as Director of Research at Lincoln to building the new social science programs, which paralleled for the lower schools what Coss and the "CC" group were doing across the street for the College. I quote from a summary interpretive publication of 1933:[18]

During the twelve years from 1920 to 1932 a program of cooperative research had been developed which yielded the following results:

A. Twenty-five studies of modern civilizations and their treatment in the school curriculum. These studies located and phrased the theme-concepts, the social trends, and the problems and issues which constituted the skeleton of the new program of social studies.

B. Experimental publication of approximately 20,000 pages of verbal, statistical, and pictorial materials covering the principal aspects of human societies. These comprised the three experimental editions known as the Social Science Pamphlets (1922–1928) and the later junior high school social science reading books.

C. The nation-wide cooperative financing and trial of the materials by public and private schools. During seven years (1922–1928) several thousand progressive administrators and teachers in 375 places experimented with the Social Science Pamphlets. They used them under various stated conditions, appraised their effectiveness as teaching materials, engaged in prolonged conference with the organization at headquarters, and evaluated thousands of objective tests.

D. The sketching of the outlines of a new educational theory—theory and practice developed together experimentally; seven pub-

[18] Harold Rugg, *Building a Science of Society for the Schools: A New Social Science Program: Man and His Changing Society.*

lications by the writer and several others by his colleagues present the record.

E. The experimental analysis of learning and growth, and the consequent formulation of a body of psychological principles of curriculum content and organization. These were incorporated in the dozen books which came to constitute the reading matter of the course. The principles were more specifically stated and applied in six other volumes known as the Teachers' Guides, and a comprehensive scheme of suggested pupil activities, based upon years of experimentation in many classrooms, and much criticism by teachers. For an account of all this see my *That Men May Understand,* and B. R. Buckingham's *The Rugg Course in the Classroom.*

I was also breaking new ground in a Teachers College course in "The Reconstruction of the American School Curriculum." Then, in 1926 and 1927, Counts, Childs, Raup, Watson, Newlon, Brunner, and Johnson came from their respective centers to join us. In the winter of 1928 we took a step that, at the moment, seemed inconspicuous and inconsequential enough. We formed, around Kilpatrick as Chairman, a little Discussion Group that met in bi-monthly dinner meetings, and we continued to meet for more than ten years. Every two weeks throughout the Depression years we carried on our cooperative study of all the foundations of education. Not only was the sky the limit—the uttermost reaches of man's changing culture of industrialism were too, and every new angle in the scholars' researches and interpretations in the sciences and the arts. We all revolutionized our personal understandings and our theories of society and the culture and of the bio-psychology of the "Whole Person," and got glimpses of the meaning of the concepts of the new field-relativity physics.

It was this new perspective that enabled fifteen of us, by 1934, to find sufficient common ground to give up our academic individualisms and unify our six prima-donna departments into one organic Division of the College—that is, the Division of Social and Philosophical Foundations. For years the history, psychology, philosophy, sociology, and economics of education, and comparative education, had been laws unto themselves, each professor teaching what he wanted to teach. This, I think, has been the chronic and besetting sin of academic life. But those who had been together in the Discussion Group began to plan our total program together; at least that was true of the major introductory courses—Education 200F—that all the masters had to take. The uprooting of old ideas and practices was torture, but the nucleus of the Discussion Group that stuck out the ten-year disciplining of minds saw the ordeal through to this practical end. With all its weaknesses, and there were many in the new year-course, in the ensuing seventeen years (1934–1951) I am confident that it jolted 25,000 education students out of their old conformities, and introduced most of them for the first time in their lives to the kind of world that has been described in this book.

XV

I have two things to say about the success and the failure of the process. The biggest positive outcome was our success in developing *the group process itself*. New minds were created by the discipline of the group dialectic. I think the crux of it is *the art of disciplined conversation,* although the actual process of discussion is essentially the group coalescing of the fruits of the hard intellectual work of the separate individuals. Mary Follett had made much of the group "creative experience" (in her book of that title). The dialectical process produced not a compromise of ideas, for that is an impossibility, but the creation of concepts of higher, and deeper meaning. At several points in the remaining pages of my book I shall stress the Group Process which is just now receiving a marked impetus through the vigorous work of the late Kurt Lewin's younger associates. There is no doubt that their Bethel (Maine) summers workshops and the work of their organized research centers, both at MIT and at Ann Arbor, have given public recognition to the importance of the group process. But too many long-time examples of the process in action have gone unnoticed; for example, the fourteen years of cooperative staff study and curriculum reconstruction at the State Teachers College at Troy, Alabama, under President Charles Bunyan Smith. There is no royal road to the rethinking and redesigning of teacher education in America but this rigorous one of study and experiment. I shall return to this matter again.

The one tragedy of the Teachers College Discussion Group was its failure to hold the strategically placed colleagues who joined with us, but left us. The process of continuing cooperative study and work over many years did not intrigue several of our colleagues for long, but especially three who came to have supreme control over the program and budget of the College and of faculty appointments and promotions: Will Russell, John Norton, and Arthur Gates. Gates, with fine spirit, struggled with our changing theories for a season. I think it was too early in our work (about 1929–1930 I recall) to understand what could be achieved, for the theories did not begin to jell until the late Thirties. I am unhappiest of all, I think, about his leaving us, for psychology is still the weakest spot in our teacher-education program and Gates's leadership is nation-wide. The teaching of Educational Psychology in hundreds of teachers colleges rigorously follows the content of the Gates, McConnell, Jersild, and Challman text. It remains primarily Thorndikian in orientation. Russell came a few times and left, never to return. That was too bad, for he was in the saddle. Norton, if I remember correctly, stayed through only one winter. The early withdrawal of these three men is to be profoundly regretted, for an understanding of the foundational point of view requires years and years of study, especially by those who have been immersed from childhood in the Conforming Way. In fact it requires study, and that is something educational administrators just do not do. They act generally on formula and mood, the latter most frequently determined by what person of prestige has last had their ears.

The foundational orientation has received progressive acceptance across the country but is constantly being denied in Teachers College. Of course this is another form of the Nature-Nurture problem; how much of the orientation of these men is hereditarian? I do not know but sometimes I think no new environmental exposure, of whatever length or pressure, would modify it.

I trust that I have not missed other influential pioneer examples of foundational reconstruction in teacher education prior to the middle Thirties, but I can find nothing else of primary importance. It is after that date that the new life appears in various centers across the country. The forces of cultural change and the increase of local popular interest in college education forced many of the teachers colleges to branch out, to develop a full liberal arts program, and to admit many students who were going into a life work other than education. Many of these little institutions became large "state colleges" in the period of 1935 to 1950. Witness Frederick Burk's little Normal School of 1900 at San Francisco, long a college of less than 600, now the San Francisco State College of 6000; witness North Texas State College at Denton and Texas Technological College at Lubbock—each is also 6000.

XVI

When I said "It's happening now!" I had in mind what has been taking place in a dozen college centers outside of Teachers College, Columbia. Two superb examples: the fourteen-year reconstruction at the State Teachers College at Troy, Alabama; and the splendid intellectual leadership of the Social Foundations Group in the College of Education of the massive State University of Illinois.

When I say to the young Teacher of Teachers, as I do constantly, "Put yourself in the Creative Path," I mean put yourself in the way of what groups like these are doing. Go there and sit in with them if you can. Read their bulletins and books. Study their courses and dig out their theories. For they are on the Creative Path. They have discovered some fundamentals—both with respect to the group process of study and thought, and with respect to experimental redesign and reconstruction of undergraduate and graduate programs of teacher education. Because the Troy experiment illustrates so perfectly what can be done in the small American teachers college, working in an underprivileged region and with typical financial difficulties, and reveals so well the steps needed in rebuilding the theory and practice of a total undergraduate program, I shall be generous in giving space to it. The Illinois Social Foundations Group has already taken over national leadership in the field of educational theory. I shall make frequent reference to both their theories and their practices on the more advanced level.

XVII

The Troy adventure grew out of the widespread interest in the state-wide school curriculum revision programs which Caswell, Hanna, Harap, and others active in The Society for Curriculum Study[19] were cultivating in the Thirties. A conspicuous example was Alabama, where 17,000 public school teachers took part, from seventy county and forty city systems, and four teacher-education institutions. The leader of the movement in the State Department,

[19] See their *The Changing Curriculum,* 1937.

from 1935 to 1937, was Dr. Charles B. Smith, who resigned in 1937 to take the presidency of the little State Teachers College at Troy. From that day to this, fourteen years as I write, Dr. Smith has stayed there, building what seems to me to be one of the most important object lessons in teacher education in America. Such continuity of personnel and group effort is of major importance. A job of educational design and reconstruction is a long-time affair.

The faculty seminars, as they called them, were the nub of the work from the beginning: study groups on needs, on the life of the surrounding community, on life on the campus, on trends in college and teacher education, on fundamental philosophy—in short, on the Whole Problem. But study requires books and materials as well as talk. Dr. Smith spent $1000 for a special faculty library on the problems of general education. The first year and a half was a "curriculum-repatterning period," followed by a "permanent period of study . . . reconstruction of the educational program as a unified whole." Thus at Troy, also, the group process has been the center. President Smith has studied and led his faculty in studying. It was hard, incessant individual study, of course, but also in the matrix of group discussion and thought. Again and again experience documents the indispensable role of the art of disciplined group thinking—in the ten years of the Teachers College Discussion Group experience, in the fourteen years at Troy, in the decade of work by the Illinois Social Foundations Group, in beginnings at many places. Years are required to uproot old attitudes; years to perceive key relationships in masses of data; years to track down key concepts. Even to design an experiment in curriculum reconstruction requires several years of continuous work. Then, more years are necessary to criticize it to the point of redesign, and then follow still more years of retrial of the newly planned program.

It is particularly important to stress this devotion to study over long periods of time, and to maintaining continuity in the staff because of the current mobility of school and college administrators in America. The bane of a good education lies in the widespread addiction to the ladder-of-opportunity idea. The ambitious president, superintendent, and professor, too, eyes on the main chance, does a conspicuous job, makes sure to publicize it, then moves on to the bigger department, school system, or college. He stays the usual two years, only to repeat the process—again and again. This lure of the glory and the power is the obstacle to profundity of thought and stability of administration and the chief enemy of the education of the Teacher of Teachers.

But Smith of Troy, and others of my acquaintance, have proved the validity of what I am saying by denying the practice. He and his people have stayed on one intellectual job of design and practice long enough to see it a long way through. I rediscovered him in 1947 when the postwar activity started up again among the college teachers of education. He and his colleagues joined our national groups, and led in setting up vigorous regional meetings in the Deep South. On my sabbatical in 1950 I spent two unforgettable days with his glutton-for-intellectual-punishment faculty. They led me through seven roundtables in one day, from eight in the morning to ten in the evening—and it was fun, and of great profit! Then after prolonged contacts with it, I discovered independent confirmation that this Troy experiment in foundations was regarded as of national importance by such reports as those of the Commission on Teacher Education.[20]

But enough about study and the group process. What kind of program did they make? First, they made a *total four-year program*, taking in the entire education of the teacher from the freshman to the senior year. This is of prime importance because of the problem of control, and I recur to it in a moment. But they really did a job in getting rid of a lot of the old academic content, bringing the study of our contemporary civilization up to date, keeping the best of the history (adding a lot of new history) and not disdaining the wise use of the Great Books. And they crossed traditional subject boundaries ruthlessly in their search for a clear organization. They really went further than any other undergraduate group I have found in the country in developing true social and bio-psychological foundations (with good beginnings in esthetics).

XVIII

I cite the Troy program not only for its conspicuous success in bringing up real educational experimentation and reconstruction

---

[20] Armstrong, Hollis, and Davis give 12 pages of their report, *The College and Teacher Education*, to a description of the work at Troy from 1937 to 1944.

in a truly underprivileged region, but also because it provides the springboard for a discussion of the *most pressing national problem in teacher education*—the problem of control. The Troy experiment shows us how completely the design and building of a total teacher-education program depends upon the educationalists having control. Troy is typical of several hundred small institutions that are really favored because *they control the whole program*. This is crucial. They could not have made any of the fundamental changes in content and could not have moved across subject lines if they had not had complete control of the freshman and sophomore, as well as the upper years.

As I said earlier, the key to the problem lies in the chronic lack of cooperation between the liberal arts departments of the sciences, history, social studies, languages, and mathematics and the education department. So important is this that I asked—and found answers to—three key questions re the findings of my sabbatical trip.

> *First:* Are colleges and Departments of Education in the Universities and the Liberal Arts Colleges as concerned with the problem of general foundations of education as the State Colleges and Teachers Colleges are?

They are not. In each of the states visited I arranged roundtables at the State University and at least one of the smaller State Colleges. The education of teachers is going on in each of these two types of institution. The State Colleges are still devoted more especially to the education of teachers, even though in recent years they have created four-year degree-granting programs in the arts and sciences. The universities have, in almost all instances, developed separate Colleges or Schools of Education within which practically all teacher education is confined. In a few state universities, conspicuously at the University of Illinois and the two Universities in Florida (Gainesville and Tallahassee), vigorous reconstruction of teacher education is under way.

A dozen times on my trip I was confirmed in concluding that the most important cooperative rethinking and reconstruction of teacher education in the United States *is being done in the State Teachers Colleges* (irrespective of name) or in private colleges in which the facilities for the education of teachers are closely integrated. In only one[21] of the eighteen state universities could I find the development of a designed undergraduate and graduate program in the education of teachers. In all the other universities at which I stopped, and I believe that the situation can be generalized for the entire country, the Colleges and Departments of Liberal Arts and Science *do not collaborate with the Colleges of Education in building a designed and unified program in the education of teachers.* Indeed, the gap between them is as wide as that traditionally widest street in the world which exists, we are constantly told, between Teachers College and the Graduate Faculty of Columbia University!

In the State Colleges I found it to be much more universally accepted that curriculum discussion and construction in teacher education is the day-to-day responsibility of a team of professors in the natural, social, and physical sciences, and the arts, as well as of the professors of the foundational and professional aspects of education. In our roundtable conferences, colleagues from these three groups assembled and worked together at the task of building programs of teacher education as naturally as the professors of education. This spirit of teamwork is, of course, the product of some years of development.

This clear distinction between the Universities and the State (Teachers) Colleges helps us to understand that, although fifty years have passed since the study of education was elevated to the curriculum of the graduate school, *the professors of liberal arts and science, with rare exceptions, still do not accept it as a respectable university discipline.* This fact confronts us now with two interrelated problems which are emerging in every college center. The first is stated by my second question:

> *Second:* In so far as an organized university discipline in Educational Foundations is beginning to appear, who is designing and constructing it: The professors of education? The professors of the arts and sciences? Is it being done by the unified effort of the entire faculty in all these three fields, all of whom are concerned with the building of the full program in the education of teachers? Or is it being done by one of those groups in isolation from the other?

[21] In the case of Iowa a special history, emanating from the pioneering work a quarter-century ago of President Walter Jessup, and continued by his successors in the Deanship of the College of Education, needs to be understood.

In the State Teachers Colleges the usual practice is for these three major divisions of the faculty to work in close cooperation, each one playing its role in the creation of the total program. Troy is a conspicuous example. In these institutions I found much teamwork in building a unified college curriculum from the freshman to the senior year—including in many cases the Masters year. The result is an increasingly better body of integrated courses of instruction.

But in the universities, and in traditional liberal arts colleges, there the vast cleavage persists between the arts and sciences on the one hand, and "education" on the other. I can see few gains toward increasing mutual respect and cooperation. The professors of the languages, mathematics, physics and chemistry, biology, general psychology, literature, music, and the graphic arts make their separate courses, select their reading materials, give their lectures, and set their examinations without the slightest collaboration with the professors of education; without, indeed, much concern over the fact that their students are soon to be the teachers of children and youth in schools and colleges. The professors of education in the Colleges or Schools of Education, in their turn, are building undergraduate and graduate programs of teacher education with little or no reference to the professors of the natural, social, and physical sciences, and the arts. But they do this *only in the junior and senior years,* for they lack control over the first two years.

This is, in my judgment, the most important problem of personnel, of theory and design, that we confront today in American teacher education. Its effect upon the program can be seen even more clearly in the answer to my third question:

> *Third:* Is the four-year undergraduate program (and the fifth year masters program) in teacher education being developed as an organized unit?

With the exception of such progressive examples as I have cited, *it is not.* In 90 per cent of the colleges today, the *general education program of the first two years is almost completely divorced from the foundational and professional education program of the higher years.* It was a rare exception to find (in such centers as Troy and San Francisco) young people introduced to the problems and the profession of education before junior year in the college. The ancient practice of devoting the first two years to a general liberal arts program of English, mathematics, sciences, and foreign language is being continued today, almost unrelated to the later needs of the young people as teachers.

The very essence of the conception of a designed "general education" is being denied. There is no real awareness of the problem of the total design of the undergraduate teacher-education program. The theory underlying General Education, including the talk about integration, has been superficially discussed for more than a generation; yet, with only a few striking exceptions, the content of the first two years of work in these general education programs has little connection with the professional and foundational education of teachers in the junior, senior, and masters years.

I must not take more space to provide additional details. Suffice it to say that nation-wide evidence supports the conclusion that those who are primarily responsible for teacher education lack sufficient control over the first two years of the college course to make an over-all, four-year design possible. Even in some of our best universities, where the study of education has made magnificent strides, the leaders in that study are still forbidden any part in the planning of the program of studies for even those freshmen and sophomores who fully intend to become teachers in American schools and will enter education courses in the junior year. This seems to many of us to be a stupid handling of a critical and difficult problem; witness the fact that the Illinois Social Foundations Group has no control over the freshman and sophomore years, even within the College of Education!

Let us not shrink from the fact that we have on our hands a difficult problem of self-education among tens of thousands of college and university liberal arts teachers who today occupy the powerful role of teachers of teachers. Not only are these academicians failing to educate prospective teachers in the foundational understandings of man, his behavior, and his society—understandings that are crucial to our times; worse yet, *because of their control over the college curriculum, they are making it impossible for progressive teachers of teachers to do it*. The condition I describe is chronic throughout the United States. Departments of Foundations of Education have no share in the control over the first two years of undergraduate work, and only partial control over the work of the last two years. The gap between the Foundations of Education, and the so-called General Education, is so great that one could drive the traditional twenty-mule-borax-team through it!

It is a truism of science, art, government, business, family life—of every phase of the culture—that no enterprise can be designed without control. Hence a total design of American teacher education which will utilize all four years of the undergraduate program, and the masters year, is today an utter impossibility. It will continue to be that until members of liberal arts departments as well as of education departments are convinced that the task of preparing a young American to teach must begin in the earliest years of the college (even of the high school) and continue, step by step, to the most advanced years of the graduate school. It will continue to be so until a team of students of education, truly cooperating in the broadest sense, takes responsibility for all the years of the college and designs a unified program of general and professional education.

XIX

Many other examples of this problem have emerged, and in such solid sources as the reports of the Commission on Teacher Education.[22] These definitely confirm my findings and supply many graphic illustrations of the difficulty of getting a faculty imbued with the liberal arts tradition to cooperate in experiments in general education, even in teachers colleges. Consider the case of the attempt of President Frank Baker and the education progressives at the Milwaukee State Teachers College (after 1938–39) to experiment with a new program in General Education which crossed the conventional subject-matter boundaries. Milwaukee "Teachers," with 1200 students, is somewhat larger than Troy, and has a staff of 100. Two-thirds of the students are women, of middle class, often of first- or second-generation immigrant families, three-fourths living in metropolitan Milwaukee, and most of them entering teaching in rural or small towns within a hundred miles. The college has a four-year program, a junior

[22] Established in 1938 by the important American Council on Education; see especially Armstrong, Hollis and Davis, *op. cit.*

college devoted to General Education, and a senior college of professional training. Many students go into occupations other than teaching.

President Baker and his faculty study groups (cooperative study was one of his basic themes also) set up an experimental broad fields program organized in the first two years in five major areas: physical science, biological science, social science, humanities, and a special experimental area called Social and Esthetic Experience. Four or five faculty members worked together in each area, each professor lecturing on his own specialty while colleagues listened and led quiz sections throughout the year. The weekly schedule included a two-hour lecture, a one-hour quiz, and one hour of illustration, demonstration, and discussion in groups. One of the most interesting phases, from the experimental standpoint, was the attempt to integrate the social and esthetic experience (the fifth area) of the student in art, music, journalism, speech, dance, study clubs, choruses, social organizations, and athletics, to find out whether greater educational good would come from relating these forms of the student's social and esthetic development to his whole life in the college. The faculty said later that the scope and complexity of the materials, ideas, and activities proved to be "too diverse for any significant correlation." (I have an idea that twenty-five years from now teacher-education faculties generally will reverse this decision.) The plan was given up, the faculty replacing the lectures and demonstrations in the humanities, and the elective courses in esthetics, with appreciation courses. Both students and instructors reported that this was an improvement.

There were similar novel undertakings in the social sciences which included significant first-hand experiences in the community, voluntary student committees working under their own elected chairmen, student-made study programs built on their own interests, student committees on planning, student-planned and executed trips to community plants, housing developments, courts. Special housing and employment studies were made in the Negro section of Milwaukee in collaboration with the Urban League; and in other areas there were similar examples of reconstructed programs.

From the beginning the predominance of the liberal arts faculty was against the experiment, and they were backed up by the examining and certifying authorities of the State University of Wisconsin, who refused to give full academic credit for the work of students in the experimental groups. They did this in spite of the evidence of the objective test records, which showed that in both freshman and sophomore years the experimental groups did better than the control (conventional program) groups—as we recall they did in the national Eight-Year Study. The experimental groups stood generally at about the 78th percentile on the tests while the control groups stood at about the 65th. Still the conservatives were adamant. Their constant complaint against their opponents was—"Lack of order" (which had been James Russell's objection to Dewey's Laboratory School). This has been the chronic criticism of classically minded, passive educationalists in opposing progressive experiments for fifty years. The Armstrong-Hollis-Davis report agrees, saying that the Milwaukee situation was not "unusual in educational circles" where experiments are stymied by conservative staff members who are suspicious of just such area attempts to reconstruct the program. I can confirm it personally for Teachers College, Columbia, and from direct report from a score of other institutions. With us for fifteen years, the so-called "subject-matter specialists" in history, mathematics, and science have opposed the major integrated course in Social and Philosophical Foundations in their advising of students, in faculty committees, and in open controversy on the floor of all-college faculty conferences. After fifty years of nation-wide discussion and experiment, and one proved success after another, the scholastic die-hards are still in control and block attempts to make a better education in both school and college.

In Milwaukee, as in other centers, the continued experimentation of the small *avant-garde* group of progressives was possible only because of the President's faith and vigorous leadership. The experimentalists wanted to quit; he held them together. Again and again, across the country, I have seen great cooperative endeavors stimulated, guided, financed, held together against the opposition of narrow and bigoted faculty classicists and ignorant citizens. But I have also seen, in case after case, a Dean or a President, nervous at any innovation—*afraid "it won't add up"*—slapping down his best professors, letting them resign to go to other places, and refusing to appoint new ones of creative imagination. *The role of the leader is crucial.*

XX

Finally, I add a few references to a dozen centers in which our colleagues are struggling to move out in new directions. Fortunately for our greatest need, I find the most favored area is the Social Foundations, the study of society and culture. I am surrounded as I write by excellent examples from a dozen states.[23] In Springfield College (Massachusetts), which has developed recently from a former YMCA college, they are

. . . seeking to weave together general and professional education on both the undergraduate and the graduate level [and] to train professional leaders for youth-serving organizations, both public and private.

From the Eastern Washington College of Education (Cheney) offerings, I pick two:

. . . *Education and Contemporary Culture* . . . an effort is here made to represent an integrated view of contemporary American culture and its relation to the schools . . . how the school was shaped by the culture and how the schools in turn help to modify the culture.

In the Georgia Teachers College at Collegeboro, Georgia, I find:

. . . *Problems of Western Civilization.* The purpose . . . is to give the student a mature understanding of the social aspects of contemporary civilization and acquaintanceship with some of its important problems.

At New Jersey State Teachers College at Montclair:

. . . *Civilization and Citizenship.* The major object . . . is to arouse in the student a vital awareness that all the varied fields of human knowledge which make up the college curriculum function in the social life—the civilization—of which we are all a part.

I cite the New Jersey State Teachers College at Newark for an important unified experiment in guidance; a case of a total faculty which built a tradition and a technique of guidance, integrated with the curriculum and teaching program, through years of continuous work.

[23] The ones cited are from the catalogues and bulletins of the institutions mentioned.

At the University of Illinois, where the Social Foundations group has no control over the first two years, the design is confined to the junior-senior and masters years. To illustrate the content of these new Illinois courses I list the main topics from a major senior course open also to graduates, entitled *Education and Social Policy.*

Part One: Education and Culture
  I. Culture and Personality
  II. Class, Welfare and Personality
  III. School and Society

Part Two: Education and the Social Order
  IV. Education and Politics
  V. Education and the Church
  VI. Education and Economics
  VII. Intercultural Education in America
  VIII. Education and World Order
  IX. Communication, Education and Democracy
  X. Education and Aesthetics in the United States
  XI. Education and the Contemporary Moral and Intellectual Crisis
  XII. Education and Democracy
  XIII. Education and Social Planning

Part Three: Educational Policy in a Period of Social Crisis
  XIV. Educational Confusion and Social Crisis
  XV. The Social Function of Education
  XVI. The Social Function of the Educational Profession
Part Four: Education and Social Change
  XVII. Group Structure and Dynamics
  XVIII. Community Analysis and Educational Strategy

In Teachers College, Columbia, on the masters level, the major introductory course required of relatively all is Education in the American Culture. In two of the three sections of this course the major topics are as follows:

  I. The Problem of Education in the Post-War World
  II. The Study of American Economic and Political Problems
  III. America in a World Society
  IV. Sources of Social and Racial Conflict in America: Stresses and Strains
  V. Democracy and the Battle for an Informed Public Opinion
  VI. The Nature of Culture and the Problem of Social Change
  VII. Social Frontiers

XXI

In the arts, or humanities, I know of nothing better in the
country than the experimental "Basic Course in the Humanities"
of Professors Neal M. Cross and Leslie Dae Lindou of the Colorado State College of Education, entitled "The Search for Personal Freedom."[24] This is a beautiful reconstruction and integration of selected materials from the world history of literature,
music, graphic and plastic arts, from the Great Greeks to twentieth-century Einsteinian mathematics, science, the modern novel,
painting, music, and Freudian psychology. But the tragic fact is
that such approaches as that of Cross and Lindou are not used
in five per cent of the colleges. Moreover it is employed primarily
only in the teachers colleges, and is studied principally by those
few students in the colleges who specialize in the teaching of the
various arts. As I said in Chapters V and VI the expressional
movement of our times has affected teaching only within the

[24] See the exciting two-volume text, published personally for the authors,
by W. C. Brown, Dubuque, Iowa.

"subject" areas of fine arts, music, literature, and drama, and only in the few progressive institutions. Superintendents, principals, and teachers outside of the arts go through undergraduate and graduate study almost unaware of the expressional age in which they are living or of the role of the expressive arts in the schools. Most important of all, I can find no single teacher-education institution in which Esthetic Foundations are being systematically developed. It is being magnificently done in a few of the newer and more progressive colleges of liberal arts such as Bennington, Sarah Lawrence, and Mills, because there they employ practicing artists as teachers—true artist-teachers. At Illinois the Social Foundations Group has recognized the importance of the problem; in their recent Document the need for such a program in Esthetic Foundations is pointed out and the desire expressed to organize it as soon as personnel is available. Sporadic examples of integrated courses in "The Arts in Education and Life" have been undertaken at Teachers College, Columbia, and my "Education and Creative America" was given for twenty-three years. Nevertheless we have failed to this day to enlist the interest and support of the Division of Educational Foundations in creating a systematic program in Esthetic Foundations.

XXII

There remains the practical problem of inducting prospective teachers into teaching. This is the action problem. Throughout this book, while we have recognized the coordinate importance of knowledge and action, we have paid much attention to the problem of knowledge. Now we must capitalize on all that has been learned concerning feeling and action, and bring it to bear on the education of teachers. In conventional terms, this is the problem of getting young people to *participate in the teaching process, while they are studying it, and also to participate in and study the life of the community.*

For fifty years since deGarmo, the McMurrys, Monroe, Thorndike, Strayer, *et al.*, made the first draft of a systematic teacher-education program, the action problem has been solved by practice teaching. It is safe to say—even with no more than a quickly scanned statistical survey—that practically every teacher-education institution in America has provided some kind of opportunity by which young people preparing to teach could observe experienced teachers at work, and also have a few weeks of actual practice themselves in the teaching of children or youth. It is the preponderant practice today *not to provide this observation and practice teaching until the senior, or last year, of the student's study*. This amounts to tacking on a kind of practical addendum to three and a half disciplinary years of academic college education, in which the reading of books and the discussion of problems has been the principal task. That does not seem to me to be even a good makeshift solution of this pressing problem.

Against this academic method a few forward-moving teachers of teachers have made beginnings in designing and putting into operation more imaginative ways of handling this problem. I have in mind experimental examples of "internships," or "apprenticeships," which have developed in some of our public and private experimental schools and colleges. Our recent roundtable discussions have made very clear—through references to "Campus Activities," "Off-Campus Activities," "Internship, Apprenticeship, and Observation," and "Study Trips" in typical selected regions of the country—that these traditional practices of conventional teacher education are being seriously called in question. At Troy, Alabama, in a unit entitled "Campus Activities," the college aims "to make clear its concern for the whole student." *Practice in teaching is being supplanted by attempts to deal with the total problem of providing active experience in directed observation and study of, and participation in, the schools, the society, and culture.* The *active* study we say, not merely reading books about it, and discussing it. This means direct, first-hand, observation and participation. As President Smith said, "Get the students out there, in the community, and get them to do something about it." An excellent illustration of experimental practice is given in which the seniors studied throughout one quarter of the school year a rural community about fifteen miles away from Troy. This seems to the staff to be "good general education for freshmen." Although not much directed observation and study in either schools or the community is carried on before the junior year, in C. B. Smith's judgment such enterprises should be used in the first year. He reiterated: "The students must go out there (meaning into the community) and meet actual social situations . . . organize a boy scout troop, or do something else."

Lacking control over the first two years, even the experimentally minded groups, such as that at Tallahassee, Florida, offer the course entitled "Internship" only during the senior year. At Texas practice teaching is provided, but not until the senior year. The preconference materials from San Francisco State report that "student teaching is given in the senior year"; they add, "through closer identification of individual college supervisors with individual public schools, and through seminars for supervising teachers and prospective supervising teachers from the public schools, we are gradually building inter-communication and rapport with regard to problems of student teachers." But in all these places—among the best examples we can find—young people remain on the campus, read and talk, *but do not get into school or community until they are ready to leave the college and begin their professional work.*

On the side of active study of the life of the community, the region, and the nation, interesting examples of new experiments are cited by Tallahassee and Gainesville, Florida, Queens College of New York City, and Troy, Alabama. The college students, preparing to teach, are taken on long bus trips through the states; through New York State in the case of Queens, and as far north as the TVA and New York City in the case of Tallahassee. This technique of directed observation via the long trip has now been tried out for a decade and a half by a few progressive secondary schools and colleges; in some this includes directed summer study tours in other countries.

Criticism of these plans in our Roundtables has stressed the lack of *direction* in both observation and intellectual analysis. There has been too much reliance upon mere action, too much moving about; observations have been too casual and there has not been enough reading, study, and critical appraisal under direction. But the fact remains that almost nowhere in American teacher education do we provide for the participation in the teaching process of the prospective teachers from the beginning to the end of their study. And the equally important fact remains that our society does not include them, while they are students, as useful functioning members of the community.

XXIII

What generalizations can now be drawn from our study of the trend toward General Education and its relations to Educational Foundations?

Three facts can be stated with finality. The *first* is that our colleges are now tending to commit themselves to some form of General Education as the characteristic core content of the first two years of the American college. This is true of the liberal arts colleges, of the state and private universities, and to a considerable extent of the teachers colleges. According to this plan three broad fields general courses replace the dozen or more separate subjects offered in the traditional liberal arts program.

—*First*, the study of contemporary civilization and its historical development—man and his society and culture; traditionally, the social sciences.

—*Second*, the study of man and his behavior and development; traditionally, the natural sciences.

—*Third*, the study of the arts of man—the humanities—man and his expression; traditionally, literature, music, graphic and plastic arts, theatre, etc.

Second, these are almost universally required courses. The nation-wide movement for freeing the college program by increasing the electives, started under the impetus of such college leaders as Harvard's Eliot more than a half-century ago, is definitely waning. The so-called general education core is coming to be regarded as a composite of the common knowledge, understanding, and orientation that is a prerequisite to the building of a democratic society. The scholars of our time are seeking for a principle of unity that will bring order into the cultural confusion of our day. It must be a principle of unity that will serve as the organizing control of the new general education programs. But, as the Harvard Report put it, the search is for a principle of "unity conditioned by difference." A principle of unity is not sufficient for a total program of education in a culture where a population of great heterogeneity holds high the Supreme Value of the Individual. That must be paralleled by a principle of diversity, which is socially powerful enough to transform egocentric and competitive Individualists into mature and cooperative Persons. This is the picture that one sees reflected in the new documents on general education. Hence, in the endeavor to build this principle of unity, conditioned by diversity, many colleges are trying out these basic core studies. This factor powerfully affects the problem of developing a program of Educational Foundations.

The third fact is that the four-year course in teacher education throughout the United States now almost universally separates, and distinguishes between, General Education and Professional Education. General Education is practically always assigned to the first two years; Professional Education is confined to the latter two years and to graduate study. In academic terms, General Education means instruction in the physical, natural, and social sciences, and the arts. Professional Education means instruction in such courses as Educational Psychology, Curriculum Development, Methods and Techniques of Instruction, Guidance and Mental Hygiene, Administration and Supervision of Schools. There is little relation between the two. In very few institutions is there a single unified control over both. Total design is impossible.

Where do the Foundations of Education stand in this changing curriculum program? Out of the progressive developments of the past fifteen years the concept, Foundations of Education, has come to denote the following departments in teacher-education institutions:

—Social foundations . . . the study of society and the culture, including the international relationships.
—Bio-psychological foundations . . . the study of man and his behavior.
—Esthetic foundations . . . the study of man's expression and appreciation.
—Historical foundations . . . the study of the critical history of society and the culture.
—Philosophical foundations . . . the study of goals of life and education, methods of inquiry and norms of behavior (logic and ethics).
—Comparative foundations . . . the study of culture and education in, and comparison with, other selected societies.

Four of these fields have established themselves in the preponderance of teacher-education institutions as general courses, some of which are to be required of all prospective teachers: the History of Education, the Philosophy of Education, the Psychology of Education, and Comparative Education. But only in a dozen, perhaps a score, of institutions do the materials of these courses meet the rigorous criteria I set up in my discussion of Frontiers of Theory in Chapter VI.

In the thirty years since World War I the single outstanding achievement of the new generation of professors of education in the experimentally minded institutions has been the development of a new program in Social Foundations. This is the systematic study of society and the culture, including its international relationships, as the primary matrix of the study of education. A few of the pioneering institutions have sought, somewhat timorously, a sixth foundation—namely, Esthetic Foundations, the study of man's expression and appreciation.

This, then, is what we mean by Educational Foundations. But is this not essentially the concept of General Education? It is certainly very close to it. The unique quality in the Foundations courses in teacher education today, as shown by our regional meetings and the pre-conference reporting and the discussions of the National Society's Philadelphia Round Table (1951), is the recurring emphasis on the common learnings, the common understandings, the common orientations held by all devoted adherents of the American way of life, including teachers of children, youth, and adults. But this is also the unique quality in General Education. Hence the indispensable role of general education for all the teachers who are to teach all of the children. It seems clear, therefore, that the Foundations program in teacher education duplicates to some extent the content of General Education—and vice versa. But because the total program is not *designed* as a whole, this duplication is hit or miss, a matter of little more than chance. *The content of a properly designed General Education will be foundational to teacher education as well as to citizenship and personal education generally.* There is one difference, however, and it is an important one. The content of the six foundations, while much of it is regarded as General Education and is required of all people, is definitely oriented toward the great task of education. In the more than one thousand teacher-education institutions in America the study of the new social sciences, natural sciences, and the humanities must be organized in the framework of child and adult education, the very desideratum of a democratic society.

CHAPTER VIII

The Case for Creative Imagination:
Theory and Program

I

This completes the statement and defense of my principal theses. Against this background we can project the tasks to which the Teacher of Teachers is now called. The first is to build a new mood about his position in our social order. The dominating climate of opinion led his elders of the first generation to improvise a program of teacher education that largely ignored both the changing civilization and the creative resources of their time. Much that they put together, with the accretions added after 1920, is now obsolete; even their history is useless to us today. The resulting loss in educational momentum could have been avoided, for imaginative students of man and culture were even then creating the disciplines on which solid foundations could have been built. Today the frontiers of both theory and practice are marked by exciting examples of reconstruction. All of this I have already set down.

II

What, then, is demanded of us? Above all else that we give up our timidity and face the present crisis in educational statesmanship. We must take our stand among those who will undertake the creative *reconstruction* of American life. We must do it now, while there is time, and we must do it with full knowledge of the penalties of our leadership.

First and foremost, the Teacher of Teachers must know that he shares equally with the Technologist in a new division of labor. The engineer's die is cast—he *is now completing the robotizing of the machine.* This is the crucial fact in our lives. The educator's

247

die is cast also—he must now *complete the humanizing of men and the building among them of an effective intelligence.* The engineer's job is now being finished, and the educator's job must come to simultaneous completion or there will be trouble.

The argument for this critical thesis centers in human work, most of which will shortly disappear from heavy industry. Since men whose stomachs will surely be full must have work for the sake of their souls and minds, masters of personality and behavior must substitute for the dying mechanical occupations an *effective* intelligence and the arts and crafts of a creative life. Most people are fitted for such new occupations and around them they can focus their working lives.

Since these must not compete with automatic industry, a way must be found to distribute to the people both the purchasing power needed to keep the system running, and the economic and social benefits of automatism. Moreover, this must be done equitably, else our children will live either in a society of robotized men, or in a greatly depressed social order.

History teaches that blind but powerful interests will fight such changes in the social system. This opposition can be defeated and the needed designs and controls can be installed within our twenty-five years of borrowed time—and within a social order in which the democratic process is preserved—*only if the people generally will authorize it and push it through.* The people will not do that unless they understand it and believe in it and want it enough to fight for it.

This sets the stage for the teachers and their leader, the Teacher of Teachers, whose function is the humanizing of men and the fostering of intelligence. He has been closer to the problem in the last two generations than any other professional and he comes to the mid-century task equipped with disciplined tools. He can now know enough, for the knowledge is assembling in the new university disciplines. He can be firmly oriented, for the outlines of sound theory are taking shape. And he can take heart for he does not work alone; a company of good companions is forming on the creative frontiers. I believe that these facts have been established in earlier chapters.

III

Lest there be remaining doubts about the imminence of the

robotizing of heavy industry, and the permanent displacement of thirty to forty million men from mechanical work, let me clinch that point. If minds are to meet we must agree that we have already moved far into the second epoch of industrial culture; in its scientific phase, we have advanced a full hundred years; in the other phases—technological, social, and educational—from thirty to fifty years. I emphasize that we are well into the *second* epoch; the products of the first stage of industrialization are *all becoming obsolete—including the educational program*. This is a basic premise: the obsolescence of much of the formal, mechanical education of the nineteenth and early twentieth centuries.

This second stage in industrialization has already interjected such novel forces into the acceleration of technological change and precipitated the effects of such a new cultural lag that we must now settle down to the task of controlling civilization *intellectually*. Whether or not the Practical Men like to hear it said, industrialism reveals, in its second stage, the earmarks of a Frankenstein, running out of control. Witness the exhaustion of the entire earth's fuels and metals in the senseless arming of the world! Witness also our politicians' inept dependence on the purchasing power of the armament industry to keep a hit-and-miss economic system running! "Out of control" is the crucial phrase. Political officialdom shuns the hated conception of planning, because it postulates the imposing of control. Yet we know that now we must design or the very conception of an industrialized democracy will become a contradiction in terms. Twentieth-century man must invent and install democratic planning and control, or his social order will survive only by becoming another totalitarian slave state.

Thirty years after Ogburn's *Social Change* we are still stymied by the most serious example of cultural lag that has yet occurred. This is the lag in the power of the creative mind to educate the people quickly enough to prevent the breakdown of the social order. To act promptly enough, I say; given a long time, there is no question of its effectiveness. The real question is whether or not it can function in our kind of society with sufficient dispatch.

As for the concept of "cultural lag," let those young anthropologists who scornfully say that the concept has become outmoded take a look at this final summing up of its effects:

First, in two centuries from Galileo to Newton, *et al.,* the creative mind gave birth to the *mechanical* laws of motion, the mechanical production of work-developing energy, and the concepts of mathematics upon which they are based.

Second, lagging more than two centuries behind, inventors thought up the gas engine and the metal machine, harnessed the two together, powered the resulting contraption with the principle of *laissez faire,* and brought about the crude mechanical (Newtonian) revolution.

Third, every phase of the material culture changed as distribution of goods became more wide spaced but so slowly that it was not evident until well into the nineteenth century. Thus two lags accumulated—technological invention behind science and the distribution of goods and services in a comparable standard of living still further behind the former two.

Fourth, still more slowly, human institutions changed: family, government, community, and corporate way of life, lagging behind science, invention, and technology, until the twentieth century of world wars and depressions.

Fifth, even more laggard was the change in men's basic concepts and loyalties and the codification of their moral values and beliefs.

Sixth and finally, the whole procession of changes has culminated today in the dangerous lag in the people's climate of opinion and the impasse of the mid-twentieth century: *Knowledge of the intellectual control of economic and political processes is out of step with our physical means of maintaining a high standard of living.*

IV

We continue to ignore these lessons of history at our peril. The idea that the creative mind must now build effective intelligence in the people and get democratic support for a program of design and control can be clarified if we take one final look at the technological nub of our problem.

In the generation which embraced the period of the two World Wars the concurrence of crucial economic and political events gave a frightening push to the explosive effects of the new electro-chemical technology. The biggest single impetus came from the simultaneous action of the private enterprisers' race for immediate profits and the call from the top military men for help in the electronic control of air warfare in the Battle of Britain. A century of creative events had paved the way: Faraday's electro-magnetic discoveries (1830's), Maxwell's masterly equation-description of the electromagnetic field and the feed-back principle (1868), Hertz's harnessing of the high frequency waves (1885), and Einstein's expression of the field-relativity concepts and the energy equation (1905) rounded out, for the moment, man's 10,000-year struggle to invent machine tools.

By 1900 the inventor himself, under the pioneering of Edison, Marconi, and Lee DeForest, took over and gave us in successive decades the electron valve (the vacuum tube) the photo-electric cell, ultra-high frequency waves in the form of radar, and the electronically operated and controlled extension of the feed-back. With the theoretical tools in hand the research engineers and mathematicians piled up new electronic tools employing circuit theory.[1]

The integration of these electronic machine tools, particularly the union of the vacuum tube with feed-back controls, now makes possible the intricate organization of the varied automatic factory. Its assembly lines are controlled through a sequential analysis which involves instructions that are coded and taped into the machine. High-speed computing machines, such as Remington-Rand's UNIVAC or the Navy's ENIAC, are really large central rooms full of tubes, photo-electric cells, condensers, thermometers, hydrogen-ion-concentration meters, from which a whole factory is operated—relatively without men.

The automatic process is being hastened by the engineers' correction of two serious errors in production design. The first error has been the failure to separate men and machines. From Neanderthal Man to the mechanical assembly of automobile frames in the A. O. Smith Corporation in Milwaukee, U.S.A. in 1925, we have mixed men and machines, although in the Smith feat we

---

[1] Witness a brief calling of their honor roll: electro-static, dialectric-heating, and induction heat processes in the mass-production of many commodities and the similar use of ultra-sonic frequencies and electric viewers . . . electronic radar-equipped navigation installations and gyro-compass radio-direction finders, which can now bring the pilot of a lost plane back to his base . . . gravity meters and temperature control indicators, giving subsurface information re oil deposits, etc. . . . electronic control of machine measurement precise to one ten-thousandth of an inch, time measurements to one part in a million . . . electronic microscopes in industrial chemistry . . . x-ray analysis of alloys, lubricating films, etc. . . . the 100,000,000-volt betraton, duplicating the operation of cosmic rays and creating matter out of energy . . . electronic fault-finders and high-speed inspection tools . . . electronic signalling devices in advancing the safety of train operation and automobile traffic . . . feed-back control of engine velocity, ship-steering apparatus . . . and many others.

eliminated 95 per cent of the men. Men have been included in mechanical production so long that they are being robotized themselves, although they are not aware of it.

The second error is the designing of a machine on the assumption that it is to make a certain complete article, or commodity.[2]

The technologists now propose to design machine tool units in terms of a single act or operation to be performed—that is, to cut, move, push, lift, pull, carry, pour, pound, screw, heat, separate, etc. Under this principle and technique, machine-tool design becomes a task of organizing and reorganizing unit tools in whatever combinations, permutations, and sequences are needed to fabricate a given product. When the market is satisfied the component tools used in making it are taken down and put together in the new organization needed to make a different commodity. Such a system is "characterized by rational functioning." Thus we stand on the verge of the complete and efficient robotizing of the machine, "well on the road to automatism." As I have been warning my educational colleagues for two decades (witness *The Great Technology*, 1933), all heavy industry will be completely automatized in another generation, with or without a shooting war. The current reports of the technologists fully bear me out.

This second phase of the technological revolution is also reducing services as well as manufacturing processes to mechanization. Two of the three distinguishable types of human response (habit, logical thinking, and creative thought or expression) have been successfully mechanized. There are innumerable illustrations of the automatization of the habitual act. Commercially practicable calculators have been used for a generation by eighth-grade graduates to total purchases in supermarkets. Writing by hand has been taken over by the electric typewriter and the stenotype machine, and Dr. Vannevar Bush of the U.S. Office of Scientific Development tells us that we shall soon have a super-secretary which will type "when talked to"—witness the Bell Telephone Laboratories' Vocoder. As for the wholesale recording of facts, handwriting or typing is being supplanted by the microfilm; soon,

[2] Leaver and Brown (*Harper's Magazine*, August, 1951, p. 93), cite a current example: The Sargrove Radio Machine which turns out 20 complete radio sets an hour. As long as there is a market the machine will continue to run; when the market is satiated the owners of the machine will stop it, let it stand idle, and it will soon become obsolescent.

we are told, we may have "The Encyclopedia Britannica in a match-box, cost one nickel . . . (and perhaps) a whole library filed in a desk." In the field of the spoken word, we have the feedback in action in the automatic telephone exchange and the wireless telephone; witness also the simultaneous sending of many messages over a single telegraph wire.

From these initial successes with the habitual processes the mathematicians and engineers have gone on to amazing achievements in mechanizing the processes of logical thought; witness the performance of the Navy's ENIAC—the electric analogue computer—which solves perfectly in one minute a quantitative problem that would occupy the time of two skilled mathematicians for six months. As Dr. Bush says:

> . . . Whenever logical processes of thought are employed—there is opportunity for the machine . . . It is readily possible to construct a machine which will manipulate premises in accordance with logic simply by the clever use of relay circuits. Put a set of premises into such a device and turn the crank and it will readily pass out one conclusion after another, all in accordance with logical law.

But note carefully: something, or some person, must put a set of premises into the device. Who? . . . what? . . . man or machine? Dr. Bush insists that *a man* is required; "*for mature thought there is no mechanical substitute . . . creative thought and essentially repetitive thought are very different things*" (my italics). The crux of creative thought is the drawing of the premise, and that can be done only by human imagination. A *creative* organism is demanded; no amount of logical analysis alone will suffice.

I find confirmation for this conclusion in the engineers' reliance upon and definition of the feed-back. In Wiener's words, the feedback relies on "control of a machine on the basis of its *actual* performance rather than its *expected* performance." But the focus of attention in the creative act is on an *expected* performance, and not merely on that; it also requires choice to select the most appropriate performance among many alternative expected ones. The human being has the capacity to make this choice, to project into an imagined form that organization which will feel right for imagined *future* ways of living. In the example of the design of the terrace for my house the task was to *imagine* the form appropriate not only to an existing architectural form, but also to an *imagined* conception of the *life to be lived there*. The owner-designer was the only one who could feel the life to be lived there, and, in the background the complex relationship "terrace-to-house-to-plateau-to-mountain-behind-to-valley-in-front," and also feel it all as a unity. No machine, since it is a mechanical assembly of parts, not an organization, can say: "I say what I see (feel, intend) my way, with a form determined by my experience, life style, purpose, drive, and tensional-attitude." Having no capacity for feeling, the machine cannot objectify what it feels.

V

These developments in our times, appraised against man's ordeal with torque and machine tools (it stretches from his discovery of the lever and the fulcrum, the wheel and the wedge, to the electron valve and the feed-back), bring us around a sharp turn in history. Such a new organization of society must now be designed that all work of mass-producing, collating, and controlling will be done by electronic machines, while men are freed for their true function—namely, to create. Vistas open before us of a Utopian society of peace and plenty. It can be a society in which men, released from routine, devote themselves to deciding which goods and services they want machines to produce, and to codifying and taping the needed premises into the chosen machines; a social order in which men will find new outlets for their imagination, create a new conception of human labor, develop the personal arts and crafts, set the goals of life in new forms of recreation and appreciation, and build beautiful villages, towns, and cities.

But these Utopian vistas are counterbalanced by pictures of the possible destruction of the whole potential by atomic warfare, or the thoughtless extension of the mixed mechanization of men and machines, or by the emergence of a robot society of idle and degenerate people. Many thoughtful men see in the confusion and contradictions of our time the signs of a degenerating society. Some are already asking: Are we witnessing the disintegration of western culture? Is that the meaning of: the moral bankruptcy of our institutions, the corruption in politics, racketeering in labor, criminal behavior in high and low places, lawlessness and violence on the city streets, the seeming degradation of morals, the growing atmosphere of frivolity and despair, the increase in the number of beds in mental hospitals, the concern of literature with pathology, the need for and sensational sale of such books as *Peace of Mind, Peace of Soul,* and *Live Longer, Look Younger,* and the retreat of distinguished liberals to theological "reason"?

Through five centuries science has brought us one disillusioning concept after another. Has man, in his brilliant conquest of ideas, merely succeeded in breaking his own heart? Our professors of philosophy, and some professors of education, steeped in positivism, sneer at the sense of the mystic significance in man. As the Authority of Aristotelian-Thomist loyalties, and the post-romantic Puritan allegiances have been given up, modern scholarship encounters great difficulty in building a substitute Authority from current human experience. Certainly philosophic leaders are not now successfully guiding our quest for certainty. The pragmatists give us only the open universe and the experimental method. The individual, growing up under stress and strain, is compelled to choose but lacks a philosophical basis for choice. Bowled over by cultural anarchy he becomes a Catholic or gets psychoanalyzed. All too frequently he finds the latter recourse of little help, for the psychiatrists, having no theory of society, try to cure with individual therapies maladies rooted in social distortions. As Frankwood Williams tried to teach us years ago, to build balanced individuals we must socialize much of our culture. In so tenuous a situation many insist that it is industrial civilization itself that is the "major psychoneurosis of our time." Little wonder then, that many men of thought sense impending world disaster.

The social-psychological task of our time is that of preserving and developing the individuality of the *person* in a disturbed society. The years ahead will be marked by intricate and difficult problems of man's psychological adjustment to the contradictions of industrial society: freedom *vs.* security, religion *vs.* science, class *vs.* mass, private *vs.* public, nationalism *vs.* world order.

VI

The crisis becomes one of creative thought applied to men. The tasks of humanizing men who have been excluded from all mechanizable occupations, of satisfying the quest for certainty, and of building understanding among the people can be managed only by competent students of personality and behavior. They must, in addition, be men of creative imagination. In the most inclusive sense that means us, the teachers of teachers.

I cannot close without striking a trial balance of the chief factors that must be reckoned with and some of the steps that certainly must be taken.

First, in case some of my readers think I am unduly concerned with the task of providing satisfying work in our lives, I shall deal briefly with that. "Your picture," I can hear them saying, "of men with full stomachs, with roofs over their heads, and no compulsion upon them to work, is fascinating. Such leisure would seem like a celestial existence." Yes, it would, indeed, for the animal-like ones among us. But a clear distinction between animals and men is that, while the former accept their lot, the latter set about improving theirs. For most men, enforced idleness would soon begin to pall, months of it would bring restlessness and despondency; years of it would be unbearable. In time it would produce a degenerate society.

One of the best descriptions of Hell I have encountered is that it is a place where there is no work. In 1932, in England, I experienced it vicariously as I looked into the eyes of those Lancashire textile workers who had been twelve years on a dole. But they were merely a few of the 150,000,000 needlessly unemployed that I had seen in a year's study of the silent cotton mills that stretched from America's New England to Japan's Shimonoseki, China's Tientsin, India's Bombay, and around again to my Massachusetts textile towns. That debauching of the human spirit was matched by the reversion to a near-animal existence in those dreadful New York breadlines of the winter of 1933. I think my body will never rid itself of these scarifying after-images of the degradation of man.

VII

We are building the case for creative imagination in a social order that now imperatively demands design and democratic control. As a next tentative step let us free our imagination for a prevision of what the occupational life of the Americans might become by the time the electronic age has matured in heavy industry. We take this flight in imagination with a clear recognition that the chances of achieving it are slim indeed. We do it however with the conviction that many of its characteristics can be introduced into our social order, in which the American democratic way is preserved, if enough of the men and women of vision will dedicate themselves to it now.

I take you for a moment, therefore, to our America as it might be in 1984, the year that George Orwell chose as the setting for his fictional picture of a coming fascist society. The world I would have you visualize is a different one from Orwell's heel-clicking, Heil-Hitlering social order of frustrated, fearful men. It is a world of free and buoyant men, radiating hope and confidence. There is life on the faces of the people and free-swinging vigor in their movements, whether we visit them in the small towns of Pennsylvania, Florida, Oregon, Maine, New York, Illinois, or California. "Just like the people in the regenerated Tennessee Valley of the 1950's!" Yes, only more so.

The 1980 Census figures show some 75,000,000 gainfully employable in a total population which in three decades has tapered off to a stable 180,000,000. Work for about half of them is much what it was in their fathers' world of the 1950's. Some thirty million devote themselves to the personal services of skilled hands and brains on the farms, in government offices, in the trucking and taxiing businesses, in the churches, schools, press, radio and movies, the managerial jobs of business, and in the technical work of the professions. In a generation there has been no revolutionary change in these services; differences from the 1950's appear only in the more common use of labor-saving gadgets and the easy, quiet dispatch with which men work. In all fabricating of the industries, in measuring and record-making, packaging and deliveries, cleaning and repairing, transporting and communicating —the quiet and smooth-acting machine is everywhere, the human beings few and far between. This situation does not occasion astonishment; it was, indeed, generally expected by thoughtful people in 1950.

As compared to mid-century conditions, few men are doing the manual labor of the huge automatic factories and mills, which are scattered in hundreds of concentrated centers. What is astonishing is that so many men are engaged in mental work in these giant automatisms: men studying the machines, and the charted records of their operation, measuring, recording and graphing facts; men in drafting and computing rooms absorbed in the problems of design; and men in electrical and chemical laboratories, testing, weighing, cutting, and trying. Taking all the basic industries the country over, there must be several millions of these interested workers. Thus the first real contrast that impresses us is that so many are in services that formerly we had thought of as "intellectual." Headwork seems to have taken far more persons than we had estimated would have been either interested or capable. The reason is that our sons found out in the sixties and seventies that our own absorption in the apparent superiority of the "verbal I.Q.'s" had misled us about the "effective" intelligence of most of the people. It is really far higher than the Thorndikian psychologists, measuring "intellect" that had been brought up in sterile backgrounds, had concluded. Millions of supposedly limited youth, brought up in an atmosphere of creativeness, have risen to their new environment and now are successfully grappling with many of the problems of society. They are well-informed men of *effective* intelligence, who are capable of sensing problems that should be solved, mathematically and electronically, by those with I.Q.'s of 140 plus. These problems embrace new types of machines, new opportunities for the machine, new organizations and sequences of processes and kinds of work for specially endowed men. These are "idea men" of a different, but equally important, order from the typical "intellectuals" of the mid-century. And—they seem to be happier men.

Their critical role in American society in 1984 is well revealed in the thrilling developments we encounter in the great river valleys, to a dozen of which we go: to the Tennessee, where we see 4,000,000 farm and town people celebrating the TVA's Semi-Centennial, 1934–1984; to the nearby Ohio and its tributary Authorities—the Allegheny and the Monongahela; to the great Missouri, where the bickerings of the intrenched business and political interests which long held back the MVA have become, under planning and control, an abundant civilization covering a dozen states; to the Columbia with its Grand Coulees and Bonnevilles, tied into a system that has become international because Canada and the United States discovered that they had to build it together; to the Colorado Authority that now guarantees work and the good life to Arizona and southern California and a citrus abundance to half the nation; to the Valleys of the Red, the Connecticut, the Hudson, and lesser rivers southward along the Atlantic coastal plain. Thus Mr. Roosevelt's dream of duplicating the TVA in other valleys of the nation has actually been surpassed. After incredible difficulties throughout a generation, the social trend has established itself and the nation's farms and towns are becoming sort of a functioning organization of planning and control. Already there is a marked regeneration in our systems of production, transportation, marketing, recreation, and education.

And are the people at work? They are indeed. Many new jobs have emerged in the continental transformation—jobs involved in rebuilding the land, rehabilitating the forests, new kinds of reportorial and interpretational work involved in the weather fact-gathering of the Valleys, river-control jobs at the hundreds of new dams, electric-plant production and distribution jobs, new types of managerial jobs concerned with farm, village, producing and marketing cooperatives, jobs in connection with hundreds of thousands of demonstration farms—jobs on County Study-Planning Councils, and new rural education jobs.

The very base of this new American life lies in the villages and hamlets; the Census report of 1980 shows some 50,000 of them. Here the rejuvenation of the handicrafts has produced a nation-wide cottage industry. Each Valley Authority has brought cheap electric power into every cottage home, 1½ cents per kwh in place of the former 5¢ of the private electric corporations and 2¢ of the TVA. The engineers' perfection of the electric motor and its accompanying electronic devices has been a boon to the wood-worker, the stonecutter, the worker in iron and other metals, the weaver, ceramics worker, tailor, rugmaker, shoemaker, village automobile and farm-machine mechanic, and of course to some 35,000,000 housewives.

That we have achieved a true cottage industry, its products valued for their unique design and fine quality, is due primarily to the leadership of a new education in the arts and crafts. This education, started in many cases by Teachers of Teachers on the Town Planning councils, has reached out in two directions within the schools and the colleges. On the one hand a widely pervasive creative climate grips the elementary and secondary schools as young teachers have built a nation-wide program of expressive arts. On the other hand, the shops, libraries, studios, and laboratories of both schools and colleges are filled every late afternoon and evening, and on weekends, with adult study and expressional groups. Auditoriums are ablaze with the light of forum meetings, while classrooms and seminar rooms hold small reading circles, discussion groups, and Neighborhood Planning Councils. The educational plant of most communities is in use 15 hours a day. This is democracy-in-action. The work in the arts and crafts in shops and studios is socially useful as well as personally satisfying; the designs have sprung from the interests and the tastes of the workers in the new cottage industries. Some of these products are being made for their own homes, some for sale in the community, while some are marketed by the local Arts and Crafts Co-operatives.

Much of this activity has sprung from the new creative mood that pervades the schools and the colleges. Little wonder therefore that there are now two million more educational jobs than there were in 1950; the nation's educational staff now numbers more than 3,000,000. A million of these are interns who serve as part-time teachers throughout each of the four years of their teacher education program. Every classroom teacher has at least two apprentices, who are registered students in the nearby teachers college; every special department in an elementary or secondary school is served by several. Instead of learning to teach merely by reading books and discussing principles, students live with children and youth from the first day of their attendance at the teachers college. Secondary schools—many of them now reflecting the conception of a new American college embracing the years 16 to 20—have turned from college preparation in the liberal arts to practicing young people in the popular creative arts and crafts and in the study of the manifold new planning jobs. American youth seem to grow up in a hospitable labor market, very different from the hostile one of their elders in the 1950's.

The new creative mood is even more evident in the graduate schools—in engineering and its basic mathematics, bio-physics, bio-chemistry, and electronics, in the social and psychological sciences and education. The ancient disciplines of the academic liberal arts are a thing of the past. The "Cybernetics" movement of Wiener, *et al.,* has profoundly advanced the process of integrating fields of knowledge—mathematics, physics, chemistry, electronics, social psychology, anthropology. As a consequence new light is constantly being thrown on the psychology of human behavior *via* the study of communication-control. Already the research discoveries of a generation have brought about a revolutionary understanding of the nature of the creative act, including the act of thought.

From the point of view of our present interest in human work, this has already increased the number of jobs on the intellectual frontier. A regime of increasing intellectual, as well as economic, abundance has quite naturally minimized the role of the profit motive in society. Talented youth are now expected to go into creative occupations, rather than into money-making. The Creative Man is coming into his own.

But how are these manifold activities tied together? The answer lies in the increasing acceptance of the notion of planning. Many of the people have now come to see that the Great Depression's National Resources Planning Board idea was on the right track. The development of the Valley Authorities was the organizing thread, for the basis of success in each one lay, as it did in the TVA, in a planning, research, and control organization. As the years passed, and the concept of valley reconstruction spread, the notion of community study and planning—often around a nucleus of school and college teachers—took root in cities, towns, and villages. The consequence is that by this year of 1984 the Study-Planning Council has come to be the key to the new American life.

This does not mean that an intellectual élite, centered in a hierarchy of Planning-Control Boards, make decisions, blue-print plans, provide the electronic machines, and give the whole enterprise to the people to carry into effect. On the contrary, the people themselves, as the conception of continuous study has grown among them, have come to see that the new life cannot be brought in unless they bring it in together. Thus slowly in the 50's, 60's, and 70's a new imaginative conception of adult education took hold in the villages and neighborhoods of the country. It was a great, slowly evolving collaborative adventure, pointed up in a national structure of design leadership. It was a two-way affair—developing from the top down, that is from Washington and the regional and state capitals, as well as up from the grass roots of the towns and villages. By the late 1970's a permanent National Planning Board was set up in Washington. Even the customary fluctuating swing of the political pendulum from Democrats to Republicans, and back, did not destroy the idea. By the late 1970's, therefore, the outlines of a truly functioning national design organization had come into being. Its headquarters at Washington, the structure ramified across the country through a hierarchy of levels: *first,* a dozen Regional Valley Authorities, the nerve centers of the nation's natural regions; *second,* the 51 State Planning Councils; *third,* the 90-odd Metropolitan Councils; *fourth,* the manifold City, Town, and Village Councils. Moreover, a liaison with similar planning organizations in many other countries has been established through the United Nations; the study-planning concept has come to grip men everywhere as the only intelligent way to manage a tenuous and interdependent world society of three billion people.

This great enterprise in national study-planning cuts other ways; as, for example, in scores of Labor-Management Study-Planning Councils through the major heavy industries. These bring together the top idea men of Big Labor, Big Business, and the Big Public. These are continuous fact-gathering and fact-interpretive Boards, their special task being to determine the level of prices and purchasing power (above the basic minimum received by all) in the light of the changing facts of production, employment, and total costs. These boards are composed of trained specialists in the study of the operation of the total economic system. The labor members are themselves the product of a full generation of college-educated, research-minded men who began to appear in labor organizations about the time of World War II. No longer do they merely bargain with management for shorter hours, higher wages, and better working conditions. On the contrary, the Management-Labor Councils continuously examine the efficiency of the entire economic system, probe its troublesome bottlenecks, both human and mechanical, improve ways of producing goods, as well as help invent the needed and more personalized kinds of work.

These Councils are led by a new breed of social engineers, and are staffed principally with competent young people, some of them still in the higher schools. Until the age of 20, all American youth are involved in some way in education, although from early adolescence they are also increasingly included in the socially useful work of the community. This is indeed the key to the new education on the higher levels, and in every phase of the culture. Creative education in the higher schools springs directly from the social engineering problems of the people. Under the national and regional leadership of the Teacher of Teachers a system of Educational Councils for Community Development has come into being. The traditional Board of Education has long since brought under its control and design all the intellectual and creative agencies of the town—the libraries, art centers, social centers, the Arts and Crafts Cooperatives, as well as the colleges and schools. In every city of any size the latter now range from nursery schools of the little children of 18 months to 3 years, to the grown-up activities of the new college for youths of 16 to 20, and the manifold adult groups. The Superintendent of Schools has become the Community Director of Education—really the "Director of Cultural Study and Reconstruction"—with a central study and planning staff which reaches into all the study-planning groups of the town.

The "Group Process" is omnipresent, the study-planning idea pervading everything educational, keying the curriculum of schools and colleges into the neighborhood and community group life. The nub of the integration in the schools is a parallel system of Junior Study-Planning Councils guided by college and secondary school youth and interns and teachers, but also including selected elementary school children. The 16- to 20-year-old group in the colleges is the center of this junior design leadership, some of whom serve as active liaison members of local Planning Councils and Study Groups. Continuous social-economic-political and esthetic surveys of the community are carried on each year as a taking-off point in curriculum development. The contemporary phases of the curriculum are keyed into the gathering and interpreting of facts and into the constant creation of new designs. Through their own leaders on the Planning Councils the young people are in touch with every phase of the creative community and national life: the operation of developments in heavy industry, the cottage industries, the arts and crafts youth units carrying on socially useful projects in home and school. There are Junior Housing Units, Junior Traffic programs, Junior Public Health Councils, and units in hygiene and sanitation, physical inspection, and preventive medicine which reach into every aspect of the health of the community. The arts departments of the schools and colleges are tied into the long-time program of Town Planning; much part-time, socially useful work for youth arises here. Nothing in the program is more important than the continuous development of local reconstruction in recreation and esthetic appreciation. The thirty years of vigorous campaigning have finally brought results in this area.

Thus at last the age-long split between the Practical Man and the Creative Man is being healed as respect has grown on both sides and a new partnership has developed between them. As this has slowly taken place our people have come to respect and to rely on the Teacher of Teachers as a fertile resource leader. They, and he, have found in the ordeal of the passing years that this creative world of human behavior is his world; that his work involves the humanizing of men on the grand scale and the uniting of the new disciplines that were barely envisaged in 1950. This is the true capitalization of the knowledge of the whole person which was assembling at the mid-century. This is the coming of age of the New Economics, the New Politics, the New Psychology, Ethics, and Esthetics. This is the Great Tradition speaking through the American Way.

VIII

Crudely improvised, and dealing only sketchily with the single task of visualizing man's future work, this is my alternative to Orwell's tyrannous "1984." "But your 1984," I can hear some of my readers say, "is as fantastic as Orwell's!" I answer: "No more fantastic than was Roosevelt's 1942 figurative picture of America as an arsenal of democracy; every one of his visionary demands (50,000 airplanes, etc.) was exceeded within three years." And would not his enemies have jeered if he had said that $75 billion a year would be put into armaments, in peacetime, six years after the close of World War II? Our 1984 is fantastic only in the same sense that the 1935 "Chart of Plenty" was with its purchasing power estimates of $130 billion a year, or Chester Bowles's "Tomorrow Without Fear" estimate of $300 billion. Already we are too close to a realization of the latter to scoff any longer.

Not fantastic, then—but breath-taking, it is! So is the fact of America, especially as one experiences it from the other side of the earth as I do now in bringing this book to a close. My Arab colleagues today insist, as did former associates in China, the Philippines, Polynesia, and other so-called retarded regions, that the fact of America is difficult to believe. We, who are so close to it, find it difficult to grasp and understand. We must stand aloof from it, mentally and emotionally if not geographically, and see it with imagination. Its actualities are tremendous; its potentialities almost beyond belief to those who have lived in a culture of scarcity. Grasped in the fullness of the cultural transformation in which it burst the bonds of its timid imitation and moved into creative maturity, it is the promise of the world. Its future focus is not on goods but on personality, not on things but on men.

Certainly we can agree that we must set our sights high if we are to have the slightest success in guiding the social trends that grip us. That is essentially what we have done. Our picture of 1984 is what we envisage as the product of another generation of systematic study-planning. The concept of Valley Authority is the TVA idea put to work throughout the country. The practice of a Mixed Economy, part-public, part-private, has been steadily increasing for three generations. The conception of cottage industries, electric-powered and endowed by labor-saving gadgets, is not alien to our craft tradition. The study-planning notion itself has deep roots among our people: witness thousands of Parent Teacher Associations . . . Town-Hall meetings . . . the federal Department of Agriculture's vast program of rural study groups . . . the Foreign Policy Association programs . . . the luncheons and dinners of the Rotary, Kiwanis, and other service clubs . . . the discussion groups of the National Association of Business Women's clubs . . . the General Federation of Women's clubs . . . Hi-Y and 4-H clubs, the Boy Scouts, the Girl Scouts, and many others. The generalization of the study-planning process for the country as a whole is backed by a planning movement that, according to George B. Galloway's *Post-War Planning in the United States*, had, in 1942, given nearly every state government a "Planning Board," staffed by competent engineers, agriculturalists, foresters, professional government workers, and research students. And the leadership of the federal government was illustrated as recently as New Deal days in the assembling of scores of top-flight study-planning men under the direction of the National Resources Planning Board. The history is clear that the technique of scientific study and design has long been adopted in government, industry, business, and in community life generally. I cannot say too often, nor too emphatically, that the study-planning process is synonymous with democracy itself.

Therefore, our imaginative flight into the future has served another purpose: it enabled us to state a social method by which the norm for our creative efforts can be achieved. Far from smacking of totalitarianism, or Communism, or what the John T. Flynns will call its "socialism," it is really the democratic group-process. For there is no short cut to the humanizing of men; there is only the long, hard, democratic way of utilizing the effective intelligence of the people in action: "You do this and I'll do that, I and We, doing it together." This process can come alive in the Valleys of America as it did in the TVA, fusing centralization of sovereignty and financing, design and total administration, with a decentralized ownership and grass-roots operation. The federal, state, and local governments will do the things for which they are best equipped; individuals, private companies, and cooperatives those things which only they can do. Thus our people discover themselves and their neighbors and, in the process, acquire vision, strength, and security. The Exploitive Tradition is foiled, the Great Tradition established.

IX

But, I can hear the faint of heart protest, the status and prestige of the educational profession is at such a low ebb that it cannot rise to the responsibilities of leadership that you demand. I have not lived on the frontier of these problems for forty years to be unmindful of the difficulties. I agree with my Illinois colleagues[3] that education is not yet a self-conscious profession in the sense of law or medicine. I know only too well that there is widespread lack of reasoned understanding of the function of the teaching profession in our society. I am aware that ours is, indeed, a house divided among itself—"segmented horizontally and vertically." There are still too many who believe that teaching is telling, and who are convinced that the "cultivation of the intellectual virtues" *via* the Great Books will produce tough fighters for the democratic way of life. And there are the tender-minded who rely too much on "the felt needs and interests of the learner," forgetting that "the ends and purposes of education can neither be determined or understood apart from the study of the culture in which the school is located."

[3] I refer here to the splendid current document of the Social Foundation group at the University of Illinois: "The Social Foundations of Education" (mimeographed).

I do not minimize the obstacles in ourselves nor the penalties that must be paid for leadership. That caution has marked the chapters of my book. These penalties run wide and deep. They affect our economic lives, our social relationships, our very inner personal living. He that steps out of the safe Conforming Way in such times as these is well advised to open his eyes wide to the precarious nature of the Creative Path. Its insecurities reach into every community, school, and college as well as into government and business. The obvious ones are economic and social. In a time when the practice of integrity invites smear and character assassination, clear thinking and forthright action threatens loss of job and income, and hence of family well-being. Academic freedom and tenure are still insecurely protected; witness the Trustee's manhandling of California's professors in the recent loyalty oath imbroglio and the gagging of speakers by the trustees and President of Ohio State. A barrage of downright lying as well as smearing innuendo is invited by any man who states a clear position on any issue of controversy. A Kilpatrick is painted by the Pasadena rabble rousers as a devil undermining the integrity of the nation's youth, and a scholarly Jessup in government as an undercover agent of the Politburo! In a society proud of its historic democratic way, any head that stands above the dead level of mediocrity is clubbed, any questioning voice is shouted down. To do a solo is suspect, security for the timid ones resides only in the chorus. Little wonder that these timid ones resort to wholesale innocence by association! In the midst of such insanities we may as well face it: to go forward in the Creative Path is a lonely task and invites risk as well as adventure.

The heartening reply to the recital of these difficulties is the parallel citing of our magnificent resources in human leadership, among which the current example of the Illinois Social Foundations group looms large indeed. The little band of California professors who refused to knuckle under went to court and whipped the patrioteers. Their mates at Ohio State who refused to lie down and be gagged were backed by teachers associations which banned that university as a meeting place until the gag should be removed; and the powerful and progressive American Association of University Professors blacklisted it. My own social science textbooks, during the years of the attack upon them, were never ousted from the schools of any community in which a few citizens led a fight for free and open public discussion and decision. And that happened in many places.

Our resources on the side of intelligence match those on the side of courage. The Teacher of Teachers can now build upon the solid university disciplines in the social and natural sciences and the esthetic arts. Because enough is known of our culture to design the content of a great teacher education, the Teacher of Teachers need no longer be bogged down in bewildered inertia. Because the key concepts of culture, behavior, and esthetics are now being assembled (witness the culture-molding process, the field-force-energy concept, the feed-back principle, dynamic cultural change and its lags, experience, integration, growth, expression, self-balance), he need no longer grope his way blindly through a mere fraction of human knowledge. Well-nigh all of it, in conceptual form, is available to him—*if he will put himself in the Creative Path*. If a determined band of American educators will do that now, the trend toward general cultural disintegration can be arrested.

Meanwhile we must not forget that the study of control and design on the economic level has priority. This includes the building of popular understanding on a nation-wide scale, the creation of a new kind of non-mechanizable work, and of a new conception of purchasing power that will equate the value of craft goods and services with the products of automatic industry.

Perhaps the most heartening factor in the mid-century scene is that the recognition of the tendencies toward cultural disintegration helps to set the great goal of our new education: *the reintegration of American culture*. This is the positive thing for which we can fight. Squarely against the confusion, lag, uncertainty, and recurring depression we can hold high before our youth a vista of the civilization of cultural health which they can now help us build. A culture of economic and spiritual abundance, and of human integrity, beckons to us on the horizon, one of creative labor and high esthetic level in which democratic government plays an optimum role, both at home and abroad.

X

Since the creative process must now become the focus of our study and planning, some of our men of theory must turn from their absorption in logic to devote their energy to a study of the expressive act. I would in no way minimize the contribution that Dewey's followers have made since 1900, in moving ahead from a concern with habit and memory to the logic of problem-solving thinking.[4] They greatly clarified "the problem"; Dewey single-handed gave men one of the best descriptions ever written of the logic of solving a problem. But in doing it he left the crucial first step—that of recognizing the problem—still shrouded in mystery. He spotted it and described it, and the Gestaltists backed him up by stressing it under the title "flash of insight." They all labeled it, and exclaimed over it, but did nothing more about it. It is now our task to unlock its secrets and put it to work in education.

We start where they left off, with the question: What is the nature of the flash of insight? To me this is the same as asking: "What is the creative act?" What does one do in recognizing a problem, in drawing a premise? For my theory I make all four—recognition of the problem, the drawing of the premise, the flash of insight, and the creative act—synonymous. Building on Dewey and the Gestaltists (and of course on Thorndike, *et al.*, Freud, *et al.*, and Cannon, *et al.*), we shift the focus of our research interests to the creative imagination. The nub is the imagined conception, the ordained relationship; and no mechanism, though it be as clever as the Navy's ENIAC, can prehend it. Even the feedback principle, which is throwing light on the logical process, is a secondary contributor.

A twofold hypothesis has been advanced in this book: *First,* that the concept is the key that promises to unlock the mystery of the creative process; *second,* that the electro-chemical power that

---

[4] My heartiest congratulations to the leaders of the Philosophy of Education Society—especially to Messrs. Raup of Columbia, Benne, Smith, Stanley and the Social Foundations group of Illinois, and Brameld and Axtelle of New York University—for their persistence in studying the methodological problem. They do well to insist that our work center on policy-making and the validation of our concepts. Congratulations also to Messrs. Margenau, Kunz, Mather, Northrup and Montagu of the Foundation for Integrated Education for their imaginative work on concepts; see their *The Nature of Concepts* (Ed. by F. L. Kunz and Schiller Scroggs; Stillwater, Okla.: Oklahoma A and M College, 1950). As a consequence of this vigorous work, logic and ethics are being cultivated by students of education. There are, however, three normative sciences—logic, ethics, *and esthetics.* Because of the current absorption in logic and ethics, men of thought, while careful to enumerate esthetics in their list of normative sciences, have tended to neglect it. Its exploration has now become imperative because we cannot move forward except through the clarification of the creative process.

fires this process resides in a fusion of specific responses in the cortex and general responses in the blood stream and endocrinological and musculature factors. A preface to this theory has been given in Chapter VI. While we are waiting for the researches of mathematicians, physiologists, psychologists, and expressive artists to integrate fields of knowledge which will expose more precisely the nature of the act, we can rebuild the curriculum with great confidence in the directive role of the key concepts. There is not the slightest doubt in my mind that these concepts are the cue to the selection of our material and to its clear organization. Fortunately, we need not wait; we can put them to work at once, and at all levels of education, from early childhood to adulthood; indeed, we shall further our knowledge of their role only as we do put them to work. So far as I can now see, this takes us out to the farthest point on the intellectual frontier of the Foundations of Education.

One additional word concerning competence in building an Esthetic Foundation for education: it can be done only by artist-educators who have made themselves masters of the expressive and appreciative acts as well as of the concepts of the basic disciplines. They must know the creative act internally, in its own terms, through having experienced it within their own bodies. Knowledge *about* creative acts is important, but it is not enough; what is needed now is the more profound feeling—understanding that comes only through expression itself. To put it differently, the Teacher of Teachers must himself first become an expressive person. He must become both artist and teacher, in the fullest sense an Artist-Teacher.

XI

Where shall we take hold? Where our competence is greatest. The prior need today, wherever vigorous new thinking and new practices are under way, is for the alert, like-minded ones among us in college and university centers to get together for prompt and thorough exchange of views. There is no question of the widespread recognition of our common need of taking thought together. But far too few of us are doing anything about it. The difficulty lies not in a lack of intellectual capacity to dig to the roots of our social problems, or to understand the essence of the scholars' multiplying researches on the scientific frontiers. I returned from the forty regional meetings in 1950 with the feeling that there is enormous potential among us for the building of a great program of education. Potential energy there is in abundance, but somehow it does not get transformed into kinetic energy of thought and action. So nothing happens.

This becomes of tragic importance when we recognize that the Teacher of Teachers is the vital agent in awakening the people to a sense of their own power and to an understanding of their problems. We are no small brigade; in the more than 1000 universities and colleges which are engaged in the education of teachers, the Teachers of Teachers constitute an army corps of more than 50,000 persons. In these teacher-education centers not less than a million young Americans are potential students, and hence potential leaders, in the study of our society, its problems, and the capacities of our people to make it work.

Yet with all this potential energy, so little happens that is really important, either to our youth or to the culture generally. Why? To borrow a figure from modern technology, teacher education is like a huge engine with all parts of the power plant assembled, but with a mechanism that will not start. It is inert; something is wrong with the sparking mechanism. Batteries are O.K., points and plugs are clean. But contact cannot be established. The spark cannot get across to explode the gas, to turn potential energy into kinetic energy, and so produce movement.

So it is with people, and so it seems with the teachers of teachers. Many of us have everything that it takes, but the gap in the starting apparatus is too great. We are regions apart—geographically, personally, and psychologically. These centers of burning enthusiasm for reconstruction, to which I referred, are too few and too far between. The creative spots, either of heroic lone individuals or small groups, appeared perhaps once in twenty times—perhaps even less often. Yet we know full well that isolation kills the creative thing. Lone persons must find their mates, work in groups, renew their energy by eye-to-eye interaction, mind stimulating mind. Some among us are fortunate for they have been brought together in groups by far-seeing leaders. These groups move the live individuals up together, give them contact, provide the sparking apparatus. But even groups can run down, repeat their cycles of concept, and wear out their power-making machinery. Then they also need to be brought near to other groups long enough for new sparks to pass across, for re-energizing.

XII

I have spoken constantly of concept and of men of concept. I close on the tragic ordeal now demanded of the men of action in education. Ideas will do no good socially unless we put them to work in society. And that brings me to the administrator of teacher education, for he stands at the piercing point where thought, control, and the possibilities of reconstructive action converge. He must help put the great concepts of society, behavior, and expression to work in programs of action. But that he cannot do unless they are *his* concepts—unless they have been made his by hard intellectual work. Indeed the key concepts must be the joint property of the President and the Professor, for either is impotent without the other. The professor is the dynamic repository of technical knowledge and design. The administrator is to lead in cooperative study, welding the professors of liberal arts and of education together within the college, and to interpret them to the trustees and the citizenry who control the budget and appointive power. But the mastery of the great concepts that "rule the world or throw it into chaos" is the obligation of both parts of the teacher-education team.

This means that the administrator, above all others, has heavy penalties to pay for his leadership. He must pay by giving up his easy and comfortable allegiance to the practical men, the easy way of feudal conformity. He must stand and pay the penalties of the hard way of study and imagination; not the easy way of the banal conformities of the political club, but the disciplined and difficult way of individual and group study. He must stop pushing precepts and people around and come to grips with profound ideas.

Indeed, educational administrators cannot put off the difficult moment any longer—they must accept the obligations of truly literate men. They must read, and study books. They must give up some of their securities and confront questions of controversy for which there are no formularized answers. If it be said that one of the penalties of leadership is the confrontation of fears, I reply as Mr. Roosevelt did, that we have nothing to fear, but fear itself.

Administrators in America *must not merely read books, they must also engage in the disciplined art of the group process.* If they are to lead their faculties in study, *they must themselves become students.* The conception of educational leadership must be drastically altered. He that leads teacher education in the next twenty-five years must pay in hard intellectual work and in creative imagination.

I have said time and again that enough is known to design and build a great teacher education. It is; but it is not known as yet by the right people. It is known only by the scholars of the Science and Art of Man, and they are not in a position to build the educational program. Moreover the knowledge must be known by all the teachers of teachers including their administrative officers. Let us not forget that the teacher-education program can be no better than the conceptual knowledge and the design of the men who build it. Concepts do not emerge full-blown from a passive listening process. They are hammered out on the anvil of creative thought.

XIII

Finally, a word with the younger Teachers of Teachers in America. The job ahead is yours. I have written this book to bring you up to date, to give you a start, and that has been no easy task. But from now on you are on your own. My generation is closing its era, coming to the end of its strength. Do not look for too much imagination from my peers. Most of them are through. Some of them never faced the problem—others have beaten a retreat to security. Those among them who had imagination blazed new trails, and much of their pioneering was good. They capitalized on the crude improvisations of Butler's men and achieved a good second statement in the social and bio-psychological foundations. But they have left undone so many things that need to be done.

My peers and I have had the adventure of the first documentation of some of the explosive ideas of the Science and Art of Man. The slack in which our guesses were made has been so great that the cost of our errors could be neglected.

But you confront the ordeal of maturity. Your concepts must be primary and right. Time is running out; even the twenty-five-year breathing space I foresee may not be sufficient for the design tasks ahead.

Two admonitions I offer: first, and to save time, capitalize on the successes and failures of your predecessors. Paraphrasing one of my great elder brothers, George Santayana: "He that ignores the lessons of history is doomed to repeat its mistakes."

And the second admonition:

Put Yourself in the Creative Path.

ACKNOWLEDGMENTS

Acknowledgment is made to the authors and publishers of the following works which have been quoted in the text of this book:

AIKEN, WILFORD M.: *Adventure in American Education:* Vol. I. The Story of the Eight-Year Study. New York and London, Harper & Brothers, 1942.

ARMSTRONG, W. EARL, HOLLIS, ERNEST, DAVIS, HELEN: *The College and Teacher Education.* Washington, D. C., American Council on Education, 1944.

BOURNE, RANDOLPH: *Untimely Papers.* New York, B. W. Huebsch, 1919.

BROOKS, VAN WYCK: *Letters and Leadership.* New York, B. W. Huebsch, 1918.

BUCKINGHAM, BURDETTE R.: *The Rugg Course in the Classroom.* New York, Ginn and Co., 1935.

CARMEN, HARRY (Ed.): *A College Program in Action.* New York, Columbia University Press, 1946.

CUBBERLEY, ELLWOOD P.: *Public Education in the United States.* Boston, Houghton Mifflin Company, 1919.

DUNCAN, ISADORA: *The Art of the Dance.* New York, Theatre Arts, 1928.

FRANK, WALDO: *Chart for Rough Water.* New York, Duell, Sloan and Pearce, 1940.

GRAY, WILLIAM S.: *General Education, Its Nature, Scope and Essential Elements.* Chicago, University of Chicago Press, 1934.

Harvard Committee on the Objectives of a General Education: *General Education in a Free Society;* Report of the Harvard Committee. Cambridge, Mass., Cambridge University Press, 1945.

Joint Committee on Curriculum, National Education Association, and the Society for Curriculum Study: *The Changing Curriculum.* New York, London, D. Appleton-Century Co., 1937.

McGRATH, EARL J. *Social Science in General Education.* Dubuque, Iowa, W. C. Brown Co., 1948.

MARIN, JOHN: *Letters of John Marin.* New York, privately printed for An American Place, 1931.

MAYHEW, KATHERINE CAMP, and EDWARDS, ANNA CAMP: *The Dewey School; The Laboratory School of the University of Chicago, 1896–1903.* New York, D. Appleton-Century Co., 1936.

MONROE, PAUL: *Cyclopedia of Education.* New York, Macmillan, 1911–1919, Vol. IV.

RINAKER, CLARISSA (Ed.): *Readings from Huxley.* New York, Harcourt, Brace and Co., 1920.

RUGG, HAROLD: *Building a Science of Society for the School. A New Social Science Program: Man and His Changing Society.* New York, Harold Rugg, 1934.

RUGG, HAROLD: *Culture and Education in America.* New York, Harcourt, Brace and Co., 1931.

RUGG, HAROLD: *Foundations for American Education.* Yonkers-on-Hudson, The World Book Company, 1947.

RUGG, HAROLD: *That Men May Understand.* New York, Doubleday, Doran, and Co., 1941.

STEINBECK, JOHN: *The Grapes of Wrath.* New York, The Viking Press, 1939.

WIENER, NORBERT: *The Human Use of Human Beings; Cybernetics and Society.* Boston, Houghton Mifflin Company, 1950.

WILD, K. W.: *Intuition.* Cambridge (Eng.), The University Press, 1938.

APPENDIX

A SELECTED LIBRARY FOR THE TEACHER OF TEACHERS

This selected library has been prepared for those who are deeply concerned with the present crisis in our culture, and commit themselves to doing something about it through education. The readings have been sifted out from a voluminous contemporary and historical literature, and organized in terms of five Foundations of Education. Under each of these major captions the study guides have been organized to fit the principal social and personal problems treated in this book.

I. ON THE BUILDING OF THE SOCIAL FOUNDATIONS OF EDUCATION

On the Nature of Our Times:
The Crisis in Twentieth-Century Culture

We begin with what many competent students are convinced is the disintegration of western "industrial democratic" culture. Robert Cooley Angell's *The Integration of American Society* (McGraw-Hill, 1941) appraises its extent. An older analysis, difficult to read but worth the struggle, is John Dewey's *The Public and Its Problems* (Holt, 1927); in the same class are Karl Mannheim's *Diagnosis of Our Time* (Paul, Trench-Trubner, 1947), and his *Man and Society in An Age of Reconstruction* (Harcourt, Brace, 1941). A more readable book for the general reader, but older and not up to date, is *Our Changing Civilization: How Science and Technology Are Reconstructing Modern Life* (Stokes, 1929) by J. H. Randall, Jr.

One of the key figures of both the theoretical analysis of twentieth-century culture and its historical development was Harold Laski. Two of his books fit here: *Reflections on the Revolution of Our Time* (Viking Press, 1943) and *The Rise of Liberalism* (Harper, 1936); the latter is the best account of the nineteenth-century "western" mind that spread economic imperialism around the world. Challenging treatments include Max Lerner's *It Is Later Than You Think* (Viking Press, 1943), Fritz Sternberg's *The Coming Crisis* (John Day, 1947), Emery Reves' *The Anatomy of Peace* (Harper, 1946), and E. H. Carr's *The Soviet Impact on the Western World* (Macmillan, 1946).

Since 1920 sociologists and anthropologists have applied their techniques to the direct study of modern industrial culture; as a consequence we have several important interpretations. For the best single symposium of the views of a score of the American students see Ralph Linton, editor, *The Science of Man in the World Crisis* (Columbia University Press, 1945), Ruth Benedict's *Patterns of Culture* (Houghton Mifflin, 1934, now in 35¢ Mentor Books), and Clyde Kluckhohn's *Mirror for Man* (McGraw-Hill, 1949). See also Melville Herskovits, *Man and His Works* (Knopf, 1948).

The pioneer scientific analysis of cultural lag was William F. Ogburn's *Social Change* (1922); see various shorter studies appearing under his editorship in *The American Journal of Sociology*. Two government-sponsored studies, guided by him in part—*Recent Economic Changes in the United States* (two volumes, McGraw-Hill, 1929) and *Recent Social Trends in the United States* (two volumes, McGraw-Hill, 1933)—roused many social-minded individuals and organizations to consider the emerging problems.

One of our best analysts is Hans Kohn, as shown by his overview, *The Twentieth Century* (Macmillan, 1949) and his somewhat older *Revolution and Dictatorship* (Harvard University Press, 1940) and the *World Order in Historical Perspective* (1942).

Do not miss one of the most profound, but much-neglected, analysts of world culture in our time—Waldo Frank. For thirty years, beginning with his beautiful and perceptive *Our America* (Boni and Liveright) in 1920, he has been digging to the bottom-most roots. His most rounded systematic account of the Great Tradition in western culture is *Chart for Rough Water* (Doubleday, Doran, 1940), but the reader should not miss the chapter on "The Atlantic World" in *America Hispana* (Scribner's, 1931) which is the best of his cultural portraits (in the low-priced edition called *South of Us* see especially pp. 309–350), as well as his *Rediscovery of America* (Scribner's, 1929) . . . *In the American Jungle* (Farrar and Rinehart, 1937) . . . *Salvos* (out of print).

On the problem of reintegration of American culture the best of my own earlier books are *Now Is the Moment* (Duell, 1943) and the latter half of *The Great Technology* (John Day, 1933).

On Domestic Reconstruction, Valley Authorities, and National Planning

The research on the problem of how to run the economic system at a full-employment, abundance level, which was first motivated in the 1930's by the Brookings Institution (Harold Moulton, *et al.*, see two of his early volumes: *America's Capacity to Produce*, 1934, and *America's Capacity to Consume*, 1934) and the National Survey Engineers (see Harold Loeb *et al.'s* Chart of Plenty, 1935), has now reached broad proportions. On the magnificent story of the TVA, nothing equals David Lilienthal's *TVA: Democracy on the March* (originally

Harper, 1944, it is now 35¢ in Mentor Books). Every teacher of teachers in America should use it; also the annual "Reports" of the Tennessee Valley Authority. The story of the TVA itself is also found in Odette Keun's enthusiastic *A Foreigner Looks at the TVA* (Longmans, Green, 1937) and in Jay Franklin's small book *The Future Is Ours* (Houghton Mifflin, 1939).

For a general overview of the "planning" problem, see George Galloway and associates, *Planning for America* (Holt, 1941). Do not miss the contrasting views in Barbara Wooton's *Freedom Under Planning* (North Carolina Press, 1945) for the positive statement and, for the negative side, F. A. von Hayek's *The Road to Serfdom* (Chicago Press, 1944). See also Galloway's *Post-War Planning in the United States* (Twentieth Century Fund, 1942). In the latter years of the Great Depression the National Resources Planning Board published positive studies of the control and use of our resources; see, for example, *Technological Trends and National Planning, Consumer Incomes in the United States, Problems of a Changing Population, Our Cities—Their Role in the National Economy, Housing: the Continuing Problem.*

On Robotizing the Machine

In this broad framework of a transforming culture we confront the twofold problem of the completion of the automatization of heavy industry and the invention of creative work for men. The conscious study of the former problem stretches now over thirty years. It begins in 1919 with Veblen and the Technical Alliance around him and the publication of his *Engineers and The Price System* (Viking, 1933). As I write (1951) Norbert Wiener's *Human Use of Human Beings* (Houghton Mifflin, 1950) has just come from the press. Read the two books together and with them, to get major steps in the thirty years of advancing thought, Bassett Jones's *Debt and Production* (John Day, 1933) and Harold Loeb's *Chart of Plenty* (Viking, 1935) and supporting documentation in his *National Survey of Potential Product Capacity* (New York City Housing Authority, 1935); see also my own *Great Technology* (John Day, 1933), and the references in this present book.

For the problem of the robotizing of the machine, in addition to the foregoing, see Wiener's *Cybernetics, Control and Communication in the Animal and the Machine* (John Wiley, 1948), especially in relation to Jones's *Debt and Production*. Wiener's autobiography, which he tells me has just been finished, should throw further light on the problem. The more recent literature of electronics and the "new physics" is needed to understand the basic concepts that are revolutionizing production and the control of the machine, and taking mechanical work away from human beings. For the lay reader's study of the field-relativity concepts see Einstein and Infeld's *The Evolution of Physics* (Simon and Schuster, 1938); for the story of the vacuum tube Lee de Forest's own story in *Father of Radio* (Wilcox and Follett, 1950) and any standard text.

II. ON THE BUILDING OF THE HISTORICAL FOUNDATIONS OF EDUCATION

An adequate theory or curriculum content cannot be designed for the Social Foundations of Education apart from a careful study of the history of modern industrial civilization and its basic history of thought. The key to the study is the history of ideas; the central concepts of the scholars' knowledge will constitute the structural outline of both theory and curriculum. The transformation of modern culture can be understood best if it is visualized as the product of a vast shift in thought that developed through two stages of a hierarchy of revolutions. It is important to distinguish the first of the two revolutions from the second.

From an enormous literature, I would begin with the writings of two American historians. The best single interpretation of the first intellectual revolution—the Newtonian-mechanical one—and its effect on the physical, natural and social sciences, is John H. Randall, Jr.'s *The Making of the Modern Mind* (Houghton Mifflin, 1926); his chapter bibliographies will be indispensable. Note carefully that Randall gives no treatment of the shift from the first to the second scientific revolution even though the latter began early in the nineteenth century. In the same category are two of Harry Elmer Barnes's many volumes: *The History and Prospects of the Social Sciences* (Knopf, 1925), *The New History and The Social Studies* (Knopf, 1927). The pioneer essays in the social sciences are J. H. Robinson's *The New History* (Macmillan in book form, 1918; original essay in 1892); F. J. Turner's *The Frontier in American History* (essay first published 1893; in book form, Holt, 1920).

For the history of western capitalism: John A. Hobson's *The Evolution of Modern Capitalism* (Walter Scott, 1926); R. H. Tawney's classic *Religion and the Rise of Captialism* (Harcourt, Brace, 1926), A. N. Whitehead's *Science in the Modern World* (Macmillan, 1925), both now available in Mentor Books 35¢; and Miriam Beard's *History of the Business Man* (Macmillan, 1938).

Among the great theories of human societies Arnold J. Toynbee's six-volume *A Study of History* (Oxford University, 1947) is indispensable; its essence can be found in the single volume composed from the six by D. C. Somervell (Oxford, 1946). In this connection see the collection of Karl Marx's indispensable writings in his *Communist Manifesto, Capital and Other Writings*, Max Eastman, editor, (Carlton, 1932). Other much-discussed theories of the history of human societies are Oswald Spengler's *Decline of the West* (Knopf,

1927–28), J. B. Bury's *The Idea of Progress* (Macmillan, 1927) and his *History of Freedom of Thought*, and W. Sombart's *Modern Capitalism*.

I personally think the most important leader of the American school of new social analysts was Thorstein Veblen. On his life and times see Joseph Dorfman's *Thorstein Veblen and His America* (Viking, 1934); among Veblen's books do not miss: *Theory of the Leisure Class* (1899), *The Instinct of Workmanship* (1914), *The Engineers and the Price System* (1919). For the best writings of his contemporaries and immediate successors, see Robinson's *The Mind in the Making* (Harper, 1921) and *The Human Comedy* (Harper, 1937); Charles and Mary Beard's four-volume *Rise of American Civilization* (Macmillan, 1929–39).

With these pioneer social-economic-political documents study the parallel appraisals of the American statement of the Great Tradition. An introductory outline can now be built from the writings of several students. Ralph Henry Gabriel's *The Course of American Democratic Thought* (Ronald, 1940) gives the economic, political, and moral-ethical aspects. The development of the literary mind is sketched in Vernon Parrington's three-volume *Main Currents in American Thought* (Harcourt, Brace, 1927–30); see especially Vols. II and III for the nineteenth century. The era of rebellion and improvisation which followed the death of Whitman is powerfully expressed through Van Wyck Brooks's early *America's Coming of Age* (1915, reprinted in *Three Essays on America*, Dutton, 1940) and in such selected essays as "The Twilight of Idols" in Randolph Bourne's *Untimely Papers* (Huebsch, 1919) and *The History of a Literary Radical* (Huebsch, 1920). The best statement, however, is that of Waldo Frank as presented in his *Our America* (1919), *Salvos* (1924), *Rediscovery of America* (1929), *In the American Jungle* (1937), and *Chart for Rough Water* (1939; all Duell). One of the most astute critics of the American literary mind is Albert Kazin; see his *On Native Grounds* (Reynal and Hitchcock, 1942). For the best critical review of the work of the symbolists see Edmund Wilson's *Axel's Castle* (Scribner's, 1941). One of the most profound analyses and clearest expressions of the long-time view of the development of the creative process in our western civilization is Horace Kallen's two-volume *Art and Freedom* (Duell, 1942).

The educational strand of American expressive development has been traced in Merle Curti's *The Social Ideas of American Educators* (Scribner's, 1935), in my own *Culture and Education in America* (Harcourt, Brace, 1931), and chapters from *That Men May Understand* (Doubleday, 1941), in the (edited) *Third Yearbook* of the John Dewey Society: "Democracy and the Curriculum" (Appleton, 1939), and most fully in my *Foundations for American Education* (World Book, 1947).

On the Improvising of the First Program
in Teacher Education (1880–1920)

It is the first thesis of my book (Chapter II) that the Teachers of Teachers made little, if any, use of this astonishing revolution in thought and feeling until after 1920. And even then only a few did, and their contributions were ignored for a long time by those who dominated the program in teacher education. Here is a rich field for research in educational history: the changing nineteenth-century climate of opinion that was making the country teacher-education conscious, the work of Susan Blow and the kindergarteners, the influence of Herbart and the Americans in the National Herbart Society, and the development of the early work in education. We need a full-length study of the development of Teachers College, Columbia, from its origins in the Kitchen-Garden Association in the 1870's and the Industrial Education Association and the New York College for the Training of Teachers in the 1880's and its final transformation in the 1890's.

As for the materials I used in writing the note in Chapter II, in addition to *experiencing* its life and program for thirty-one years, the major steps of its origin are well summed up in papers presented in the *Teachers College Record* for 1900 and the next few years. The student who wishes to check my analysis of the improvising of the first program should scan the first basic textbooks against the major essays and books which were coming at the same moment from the researches of the new students of society. Compare, for example, such books as Monroe's (or Dexter's) *History of Education,* O'Shea's *Education as Adjustment,* Ruediger's or Henderson's *Principles of Education.* Scan and compare the books by Veblen, Robinson, Turner, *et al.,* with volumes of the new educational "series" edited after 1880. See, for example, Butler's "The Teacher's Professional Library," James E. Russell's "The American Teacher Series," Paul Monroe's "Textbook Series in Education" and his "Brief Course Series in Education," W. C. Bagley's "The Modern Teachers Series," and Cubberley's "Riverside Textbooks in Education." Compare the latter with Dewey's *Democracy and Education* (1916) and Kilpatrick's *Project Method* (a pamphlet published in 1918 by Teachers College, Columbia); see also the new biography, William Heard Kilpatrick, by Samuel Tenenbaum (Harper, 1951).

Contrast what the two groups took from the controversial literature over Darwin's evolutionary thesis: read Butler's *The Meaning of Education,* and any of the books I have named by Monroe, Dutton, Dexter, O'Shea, Henderson, or Ruediger against the direct eye-witness studies of society by Veblen, Turner, Robinson, Boas, and Beard. Feeling for the Puritan allegiances of the first teachers of teachers can be got from Levermore's biography, *Samuel Train Dutton* (Macmillan, 1922).

For still more contrasting data study the foregoing materials of Butler's men together with those that pictured the progressive move-

APPENDIX 283

ment initiated even earlier by Francis W. Parker, by John Dewey in the 1890's, and by J. L. Meriam at Missouri in 1904; see the latter's *Child Life and the Curriculum* (World, 1920). For the Dewey group at the University of Chicago (1896–1904) see Mayhew and Edwards's *The Dewey School* (1936). The detailed sources for the study of the Dewey School, however, are to be found in the *University Record* from 1897 to 1899, the *Elementary School Record* of 1900 and 1901, and the *Elementary School Teacher* from 1902 to 1904. Other sources which should be explored are *Transactions of the Illinois Society for Child Study* for the years 1895 and following; the *Yearbooks* of the National Herbart Society for various years beginning with 1895.

In beginning the study of the contribution of Francis W. Parker, and of his famous Practice School at Chicago, 1883–1901, and the school named for him founded in 1901, see Ida Heffron's *Francis Wayland Parker* (Deach, 1934), Parker's own book *Talks on Pedagogics* (Kellogs, 1894), the many *Yearbooks* of the Francis W. Parker School of Chicago, and my *Foundations for American Education* (World Book, 1947).

The limitations in the writers of the Conforming Way also stand out to one who reads the early story of the Creative Path in Van Wyck Brooks's *America's Coming of Age* (Huebsch, 1914), Randolph Bourne's *Untimely Papers* (Huebsch, 1919), and Waldo Frank's *Our America* (1920). My own *Culture and Education in America* (Harcourt, 1931) puts the story together as I had seen it developing in the years after 1918. I restated it more completely in the middle chapters of *That Men May Understand* (Doubleday, Doran, 1943) and in *Foundations for American Education* (1947).

III. On the Building of the Bio-psychological Foundations of Education

We provide an effective bridge between the Social and the Bio-psychological Foundations, by dealing first with the recent and profitable study of *the personality-molding processes of the culture.*

1. The Culture-Molding Process

The best brief introduction to the problem is Cole and Bruce's *Educational Psychology,* especially Chapter VIII (World, 1950). From it we turn first to the anthropologists and sociologists, then to the psychologists and psychiatrists.

Much light is thrown on the culture-molding process by the social anthropologists' studies of primitive cultures. See, for example, Ruth Benedict's *Patterns of Culture* (Houghton, 1934, available in a 35¢ edition) and Margaret Mead's *From the South Seas* (Morrow, 1939), a reprint of three of her earlier volumes, and her edited volume, *Cooperation and Competition Among Primitive Peoples* (McGraw-Hill, 1937). Abram Kardiner's *The Individual and His Society* (Columbia University Press, 1939) and his *The Psychological Frontiers of Society* (Columbia University Press, 1945) are both a psychiatrist's interpretation of the effect of cultural factors in primitive societies on the development of personality.

There are many excellent eye-witness studies of the culture-molding process in American communities. For the effect on Negro children, I think the best is Allison Davis and John Dollard's *Children of Bondage* (American Council of Education, 1940); see also their *Caste and Class in a Southern Town* (Yale Press, 1937) and Davis, Gardner, and Gardner's *Deep South, a Social-Anthropological Study of Caste and Class* (University of Chicago, 1941).

For the effect of the "backward" mountain community on personality development see Mandel Sherman and John Henry's *Hollow Folk* (Crowell, 1933), and *Children of the Cumberland* (Columbia University Press, 1946) by Claudia Lewis. The effect of Middle-West rural community life is clearly depicted in James West's *Plainville, U.S.A.* (Columbia University Press, 1945), and city life in the Lynds' *Middletown* (Harcourt, Brace, 1929) and *Middletown in Transition* (Harcourt, Brace, 1937). The problems of class and life histories of individuals in various classes of a small and old New England community are treated in Warner and Lunt's *The Social Life of a Modern Community* (Yale University Press, 1941).

For the more basic theoretical treatment see Kurt Lewin's *A Dynamic Theory of Personality* (McGraw-Hill, 1935), especially Chapter III and pages 250–254—a pioneer analysis. For penetrating psychiatric studies of motivation and the culture, see Chapters X and XV of Karen Horney's *The Neurotic Personality in Our Time* (Norton, 1937), her *Our Inner Conflicts, A Constructive Theory of Neurosis* (Norton, 1945), and Erich Fromm's excellent *Man for Himself* (Rinehart, 1947). Margaret Mead's *And Keep Your Powder Dry* (Morrow, 1942) is an anthropologist's analysis of patterns of culture in America today. A nontechnical discussion of recent studies is given in Clyde Kluckhohn's *Mirror for Man* (McGraw-Hill, 1949), and a fine symposium in Kluckhohn and Henry A. Murray's *Personality in Nature, Society, and Culture* (Knopf, 1949).

For good case studies of the influence of parent behavior on child development see Baldwin, Kalhorn, and Breese's *Patterns of Parent Behavior* (Psychological Monographs, American Psychological Association, 1945), and for diary records see *Helping Teachers Understand Children* (American Council on Education, 1945). Important life histories of child personalities can now be found in the reports from the Institute of Child Development. For fine interpretations see Harold E. Jones's *Development in Adolescence: Approaches to the Study of the Individual* (Appleton, 1943), and Chapter XXXIII of Barker, Kounin, and Wright's *Child Behavior and Development* (McGraw-Hill, 1943); see also *Biographies of Child Development: the Mental Growth Careers of Eighty-four Infants and Children,* by

Arnold Gesell, Catherine S. Amatruda, Burton M. Castner, and Helen Thompson (Paul B. Hoeber, 1939).

2. On Growth and the Development of Personality

We should note first the two key ideas that pervade the enormous scientific literature of growth: growing whole and interrelatedness. Many "Child Development Institutes" have now produced continuous growth studies covering ten to twenty years. The enormous literature is summarized and interpreted in so many places that I shall not duplicate it here. By far the best symposium of interpretation, in a single volume, in Barker, Kounin, and Wright's *Child Behavior and Development* (McGraw-Hill, 1943). The mate to it is the Cole and Bruce *Educational Psychology,* Chapters 3 and 4 (World, 1950), based on Lawrence Cole's forthcoming major "principles of psychology" (probably World, 1952 or 1953); other good cooperative interpretations can be found in Leonard Carmichael's *Manual of Child Psychology* (Wiley, 1946).

3. On the Growth of "Intelligence"

In this controversial field, I urge the critical exploration of the role of "effective" intelligence, as distinguished from "test-measured intelligence," and as discussed in this book. Cole's material, as given briefly in Chapters 3, 5, and 8 of Cole and Bruce, is by far the most perceptive discussion. With that see the respective chapters referred to in Barker, Kounin, and Wright's *Child Behavior and Development* and in Carmichael's *Manual of Child Psychology.* For studies of the "effective" intelligence of World War II soldiers see the United States Office of Strategic Services' *Assessment of Men* (Rinehart, 1948). For a direct study of the effects of social class on "test-measured" intelligence, see W. Allison Davis' *Social Class Influences on Learning* (Harvard, 1948). On the relation of intelligence to race differences see Otto Kleinberg's *Race Differences* (Harper, 1935).

On the relation of intelligence to the nature-nurture problem, the most comprehensive statement of opposed views is the National Society's two-volume *Thirty-Ninth Yearbook,* "Intelligence: The Nature and Nurture" (Public School Publishing Company, 1940). For the environmental point of view see George D. Stoddard's *The Meaning of Intelligence* (Macmillan, 1943), Chapters XIII–XVI; Cole and Bruce have a balanced interpretation.

4. On Emotional Behavior and the Development of Personality

The original pioneer studies on the physiology of the emotions are Charles Darwin's *Expression of Emotions in Man and Animals* (1872) (Appleton, 1910) and William James's *Principles of Psychology* (Holt, 1890). John B. Watson's famous studies are reported in his *Behaviorism* (Norton, 1930), and in his chapters in Murchison's *Psychologies of 1925* (Clark, 1926).

The "must" physiological studies are Walter B. Cannon's *The Wisdom of the Body* (Norton, 1932) and his *Bodily Changes in Pain, Hunger, Fear, and Rage* (Appleton, 1929); also R. G. Hoskins's *The Tides of Life* (Norton, 1933) and his *Endocrinology* (Norton, 1941). See also Wolf and Wolff's *Human Gastric Function* (Oxford, 1943), and Helen F. Dunbar's *Mind and Body, a Study of the Interrelationships within the Personality* (Random House, 1947).

Barker, Kounin, and Wright's *Child Behavior and Development* has three chapters, XVIII, XIX, and XX, bearing directly on the problem of emotion. Basic volumes dealing with emotional development and school education are Daniel A. Prescott's *Emotion and the Educative Process* (American Council on Education, 1938); Caroline B. Zachry's *Emotions and Conduct in Adolescence* (Appleton-Century, 1940); Peter Blos's *The Adolescent Personality* (Appleton-Century, 1941); and Elsie Smithies' *Case Studies of Normal Adolescent Girls* (Appleton, 1933). Carl R. Rogers' *The Clinical Treatment of the Problem Child* (Houghton-Mifflin, 1939) deals with children troubled by emotional problems. Virginia Mae Axline's *Play Therapy* (Houghton-Mifflin, 1947) is rich in concrete cases.

5. *On Motives and the Development of Personality*

Here the resources draw heavily on both physiological and psychological studies. The cue is "needs" (tensions), both physical and psychological, and the two must be carefully distinguished. On primary physiological needs, in addition to those already mentioned, see Paul T. Young's *Motivation of Behavior: The Fundamental Determinants of Human and Animal Activity* (Wiley, 1936). For a basic study of drives, see Curt P. Richter's "Biology of Drives" in *Psychosomatic Medicine,* 3 (1941), pages 105–110; also, his "The Internal Environment and Behavior" in *American Journal of Psychiatry,* 97 (1941), page 878, and other articles in the *Quarterly Review of Biology* and in *Comparative Psychological Monographs.* In such sources, see articles by R. M. Yerkes, reporting studies of the female sexual cycle in animals; see also Kurt Goldstein's *Organism; A Holistic Approach to Biology Derived from Pathological Data in Man* (American Book, 1939).

The pioneer study of interest and effort for teachers is Dewey's *Interest and Effort in Education* (Houghton, 1913); see also Chapter X of his *Democracy and Education,* and Mayhew and Edwards' *The Dewey School* (Appleton, 1936).

6. *On Learning and Thinking*

The scientific literature has been so frequently and recently summarized and interpreted that I shall not duplicate it here.

The theoretical problem falls into clear organization if we focus on three schools of thought: two connectionist views—Conditioning of Response, and Trial-and-Error—and a third, the organic and "field" theories. By far the best cooperative symposium is the *Forty-first Yearbook:* "The Psychology of Learning," Part II (1941) of the National Society for the Study of Education. With that I would put Robert Woodworth's *Contemporary Schools of Psychology* (Ronald Press, 1931). Hilgard's *Theories of Learning* (Appleton, 1948) is excellent but to me the indispensable single volume for the Teacher of Teachers is Cole and Bruce, referred to above, Chapters 10–15.

7. On the Role of the Developing Self

In James's days "Self" psychologies were academically respectable; his famous chapter on the Self in the *Principles* (Holt, 1890) was long the classic. Then the statisticians, factorial analysts, *et al.*, drove it out of fashion. But the accumulating studies of the students of personality are bringing it back. The basic data are in the fifty years of psychoanalytic and psychiatric literature. The original classic is still Sigmund Freud's *General Introduction to Psychoanalysis* (Garden City, 1938); see especially his discussion of "the anatomy of personality." A good selection is *The Basic Writings of Sigmund Freud* available in the Modern Library. A final summing up was given in *An Outline of Psychoanalysis* (Norton, 1949).

Of the pioneer Americans in this area, the early writings of William Alanson White stand out; see his *Mechanisms of Character Formation* (Macmillan, 1916); among the statements of current American psychiatrists, two of Karen Horney's books are important: *The Nature of Our Inner Conflicts* (Norton, 1945) and her *Self-Analysis* (Norton, 1942). Otto Fenichel's *Psychoanalytic Theory of Neurosis* (Norton, 1945) is a representative psychoanalytic treatment; see also Louis Schneider's *The Freudian Psychology and Veblen's Social Theory* (King's Crown Press, 1948). For a wealth of material on the self see Erich Fromm's *Man for Himself* (Rinehart, 1947), especially his analysis of the "productive" personality.

A wide ranging school of "personality" psychologists has recently brought out interpretations which are indispensable to us. See two of Henry A. Murray's books: his *Explorations in Personality: A Clinical and Experimental Study of Fifty Men of College Age* (Oxford University Press, 1938), and Kluckhohn and Murray's *Personality in Nature, Society, and Culture* (Knopf, 1949). Mature treatments are given in Gardner Murphy's *Personality: A Biosocial Approach to Origins and Structure* (Harper, 1947), Gordon W. Allport's *Personality, A Psychological Interpretation* (Holt, 1937), Andras Angyal's *Foundations For a Science of Personality* (Commonwealth Fund, 1941), and M. Sherif and H. Cantril's *The Psychology of Ego Involvements* (Wiley, 1949).

Coming directly to personality problems and the school, W. Allison Davis and Robert J. Havighurst's *Father of the Man: How Your Child Gets His Personality* (Houghton-Mifflin, 1947) is full of suggestions; Sections II, III, and IV and Chapter XX of John J. B. Morgan's *The*

Psychology of the Unadjusted School Child (Macmillan, 1930) will help; H. E. Bullis and Emily E. O'Malley's *Human Relations in the Classroom; Kindergarten-Twelfth Grade* (Delaware State Society for Mental Hygiene, 1947); also see Eugene Lerner's (edited) monograph: *Methods for the Study of Personality in Young Children;* Virginia Axline's *Play Therapy* (Houghton-Mifflin, 1947) for its wealth of self-revealing behavior of children; and Willard Olson's *Child Development* (Heath, 1949), particularly Chapters VIII, IX, X.

On the college level, Clements Fry's *Mental Hygiene in College* (Commonwealth Fund, 1942) deals with personality factors in the adjustments of young people; Fry and Haggard's *The Anatomy of Personality* (Harper, 1936), is packed with eye-witness pictures of life styles.

8. On the Mature Person

Here is a guiding theme for the building of the Bio-psychological Foundations and a great aim for educational reconstruction; that theme has, indeed, guided my psychological writings during the past twenty years. It is the frankly espoused goal of the Cole and Bruce *Educational Psychology;* scan the concluding pages of most of their chapters and see especially Chapters 9 and 19, and pages 43–47. Of the books mentioned earlier see Fromm's *Man for Himself,* and Horney's *Self-Analysis.* For the pathways to the mature life as given by several great moderns see Bertrand Russell's *The Conquest of Happiness* (Liveright, 1930); Max Otto's *Science and the Moral Life* (New American Library, 1949); John Dewey's *Human Nature and Conduct* (now in Modern Library) and Boyd Bode's *Democracy as a Way of Life* (Macmillan, 1939). Harry A. Overstreet's *The Mature Mind* (Norton, 1950) has attained a spectacular popular use.

9. On Studying and Guiding Personality Development

Helping Teachers Understand Children, by Prescott, *et al.,* of the Commission on Teacher Education (American Council, 1945) comes close to being the best single volume for teachers. Fritz Redl's *Understanding Children's Behavior* (Teachers College, Columbia University, 1949) is deeper. Do not miss Willard C. Olson's *Child Development* (Heath, 1949).

For the sociometric technique see J. L. Moreno's *Who Shall Survive?* (Nervous and Mental Disease Publishing Company, Washington, D. C., 1934); see also *How to Construct a Sociogram* (Teachers College, Columbia University, 1947).

On projective techniques, a basic book is Lawrence K. Frank's *Projective Methods* (Thomas, 1948). See the United States Office of Strategic Services's *Assessment of Men* (Rinehart, 1948) and Henry A. Murray's *Explorations in Personality: a Clinical and Experimental Study of Fifty Men of College Age* (Oxford University Press, 1938).

And on "nondirective therapy" read the pioneer himself—Carl R. Rogers' *Counseling and Psychotherapy* (Houghton-Mifflin, 1942).

IV. ON THE BUILDING OF ESTHETIC FOUNDATIONS OF EDUCATION

An important caution as we approach this vital area: It is impossible to build a theory of esthetics apart from a basic theory of human behavior. Hence the sources already noted in psychological foundations are just as important to the Teacher of Teachers' theory of esthetics as are those in this section. Assuming, therefore, that my readers will combine the suggestions given here with those of Section III, we can be brief.

The nub is the creative process, and the question: "What takes place in the creative act?" might well guide the study. The sources lie in a dozen disciplines—physiology and its components, the organic-field psychologies applied to the various expressive arts and, to a limited extent, in the philosophy of esthetics.

We turn, first, to important attempts at synthesis. For the direct application of Gestalt psychology to a theory of esthetics, Gyorgy Kepes' fine *Language of Vision* is indispensable. The parallel source applying psychoanalysis to the graphic and plastic arts is Otto Rank's *Art and the Artist* (Knopf, 1932), and to creative writing, F. J. Hoffman's *Freudianism and the Literary Mind* (Louisiana State University Press, 1945).

The classic pragmatic interpretation of the graphic arts is Dewey's *Art as Experience* (Minton, Balch, 1934); briefer statements, of lesser stature, are Irwin Edman's *The World, The Arts and The Artist* (Norton, 1928) and his *Arts and the Man: A Short Introduction to Esthetics* (Norton, 1939).

In each of the expressional arts we now have mature students who *know* their media because they passed them through their organisms as practicing artists. Sheldon Cheney is by far our best interpreter of the modern expressional movement in the graphic and plastic arts, architecture, and the theater, see especially his *Expressionism in Art* (Tudor, 1948), which also contains the most profound single analysis of the "movement" concept in art. From the writing of articulate painters themselves see especially Hans Hofman's *Search for the Real* (Addison Gallery, 1948), Gleize's *Cubism* (Unwin, 1913); also Adolph Hildebrand's *The Problem of Form in Painting and Sculpture* (Stechert, 1932), and *Concerning the Spiritual in Art*, by Wassily Kandinsky (Wittenborn, Schultz, 1947).

Leo Stein's *A-B-C Esthetics* (Liveright, 1927) and *Appreciation, Painting, Poetry and Prose* (Crown, 1947) are two profound analyses of creative expression and appreciation by a man who was close to the greatest modern artists most of his life.

For twenty-five years Robert Edmond Jones worked as one of our sensitive stage designers; then he wrote the most perfect study of the creative theater America has produced—*The Dramatic Imagination: Reflections and Speculations on the Art of the Theatre* (Duell, 1941). The best introductory history of modern expressional painting is Cheney's *Story of Modern Art* (Viking, 1941).

From autobiographical writings of distinguished artists on the creative process, see the collection of excerpts entitled *Artists on Art*, edited by John Goldwater (Pantheon, 1945). For statements of our musical composers see Henry Cowell's *American Composers on American Music* (Stanford University, 1933). For the dance see Isadora Duncan's *My Life* (Boni and Liveright, 1927). From the views of one of our greatest modern painters, John Marin, see Dorothy Norman's *The Selected Writings of John Marin* (Pellagrini and Cudahy, 1949); also Mackinley Helm's biography, *John Marin* (Pellagrini and Cudahy, 1948).

The building of an indigenous and original House for the American is pictured in the autobiographies of our two greatest architects: Louis Henry Sullivan's *Autobiography of an Idea* (Norton, 1924) and Frank Lloyd Wright's *Autobiography* (Duell, 1943). For the philosophy of the latter see *Frank Lloyd Wright on Architecture, Selected Writings, 1894–1940*, edited by Frederick Gutheim; also Henry-Russell Hitchcock's *In the Nature of Materials: Wright's Buildings, 1887–1941* (both Duell, 1942). An interpretation of American culture as revealed through the development of its architecture is given in Lewis Mumford's fine *Sticks and Stones: A Study of American Architecture and Civilization* (Norton, 1934). The contemporary phase is well shown in the development of "industrial design"—design for an industrial civilization. For the initial work of the Bauhaus group in Weimar, Germany, see Walter Gropius, *The New Architecture and the Bauhaus* (Museum of Modern Art, 1937). For the development in America see Norman Bel Geddes' *Horizons* (Little, Brown, 1932), Walter D. Teague's *Design This Day* (Harcourt, Brace, 1940), and Sheldon and Martha Cheney's *Art and the Machine* (Whittlesey House, 1936).

Although, among the "professed" estheticians, the textbooks of most of the professors of the Philosophy of Esthetics will be of little use, there are a few historic exceptions. George Santayana's *Sense of Beauty* (Scribner's, 1896) will probably repay your prolonged struggle with his special vocabulary. Perhaps Benedetto Croce's *Aesthetics* (Macmillan, 1922) also, although for that my praise is faint indeed. Max Schoen's *Art and Beauty* (Macmillan, 1932) is certainly valuable, and Horace Kallen's two-volume history, *Art and Freedom* (Duell, 1942), to which he gave twenty-five years of research and thought, is eminently so. Very important for its flashes of understanding of the role of "movement" in expression is a too-much ignored essay by Louis Danz, *The Psychologist Looks at Art* (Longmans, 1935).

1. On Modern Literary Criticism

The Teacher of Teacher's study of modern literary criticism should be founded on the truly great classic—Samuel T. Coleridge's *Biographia Literaria* (1717).

As Chapter V makes clear, a new and powerful criticism has emerged since World War I. The best single guide and interpretation is Stanley Hyman's *The Armed Vision* (Knopf, 1948); and do not miss Harry Slochower's *No Voice is Wholly Lost* (Creative Age, 1945), or, for the American novel since Howells, Alfred Kazin's *On Native Grounds* (Reynal and Hitchcock, 1942). Its impetus was provided by the pioneering of Brooks, Bourne, and Frank (1915–1919) to which I have already referred. An early classic is T. S. Eliot's *The Sacred Wood* (Methuen, 1920). Of these four, only Frank has remained to this day a true critic; see especially his *Our America* (1919), *Salvos* (1924), *Re-discovery of America* (1929), *In the American Jungle* (1936), *Chart for Rough Water* (1939). The best psychological analysis is C. K. Ogden and I. A. Richard's early *Meaning of Meaning* (Macmillan, 1922). An excellent historically organized critique of the symbolists from Poe to World War I is Edmund Wilson's *Axel's Castle* (Scribner's, 1931). From the 1920's, also, do not miss John Livingston Lowes's much-used *The Road to Xanadu* (Houghton-Mifflin, 1927). The main shifts in critical point of view through the 1920's and 1930's are well illustrated in I. A. Richard's five volumes, 1924–1935: *Principles of Literary Criticism* (Harcourt, Brace, 1924), *Science and Poetry* (Norton, 1926), *Practical Criticism* (Paul, Trench, Trubner, 1929), *Mencius on the Mind* (Paul, Trench, Trubner, 1932), and *Coleridge on Imagination* (Harcourt, Brace, 1935).

The "scientific and positivistic" attack on the "artist's" point of view is well represented by Max Eastman's *The Literary Mind* (Scribner's, 1931) and Charles Morris' *Foundations for the Theory of Signs* (University of Chicago Press, 1938). The orientations of David Daiches' four volumes is not too dissimilar: *Literature and Society* (Gollancz, 1938), *The Novel and the Modern World* (University of Chicago Press, 1939), *Poetry and the Modern World* (University of Chicago Press, 1940), *A Study of Literature for Readers and Critics* (Cornell University Press, 1948).

But the true nucleus of the new generation who produced our modern criticism after 1930 is made up of a dozen Americans and Britishers. I suggest eight as the important sources for the Teacher of Teachers, six from the United States and two from England. Of the Americans an increasingly profound contribution has been coming, between 1935 and 1950, from Kenneth Burke, as shown in his five volumes: *Permanence and Change* (The New Republic, 1935), *Attitudes toward History* (two volumes, The New Republic, 1937), *The Philosophy of Literary Form* (Louisiana State University Press, 1941),

A Grammar of Motives (Prentice-Hall, 1945), and *A Rhetoric of Motives* (Prentice-Hall, 1950).

The much-respected elder critic of the group is John Crowe Ransom; see especially his *The World's Body* (Scribner's, 1938) and *The New Criticism* (New Directions, 1941). The real contrast between the scientific-positivistic and the poet's point of view is, I think, given best in Allen Tate's volumes, especially in *Reason in Madness* (Putnam, 1941). Two other important volumes are Cleanth Brooks's *Modern Poetry and the Tradition* (University of North Carolina Press, 1939) and R. P. Blackmur's *The Expense of Greatness* (Arrow Editions, 1940). Harvard's sociologist-philosopher of the arts, Pitirim Sorokin, presents a similar critique in his *The Crisis of Our Age* (Dutton, 1941).

Of the English "modern critics," do not miss Christopher Caudwell's three volumes: *Illusion and Reality* (Macmillan, 1937), *Studies in a Dying Culture* (John Lane, 1938), and *The Crisis in Physics* (John Lane, 1939); C. Day Lewis' *A Hope For Poetry* (1936) and *The Poetic Image* (1947, both Oxford); or William Empson's *Seven Types of Ambiguity* (Chatto and Windus, 1947).

2. On the Creative Process and Its Application in Education

My own quarter century of work (a full treatment is expected in 1953) has thus far been reported only in articles, and in chapters of books. Half of *The Child-Centered School* (World Book, 1928) was devoted to examples and interpretations from the exciting practices of progressive schools in the 1920's. My first full-length criticism of the inadequacy of the Dewey-Kilpatrick-Bode theory of education on the esthetic side (and, up to the present volume, my best) was *Culture and Education in America* (Harcourt, 1931). About the same time I put the artist in America in his expressive setting in a chapter of the Norman-Frank-Mumford-Rosenthal-Rugg *America and Alfred Stieglitz* (Literary Guild, 1934) which I find today I would change little. In a sense my essay, *Now Is the Moment* (Duell, 1943) written to save my own soul, not others, is my best writing, and gives me a chance a decade later to say I told you so! Esthetics is put more clearly in the framework of the foundations of education, than in any others of my writings up to the present volume, in *Foundations for American Education* (World Book, 1947).

One of our most important educational interpretations is Hughes Mearns's one-hundred page "Introduction" to his *Creative Youth* (Doubleday, 1925); see also his *Creative Power* (Doubleday, 1929); and *Creative Adult* (Doubleday, 1941). I regard Rosabell Macdonald Mann's *Art as Education: The Study of Art in the Secondary Schools* (Holt, 1941) as the most sensitive and profound writing that has come from teaching practice in public schools. Do not miss it. Among the publications from private art schools see Ralph Pearson's *New Art Education* (Harper, 1941). From the writings of teachers on children's

creative activities, see Rose H. Alschuler and La Berta W. Hattwick's
Painting and Personality: A Study of Young Children (University of
Chicago, 1947, two volumes). Of Herbert Reed's endless publication
of "art" books see *Education Through Art* (Pantheon Books, 1949).

V. On the Building of New Philosophical Foundations of Education

It is obvious that this volume has been written from a definite
philosophy of life and education; the concepts, beliefs and values,
what I approve and detest, cleave to and shun, have been explicitly
stated in the brief outline of my theory of teacher education in
Chapter VI. Moreover, the chief documentary sources which I have
used during the past thirty years have been cited in the preceding
sections. In addition to them, however, every generation needs to build
on the best philosophizing of its predecessors. I pick, therefore, a few
of the classic statements of modern times that have cumulatively
helped me most.

First, a few fine orienting interpretations. For the point of view
maintained in the *Teacher of Teachers,* by far the most valuable
"introduction" to the philosophy of education, with the best selected
reading lists, is Theodore Brameld's new and provocative *Patterns of
Educational Philosophy* (World Book, 1950). I think it is the best single
volume on educational philosophy since Dewey's *Democracy and
Education* (1916). To supplement it, for general orientation, I suggest
some of the following: Bertrand Russell's *A History of Western Philosophy* (Simon, 1945), Will Durant's *The Story of Philosophy* (Simon,
1927), Harold Larrabee's *What Philosophy Is* (Macy-Masius, 1928),
and there are excellently chosen excerpts in Randall and Buchler's
Readings in Philosophy (Barnes and Noble, 1946). For beginners in
this field see A. K. Roger's old but excellent *A Student's History of
Philosophy* (Macmillan, 1907). A recent, somewhat popular, but helpful comparison of basic orientations of western and eastern cultures is
F. S. C. Northrup's *The Meeting of East and West* (Macmillan, 1947).
For the more especially American viewpoint see H. W. Schneider's
A History of American Philosophy (Columbia University, 1946),
Morris R. Cohen and Ernest Nagel's *Introduction to Logic and the
Scientific Method* (Harcourt, 1934), and G. T. W. Patrick's *Introduc-
tion to Philosophy* (Houghton-Mifflin, 1927).

Four rival philosophies of education guide the teaching of teachers
today: (1) The "Progressive," held by Dewey and his followers of
the progressive education movement since 1890; (2) The "Essentialist," maintained during the past fifty years by the leaders of the established liberal arts philosophy and in education especially by H. H.
Horne, W. C. Bagley, Izak L. Kandel, Michael Demiashkevitch, and
Robert Ulich; (3) The Neo-scholastic view—the self-styled "Perennialists"—led since 1930 by M. J. Adler and Robert M. Hutchins and

their colleagues at Chicago and St. Johns and by the philosophers of Thomism; (4) What Brameld calls the "Reconstructionist" view, as developed more recently by the younger leaders of the "Social Frontier" group; to name a few—Brameld and Axtelle of New York University, B. Othanel Smith and Kenneth Benne of Illinois, and Childs and Raup of Teachers College. Of these four outlooks my own is most approximately represented by that of social reconstruction, but definitely built around a more personally creative philosophy.

1. For the Progressive Point of View

The pioneer and still basic book is Dewey's *Democracy and Education* (Macmillan, 1916); a small and much later restatement of it is his *Experience and Education* (Macmillan, 1938). Key interpretations by his older students are William H. Kilpatrick's *Selfhood and Civilization* (Macmillan, 1941); Boyd H. Bode's *How We Learn* (Heath, 1940); John L. Childs's *Education and Morals* (Appleton, 1950); Bruce Raup's *Education and Organized Interests in America* (Putnam's, 1936). In 1933, the group, with H. Gordon Hullfish and Vivian T. Thayer, wrote the definitive *Educational Frontier* (edited by Kilpatrick, Appleton); do not miss it.

An effective sympathetic critic of the progressive philosophy has been I. B. Berkson; see his *Education Faces the Future* (Harper, 1943), Chapters 10, 11, and 15; also his *Preface to an Educational Philosophy* (Columbia University Press, 1940). The history, theory, and practice of progressivism can be found in my *Foundations for American Education* (World Book, 1947), Chapters 17 and 18. The most elaborate statement of both theory and practice of the progressive schools is the five volumes of the so-called "Eight-Year Study" of the Progressive Education Association, Commission on the Relation of School and College, entitled *Adventure in American Education* (Harper, 1942–43).

By far the best textbook is Brameld's *Patterns of Educational Philosophy* (World Book, 1950).

2. On the Essentialist Point of View

For two outstanding idealist statements of the essentialist position see Horne's *The Philosophy of Christian Education* (Revell, 1937) and Robert Ulich's *Fundamentals of Democratic Education* (American Book Company, 1940)—a more scholarly treatment. Herman H. Horne's *The Democratic Philosophy of Education* (Macmillan, 1932), an excellent comparison of progressivism and essentialism, analyzes Dewey's *Democracy and Education;* see Michael Demiashkevitch's *An Introduction to the Philosophy of Education* (American Book Company, 1935), especially Part 3.

For the ideas of the essentialist leader in the 1920's and 1930's see William C. Bagley's *Education and Emergent Man* (Thomas Nelson, 1934) and *Education, Crime, and Social Progress* (Macmillan, 1931).

Perhaps the most publicized statement is The Harvard Report, *General Education in a Free Society* (Harvard University Press, 1945). Three popular essentialist attacks on the progressive views on education are Mortimer Smith's brief *And Madly Teach* (H. Regnery, 1949), Bernard I. Bell's *The Crisis in Education, a Challenge to American Complacency* (McGraw-Hill, 1949), and Albert Jay Nock's *The Theory of Education in the United States* (Harcourt, 1932).

3. On the "Great Books," Perennialist, Philosophy of Education, Written by Scholastics in Modern Dress

Ten of their books and many articles are interpreted in my own *Foundations for American Education*, pages 613–627. I give here a few key sources which will give the essence of the point of view.

Books by Hutchins are *The Higher Learning in America* (Yale University Press, 1936), *Education for Freedom* (1943); thirty-four articles by Hutchins, 1932 to 1942, appear in popular magazines. The best analysis of Hutchins is Harry D. Gideonse, *The Higher Learning in a Democracy* (Farrar and Rinehart, 1937). There are many articles on Hutchins, a few of which are A. N. Whitehead's "Review of Higher Learning in America," in 1936, and John Dewey's "Remaking Higher Education," *Social Frontier*, January, 1937; Hutchins (reply), "Grammar Rhetoric and Mr. Dewey," *Social Frontier*, February, 1937; Dewey (counterreply), "Was President Hutchins Serious?" *Social Frontier*, March, 1937. Books by Adler are *What Man Has Made of Man* (Longmans, Green, 1937), *How to Read a Book* (Simon and Schuster, 1940), and *How to Think About War and Peace* (Simon and Schuster, 1944).

For succinct statements on perennialist education see *Forty-first Yearbook* of the National Society for the Study of Education, "Philosophies of Education," Chapters by Adler, W. J. McGucken, W. F. Cunningham, J. D. Redden, and F. A. Ryan.

4. On the Reconstructionist View

Brameld's *Patterns of Educational Philosophy* is the basic book, especially pages 387–758; the first three chapters set the stage. "Social Reconstruction as a Basic Curriculum Theory," the concluding Chapter 29 of the Smith-Stanley-Shores *Fundamentals of Curriculum Development* (World, 1950), and their Part II, Chapters 6 to 10 inclusive, is the most profound analysis of the philosophy of "Basic Curriculum Issues" in print; do not miss it. Cole and Bruce's *Educational Psychology* is the corresponding parallel "psychology" for the reconstructionist philosophy. As for my own writings, while a strong advocate of progressivism in philosophy, I have been seeking to document the social reconstruction view as a necessary supplement to it for twenty-five years. In addition to the *Teacher of Teachers*, *Foundations for American Education* is the most inclusive statement; see also its selected bibliographies. The view is not complete without

The Great Technology (John Day, 1933), *That Men May Understand* (Doubleday, 1944) and *Now Is the Moment* (Duell, 1943). The chief gap is in esthetics, to be supplied soon in a major volume on the "Creative Process."

On reconstructionist beliefs about value see earlier references to Murphy's *Personality*, Lynd's *What Knowledge is of Most Worth?*, Horney's various books, and Allport's *Personality*. One of the best single statements is Erich Fromm's *Man for Himself*.

Goal-seeking is well interpreted in Gardner Murphy's *Personality*. On the unrational traits see Sigmund Freud's *A General Introduction to Psychoanalysis* (Liveright, 1920) and Karl Marx's *Capital, The Communist Manifesto and Other Writings* (Eastman, editor, Modern Library, 1932). On ideologies and utopias, see Karl Mannheim's *Ideology & Utopia* (Harcourt, 1936). On the problem of arriving at social consensus see Kurt Lewin's *Resolving Social Conflicts* (Harper, 1948) and Raup, *et al.*, *The Improvement of Practical Intelligence* (Harper, 1950).

VI. ON THE RECONSTRUCTION OF THE LIFE AND PROGRAM
OF THE SCHOOL (THE CURRICULUM)

On the basic principle that the curriculum shall be designed from the culture, every reference cited in Section I, "Social Foundations," is important for this Section. In addition to these, several key educational books bridge the gap between society and the life and program of the school. By far the most important is the Smith-Stanley-Shores *Fundamentals of Curriculum Development*. The second in order is *Democracy and Curriculum* (Third Yearbook of John Dewey Society). The first of many "Committee" statements was the (1926) *Twenty-sixth Yearbook* of the USSE–"Foundations of Curriculum-Making" (two volumes). The culmination of the movement which it launched is the Smith-Stanley-Shores volume, my own *Foundations for American Education*, Brameld's *Design for America*, and William Van Tyl's *Economic Roads for American Democracy* (McGraw-Hill, 1947)–a high school text.

On the source of authority in curriculum building the best general statement is Kenneth D. Benne's *A Conception of Authority* (Teachers College, Columbia University, 1943). For the principal opposed doctrines in American education see Freeman Butts's *The College Charts Its Course* (McGraw-Hill, 1947), pages 1–51, or his *Modern Philosophies of Education* (McGraw-Hill, 1939), pages 24–100. For the Catholic position that the teacher derives his authority from supernatural sources, see Jacques Maritain, *Education at the Crossroads* (Yale University Press, 1943), pages 1–28, and William McGucken, "The Philosophy of Catholic Education" in the *Forty-first Yearbook* of the National Society for the Study of Education, Part I, "Philosophies and Education," pages 251–288; the most thorough analysis of the case for the separation of church and state in education is Butts's *The American Tradition in Religion and Education* (Beacon Press, 1950).

For discussions of values in relation to our educational task see Raup, Benne, Axtelle, and Smith, *The Improvement of Practical Intelligence* (Harper, 1950). "The Public Schools and Spiritual Values," *Seventh Yearbook* of the John Dewey Society (Harper, 1944); my own *Foundations for American Education* (Chapter XV), and my (edited) *Readings in the Foundations of Education,* Vol. II; see also Part I, the Educational Policies Commission's *Education of Free Men in American Democracy* (National Education Association, 1941).

On Principles of Selecting Curriculum Content

Assuming such basic references on theory as Cohen and Nagel's *An Introduction to Logic and the Scientific Method* (Harcourt, 1934, especially pages 191–222, 273–288, 323–375), I present a few items grouped in terms of opposed schools of thought:

First: the disciplinary, "great books," subject approach. For the classic treatments of the liberal arts devotees see Irving Babbitt's *Literature and the American College* (Houghton-Mifflin, 1908); Norman Foerster's *The Future of the Liberal College* (Appleton-Century, 1938); Everett D. Martin's *The Meaning of a Liberal Education* (Norton, 1926); and the Harvard Committee's *General Education in a Free Society* (pages 103–176). Mark Van Doren's *Liberal Education* (Holt, 1943, pages 71–168) and Robert M. Hutchins' *The Higher Learning in America* (Yale University Press, 1936, pages 59–87) are the perennialists' best statement of the case for the "great books" principle. Bode's *How We Learn* is a good criticism of it; see also my *Foundations for American Education* (pages 613–627). Arthur I. Gates, *et al., Educational Psychology* (Macmillan, 1942), pages 504–542, is a good "connectionist" summing up of the modern views in psychology on mental discipline; put with it Boyd H. Bode's chapter (pages 43–72) of his *Modern Educational Theories.*

Second: on building the curriculum on the job-analysis of social practices, see W. W. Charters, *Curriculum Construction* (Macmillan, 1925) and Franklin Bobbitt's *How to Make a Curriculum* (Houghton-Mifflin, 1924), pages 1–62. Bode's *Modern Educational Theories* (Macmillan, 1927, pages 95–121) is a devastating criticism of it.

Third: on the survival-of-social-institutions conception, see (1) H. C. Morrison's *The Curriculum of the Common School* (University of Chicago Press, 1940), pages 1–35, and his *Basic Principles of Education* (Houghton-Mifflin, 1934); (2) William C. Bagley's *Education and Emergent Man* (Nelson, 1934); and (3) for the theory of the approach see Joseph Justman's *Theories of Secondary Education in the United States* (Teachers College, Columbia University, 1940), pages 22–32, 71–88, 144–168, 227–339, 410–423.

Fourth: on the social-problems-and-trends approach, the classic study is Dewey's *Democracy and Education*. See my *Culture and Education in America,* and *That Men May Understand,* especially Chapters X and XI; also *American Life and the School Curriculum* (Ginn, 1936). Harold Hand's (editor) *Living in the Atomic Age* (University of Illinois, 1948) is a fine resource unit and William Van Tyl's *Economic Roads for American Democracy* (McGraw-Hill, 1947) an excellent textbook.

Fifth: on the activity-child-interest approach, several books already mentioned are of first importance: John Dewey's *School and Society* and his *Child and Curriculum;* Mayhew and Edwards' *The Dewey School;* J. L. Meriam's *Child Life and the Curriculum;* W. H. Kilpatrick's *The Project Method* and *Remaking the Curriculum;* Ellsworth Collings' *An Experiment with a Project Curriculum,* and Rugg and Shumaker's *The Child Centered School* (World Book, 1928).

Finally, *sixth:* on the core curriculum, many of the references already given, dealing with the social reconstruction and social problems approach, are useful. For new examples see my *Culture and Education in America* (Harcourt, 1931), J. Paul Leonard's *Developing the Secondary School Curriculum* (Rinehart, 1946), Harold Alberty's *Reorganizing the High School Curriculum* (Macmillan, 1947), *Exploring the Curriculum* (Harper, 1942) by H. H. Giles, S. P. McCutchen, and A. N. Zechiel, and The Progressive Education Association's *Thirty Schools Tell Their Story* (Harper, 1943).

Index of Names

Abbott, Frank, 69
Adler, Alfred, 101
Adler, Mortimer J., 62, 209
Aikin, W. M., 215
Aldrich, Thomas Bailey, 46
Allport, Gordon, 87, 101, 104
American Legion, 209
American Place, 111
Anderson, Margaret, 128
Anderson, Sherwood, 116, 117, 122
Angell, James R., 25, 69
Armstrong, Hollis, and Davis, 62, 236

Babbitt, Irving, 133
Bagley, William C., 29, 43-44, 45, 49, 62
Baker, Frank, 235-236
Baker, Franklin T., 29
Baldwin, J. Mark, 51, 53, 55
Barnard, Frederick A. P., 30
Barnard, Henry, 26
Barr, S., 62
Bauhaus, 189
Beard, Charles, 46, 52, 70, 71, 72, 108, 178
Bechterev, 54, 56
Bel Geddes, N., 189
Bellamy, Edward, 72, 85
Benedict, R., 86
Benne, K. D., 189, 191, 207
Bennett, Hugh, 79
Bentley, Madison, 55
Bergson, 138, 180
Berkeley, 73
Bernard, Claude, 69, 74
Bigelow, Karl, 62
Bigelow, Maurice, 29
Bliven, Bruce, 121
Blow, Susan, 24
Boas, Franz, 43, 46, 52, 69, 74, 85
Bode, Boyd H., 36, 55, 60, 62, 74, 96, 109

Bourne, R., 58, 116, 129, 132, 133, 135-136
Bowles, Chester, 81, 264
Brameld, Theodore, 61, 94, 207, 269
Brooks, Cleanth, 121
Brooks, Van Wyck, 44, 58, 116, 129, 132, 133-135
Brubacher, John S., 191, 207
Brunner, Edmund de S., 225
Buchanan, Scott, 62, 209
Buckingham, B. R., 225
Burke, K., 121, 143
Burnham, W. H., 69
Burton, W. H., 207
Bush, Vannevar, 9, 10, 82, 178, 252
Butler, Nicholas Murray, 24, 25, 31, 33, 34, 38, 43, 45, 47, 49, 60, 67, 68, 69, 132, 224
Butts, R. Freeman, 53, 207

Cahill, Holger, 79
Caldwell, E., 128
Cambridge Metaphysical Club, 67
Cannon, W. B., 54, 107, 173-174, 269
Cantril, H., 85
Carter, James, 20, 26
Cattell, J. McKeen, 34, 55, 70
Cézanne, 58, 69, 70, 111
Charcot, 69
Charters, W. W., 30, 43, 207
Childs, J. L., 225
Clemenceau, 71
Coffman, Lotus D., 30, 207
Coghill, Lashley, 111
Cole, Lawrence E., 57, 89, 93, 172
Committee on Personnel in the Army, 68
Commons, John R., 71
Comte, August, 51, 53, 74
Cooke, Morris, 79
Cooley, C. H., 53
Copernicus, 131
Coss, J., 209
Counts, G. S., 225

299

Herbart, 24, 35, 53,
Herskovitz, M., 87
Hertz, 251
Hervey, Walter S., 31, 32
Hobbes, 73
Hobson, John A., 52, 68, 71
Hollingshead, 89
Holmes, Mr. Justice, 39, 51, 68-69
Horn, Ernest, 30
Horne, Herman Harrel, 60
Howe, F., 121
Howells, W. D., 117
Hull, Clark L., 56, 96
Hume, 73
Huntington, Emily, 31
Hutchins, R. M., 62
Huxley, T., 219, 220
Hyman, S., 140-141

Ives, Charles, 58, 70, 108, 121, 199

James, William, 53, 57, 69, 73, 74,
    92, 96, 104, 172, 185
Jastrow, Joseph, 69
Jefferson, 20, 40
Jessup, Walter, 30
Johnson, F. E., 225
Johnson, Henry, 29
Jones, B., 55, 78, 79
Jones, H. M., 219
Jones, R. E., 129
Jordan, 216
Joyce, James, 128
Judd, Charles H., 29, 43, 55, 85-93,
    95-97, 101, 207
Jung, C. J., 180

Kazin, A., 123
Kennerley, Mitchell, 111
Keynes, 71, 79
Kilpatrick, William Heard, 36, 60,
    61, 62, 96, 104, 206, 224
Kitchen-Garden Association, 31
Koffka, 96
Köhler, W., 96, 172
Kunz, F., 191, 269

Ladd-Franklin, Christine, 69
Lamarck, 45
Laski, H., 68, 71
Lasswell, H., 85
Lazarsfeld, Paul, 85
Leaver and Brown, 252

Lewin, K., 101, 177, 182, 185, 226
Lewis, S., 116, 117, 122, 131
Lilienthal, David, 79
Lincoln School Social Science Re-
    search Group, 210
Lindou, L. D., 240
Linton, Ralph, 74
Lippmann, Walter, 71, 85, 87, 88
Lipps, T., 178, 183
Lloyd George, 71
Locke, 73, 89, 104
Lodge, Gonzalez, 29
Loewy, R., 189
London, Jack, 123
London School Group, 68
London School of Economics and
    Political Science, 69, 71
Lowell, J. R., 46
Lund, S. E. T., 207
Lyell, 45
Lynd, Robert and Helen, 55, 88
Lyons, R., 207

Mach, 73
MacLean, M., 213, 218
MacVannel, John A., 59
Mann, Horace, 20, 24, 26
Marconi, 251
Margenau, H., 188, 191, 269
Marin, John, 58, 69, 70, 111, 184,
    199
Marshall, Leon, 71
Martin, J., 184, 185
Masters, E. L., 143
Mather, K., 269
Matisse, 58, 69, 70
Maxwell, J. C., 55, 81, 82, 131, 250
Mayberry, G., 133
Mayhew and Edwards, 181
McCullough, W., 173
McGrath, E. J., 221
McKeon, R., 62, 209
McMurry, Charles, 28
McMurry, Frank N., 25, 28
Mead, George H., 69
Melville, H., 109
Mencken, H. L., 129
Meriam, Junius L., 30
Merriam, Charles E., 79
"Metaphysical Club" (1869-1874),
    68
Michaelson, 69
Mitchell, Wesley, 79

Index of Subjects